SOMETHING IN THE WAY
SHE MOVES

Wendy Buonaventura

SOMETHING IN THE WAY SHE MOVES

Dancing Women from Salome to Madonna

DA CAPO PRESS
A Member of the Perseus Books Group

Cataloging-in-Publication data for this book is available from
the Library of Congress.

First Da Capo Press edition 2004
First published in the United Kingdom as
I Put a Spell on You.
Reprinted by arrangement with Saqi Books.

ISBN 0–306–81348–3

Published by Da Capo Press
A Member of the Perseus Books Group
http://www.dacapopress.com

Da Capo Press books are available at special discounts for bulk
purchases in the U.S. by corporations, institutions, and other
organizations. For more information, please contact the
Special Markets Department at the Perseus Books Group,
11 Cambridge Center, Cambridge, MA 02142,
or call (800) 255-1514 or (617) 252-5298,
or e-mail special.markets@perseusbooks.com.

1 2 3 4 5 6 7 8 9—07 06 05 04

for Nick –
more than words can say

Acknowledgements

I would like to thank Rebecca Lisle for her invaluable comments on the manuscript; Medea Mahdavi, who introduced me to the beauty of Persian arts, and my other fellow-dancers Hazel Kayes, Caroline Wright, Venus Saleh and Karine Butchart. I owe thanks as well to Martin Weitz, Lynne Ingram, Sue Way, South West Arts and the Lisa Ullman Travelling Scholarship Fund. I am also very grateful for the library at London's Laban Centre, where I spent many happy afternoons. Last of all, thanks to the poker group for hours of entertainment and for putting up with my bad behaviour.

Contents

Introduction: She Moves   9

And God Created Devil-Woman   17

Sexual Imposters   39

Revolution on the Dance Floor   65

Forbidden Fruit   95

Twentieth-Century Goddess   135

Black Bottoms   171

Battle of the Sexes   207

Danse Macabre   233

Dance of the Seven Veils   261

Afterword: Still Moving ...   285

Sources   291

Further Reading   297

Index   303

Introduction: She Moves

Oh baby! When she moves I go crazy:
She looks like a flower but she stings like a bee,
Like every girl in history.
Rosa/Afansieff/Child

Many years from now, when our civilization has crumbled into the dust, archaeologists may dig up a newsagent's shop. There they will find worm-eaten magazines with faded photos of nude women on the cover: cheerful, buxom blondes and dark temptresses, advertising their wares from between parted legs. They may think that these iconic images on the top shelf, the shelf closest to heaven, belonged to religious magazines. And from this they may deduce that we were a goddess-worshipping civilization in which women enjoyed high social status; that these images, which throw into relief the nurturing and reproductive parts of the female body, indicate reverence for women's life-giving power. Then they'll discover something else: that there's a world of difference between the smiling invitation on the faces of the blondes with their huge silicone breasts and the 'Enter at your peril' challenge on the faces of the dark-haired models lying there with their legs open.

The female body has been an object of sexual obsession throughout history, the focus of dreams and fears. The fashion and beauty business, organized religion, the entertainment world, the media and the medical establishment have all staked their claim to this fertile territory. Women have long been assumed to reveal their true nature through their bodies, and aside from giving birth this is most in evidence when they dance. According to many historians and other commentators, the main purpose of dance is either to stimulate sexual appetite or act as a substitute for sex. At different periods throughout history, dancing has been banned by governments who feared its potential as a source of social chaos. Professional dancers have been seen as the most dangerous of all women, a reflection of the idea that men are powerless to resist temptation when it's put on display.

It was only when I, a dancer myself, began delving into the subject that I realized to what extent female dancing has been regarded as confrontational and subversive. The more I explored, the more fascinated I became by this aspect of an activity which enables us to release pent-up energy and express ourselves in a language beyond words. I discovered that in every culture restrictions have been placed on women dancing, even in private. And the social position of women who went out and danced for a living was precarious.

Fear of the disorder that would result if women made a public spectacle of their bodies led to them being banned from the stage, giving rise to a drag tradition which flourishes to this day. When Italy's *commedia dell'arte* first featured women in the sixteenth century it was thought the height of daring. In China it was only in the 1930s that women were accepted on the stage. Until then their place had been taken by men in drag, who sent their audience wild as they sashayed across the stage, hand on hip, flicking a coquettish hanky in the air.

Given its tremendous power to arouse our emotions, it isn't surprising that dancing has been outlawed as a dangerous social force. The cancan is one of many dances that governments have tried to suppress over the years. The Spanish saraband – a seventeenth-century women's dance accompanied by what was described as 'licentious' singing – is another. The authorities claimed it caused more evil than the plague and tried to ban it in places of public entertainment. The Hawaiian hula was prohibited by outsiders, religious busybodies bent on taking control of other people's culture as well as their land. Even the waltz was thought scandalous and banned from 'polite' society in its early days. As one moral guardian put it, 'The waltz is a dance of quite too loose a character and unmarried ladies should refrain from it altogether, both in public and private.'

The dance floor is one of the main venues where people meet and talk for the first time and the waltz created a cultural revolution in Europe by allowing the classes to mix socially. The main fear behind banning dance, though, is that it might encourage sexual activity. Many dances which today look completely innocent were seen as erotic in their time, especially if they included pelvic movements. In 1828 a French traveller wrote that the vigorous hip movements of African women were 'so lascivious, so lubricious that it's impossible to describe them', adding, in some bewilderment, 'It's true the negresses don't appear to have the depraved intentions one would imagine … one sees children of six performing this dance, certainly without knowing what they're leading up to.'

It goes without saying that creating a sexual display isn't necessarily what someone has in mind when they get up and move, urged on by the seductive power of music. But for people obsessed with sex even piano legs or the sight of a woman's face can send the pulses racing. How much more troubling is the spectacle of a woman moving her body rhythmically to music!

In the nineteenth century the hoops of a woman's crinoline, swinging from side to side as she waltzed round the ballroom floor, were hugely suggestive. And if all those yards of material made it difficult for men to get too close, at least they could entertain themselves watching the tide of skirts go billowing past, hems swinging up to reveal the women's trim black ankle boots.

Social and sexual revolutions are reflected in changing styles of dance and fashion, and women's clothes have often been designed around dance to allow freedom of movement. Trailing skirts made it difficult to dance the tango, as did whalebone corsets which kept the torso rigid. So it was that the tango gave rise to rubberized corsets and divided skirts. And – though this contradicts popular legend – the cancan, in which women lifted their petticoats to show their legs, was a dance which encouraged them to wear long white culottes under their skirts. Until then, it was largely whores who wore knickers. The cancan must be the rudest dance of all time and the original *cancaneuses* performed, not for money, but for their own pleasure. They held their legs above their heads, exhibiting their crotches, kicked the hats off the heads of wealthy gents who came to ogle them and laughed in their faces.

The nineteenth century was a time of turbulent change and it saw a continual uproar on the dance floor. Western women were becoming prominent stage performers and beginning to express themselves with real wildness in the public arena. It's no accident that a number of defiant, subversive dances flourished during the first industrial age, when huge numbers of people were congregating in the rapidly expanding cities of Europe and America.

Some nineteenth-century dances which created a scandal in their own country were only accepted after being tamed abroad and brought back home. The cancan and tango were two which attempted to cross borders, only to be halted at customs and turned back. In the middle of the twentieth century even the formal manoeuvring of ballroom dancing was found subversive in the communist bloc. In 1834 Cairo's female dancers were banned from plying their trade in public and sent up the Nile to Esna, and at the end of the twentieth century they were once again subjected to threats and beatings by religious fundamentalist groups.

Men and women were thought to be at risk from dance for different reasons. When the waltz was discouraged it was argued that women were such delicate creatures their weak constitutions couldn't cope with all that strenuous whirling. Even in the role of observer they were considered susceptible to the suggestive aspects of dance. It was young girls, rather than their brothers, who were forbidden to attend the opera house if a ballet was included on the bill. At that time ballet was far from being high art enjoyed by a cultural elite. The opera house was a shop window for women looking to sell themselves to the highest bidder and ballerinas were mistress, rather than wife, material. They were also more eagerly sought after than today's rock stars.

The nineteenth century was a period when women were struggling to assert their independence and they demonstrated their rebellion on the dance floor. During this period the Argentinian tango was born. The melancholy, combative tango began life as a duet of male immigrants in low dives and brothels, and later evolved into a mixed-couple dance. In time it became a fascinating reflection of the battle for social and sexual mastery in a community where men hugely outnumbered women.

Among the well-heeled, private dancing – if done in the right setting and with decorum – was acceptable. Indeed, in Europe and America a young girl could show herself to her best advantage, dancing in front of potential suitors. In the Middle East she could do the same, dancing at female-only gatherings before potential mothers-in-law.

As a profession, however, dance was something else. In many cultures women weren't supposed to show their charms in public. Entertainers played a vital role in celebrations, yet they had no more status than servants. Fifty years ago, no well-bred Indian girl would have dreamed of taking up dance as a career. To do so would have meant losing her honour. For thousands of years, lacking a place in public life, women in the Arab world have entertained each other in private. In the process they've developed a dance full of sensuality and subtle humour. Yet in many Islamic countries (and even outside them) Muslim nervousness about the sensuality of women's dancing can cause ructions.

I experienced this recently when I revived my theatre piece *Dancing Girls*. This show looks at Orientalist perceptions of Egyptian life through travellers' meetings with dancers. It was booked into a Liverpool arts centre and was publicized with extracts from reviews that it had garnered the first time around. The publicity fell into the hands of a Muslim fundamentalist group, who produced a leaflet protesting against the show's sexual content (about which they could only fantasize, not having seen it). A Yemeni woman connected with the production had a stone thrown through her window, another received a threatening and abusive phone call from a man too cowardly to identify himself. A leaflet was produced and distributed at the local mosque where, I heard, the subject dominated Friday prayers that week. In an attempt to defuse the situation, the imam told his flock to boycott the show. A few isolated individuals still threatened to come along and disrupt the performance but, as it happened, it was already sold out and the evening passed off without incident.

In Egypt today dance is still not an honourable career for women and only those at the very top of their profession are respected and not assumed to be whores. Yet Egypt is only one country which uses dancing girls to symbolize the passion and sensuality of its culture in order to attract tourists: postcards and travel brochures show pictures of the Sphinx side by side with cabaret dancers in glittering, baby-doll costumes. Spain trades on the passion of flamenco women and Paris advertises itself with an interesting juxtaposition of the Eiffel Tower and the uplifted, open legs of cancan dancers.

Throughout history men's fascination with female sexuality has been equally matched by the fear of it, resulting in valiant efforts to control women. Locking them up in madhouses, confining them in corsets and cumbersome skirts, clitoridectomy, cosmetic surgery: these are only some of the attempts, and women have both defied and colluded with them. The current mania among women for surgically altering their bodies, pumping them full of silicone and the virus Botox, is only the most extreme form of this collusion.

How has it come about, the perception of women as dangerous creatures whose bodies are so poorly designed they need constant modification? And what stimulated this obsession with the female body in the first place?

Perhaps it stems from the fact that, in many cultures, the worship of a single male god replaced religions in which both male and female deities were once honoured for their powers. Under male-centred monotheism women were taken out of the creative picture. They no longer played a part in shaping our world, nor was there a place for them in religious ceremony. Ever since then, man has been the measure of all things. Man, with his intellect, is the arrow shooting forward and woman, with her messy biology, is something of a liability.

As we know, women's bodies have been used to sell everything from cars to financial services. And it isn't only tabloids and sex magazines confined to the top shelf that rely for sales on displaying a woman on the cover.

Years of idealizing men have had little effect on diminishing the obsession with female icons. If anything this obsession has become more exaggerated, as if in subconscious protest at women having been airbrushed out of the religious picture altogether. Music and dance once played a central part in religious worship. When this changed and dance evolved from a sacred rite into a form of entertainment, its female exponents came to replace the vanished goddesses of paganism. They were the visual embodiment of the sensual aspect of our experience; and they were the first performers to be worshipped by the public.

Among all the dancers whose names have come down to us, the one who most merits the title goddess was at the height of her fame in the early years of the twentieth century. The most celebrated Western woman of her time, she inspired the sculptor Auguste Rodin to comment, 'Isadora Duncan's art has influenced my work more than any other inspiration that has come to me. Sometimes I think she is the greatest woman the world has ever known.'

Isadora was loved by artists and public alike for her dancing, but she's remembered most of all for her wildness. She helped redefine the female image for the modern age and she did it through the expressive power of her dancing. A woman of strong emotions and even stronger convictions, the word 'caution' wasn't in her vocabulary, and in her private life she challenged every social convention. She was more than a rebel; she was a revolutionary who offered up sensual expression of the body as a cultural endeavour. And this was in an age when female performers were assumed to inhabit the same underworld as criminals and whores.

Performing in Boston once, she accidentally revealed her breast and there was a great uproar. As the audience made for the exits she stepped down to the footlights and ripped open her costume. 'This is beauty!' she declared.

'My body is beautiful. My movements are beautiful. Not like your half-clad chorus girls.' As the last members of the audience scuttled down the aisles she called after them, 'You were wild once! Don't let them tame you!'

This book celebrates the spirit of Isadora and other dancers who have defied the rules to strut their stuff on the public stage. It looks at how women have found, in dance, a way of accommodating social constraints and subverting their sting; and at how dance has given them independence and a way out of poverty. It also looks at how the battle of the sexes has been played out on the dance floor.

And God Created Devil-Woman

Woman is a narrow pit who lies in wait for her prey.
The Old Testament, Book of Proverbs

For the first time in over twenty years as a dancer, I recently found myself having a brush with the Church. A TV station had broadcast a documentary about my show *Mimi La Sardine*, which included footage of rehearsals in a church hall. When I phoned to book the hall again I was told I'd been banned. A member of the church committee had seen the film and objected to the dancing. But what had he objected to? No one could give me an answer, for though they'd decided to ban me, no one else connected with the church had seen the programme. I found another place to rehearse, sent them a copy of the film and meanwhile took another look at it. I came to a sequence which showed my company rehearsing the wild hair-tossing, spinning movements of a trance dance.

Trance dancing is one of the oldest dances and is still used all across Africa as a form of healing by people suffering from mental and emotional problems. Simple movements are repeated, to an unwavering rhythm, in non-stop motion which may go on for many hours. Anyone who submits to the repetitive movement and driving rhythm may, after a while, go into a true state of trance, which induces a sense of ecstasy and transcendence. At the very least, like other vigorous, sweaty activities, this kind of dancing makes you feel fully, nerve-tinglingly alive and leaves you with a sense of profound well-being.

In an interview for this part of the programme one of the dancers said:

> It's almost a religious experience – if a religious experience is when

you let go, you feel the earth under your feet, you feel safe and secure and trusting in your body. When it really is flowing, I feel fluid, boneless. I can feel every inch of my body, every cell. I'm constantly checking in with myself: Am I here? Can I feel this? I could push this. I'll just try this a bit further. And it's not just push, push, push and beat yourself up if you don't get there. It's more a feeling of open up, softer, trust, release.

It was some weeks before my suspicion was confirmed that this was the scene which had caused all the trouble. But the committee didn't spell out just why an expression of confidence and feeling good about the body was so disturbing to them. They didn't say that trance dancing is the work of the devil and unless we mended our ways we would burn in the fires of hell. They wrote instead that the spiritual connotations of this type of dance were contrary to Christian belief and continued with a quotation from the Bible which begins, 'Come to me, all you who are weary and burdened, and I will give you rest.'

Christianity isn't the only religion to think it has a monopoly on spirituality. Judaism and Islam are also based on the belief that they alone can connect us with the realm of ecstatic experience. And in their own way all three faiths are wary of dance, which can free us and put us in touch with our spirituality without their controlling assistance.

In the European tradition the spirit or soul is held to be a quiet thing, to be discovered through thought and contemplation rather than physical means. In Africa, on the other hand, people use the joyous, life-affirming nature of dance to connect with the soul. And nowhere is the location of spirituality in dance more evident than in trance dancing. This makes it especially dangerous to organized religion, which holds that the source of spirituality is not rooted in ordinary human experience, but in a cerebral discourse with a great father god in the sky.

When Princess Diana died in 1997, and people all over Britain fashioned shrines with flowers and photos and candles, the Church elders sat up. There is something religious in all this, they said. How can we harness people's deep spiritual impulses and bring them back to our empty churches? Too late! For in people's spontaneous rituals to Diana, they were honouring a woman who, for various reasons, had come to mean more to them than the icons of a male-dominated religious faith.

Shortly after Diana's death I was in Tunisia, taking part in a dance documentary, when I was given a poignant reminder of her. One day I went with the crew to watch them shoot a trance ceremony in a remote village. Every Thursday women gathered at the tomb of their local saint to ask for his help with their problems. Before the dancing began a sheep was sacrificed. I watched as a group of men and women were filmed walking down the dirt track, leading the sheep on a frayed length of rope. Drawing near, the cameras picked out a young lad walking beside the animal. He was wearing an open jacket revealing a T-shirt with a giant image of Diana's face on it. When this was noticed the filming stopped and the director ordered the boy to zip up his jacket. It was a pity that he chose to hide this little bit of *ciné-vérité*: alongside the tribute to a long-established male saint we were seeing the image of a new female icon, one to whom ordinary people had been moved to pay extraordinary tribute.

During her life the public projected onto Diana all the attributes of an ancient goddess. She took on the healing role traditional to gods, saints and royalty, a role which royalty has long since abandoned. She came to represent love and suffering and, like many a pagan goddess, she died in her prime, in her case hounded down by the press.

The night before her funeral the atmosphere in London's Mall near the chapel where her body lay was one of carnival. Nobody slaughtered a sheep – and Britain is no longer a country where people of all ages dance spontaneously to express sorrow and joy, so there was no dancing. But in the warm midnight air the crowd swarmed in a pagan mingling of life and death, mourning and celebration. People stood and chatted and drank beer. They crouched down to take a look at the makeshift shrines, their faces illuminated in the flickering candlelight. I watched a group of leather-clad bikers walk to the head of a long queue where people were lining up to sign the condolence book. They unscrewed their flasks and began going down the line, handing out cakes and steaming cups of coffee to those who had been waiting there for hours.

It made me think of the festivals of ancient times, when the entire community united to mourn and celebrate powerful female deities who were thought to hold the secrets of life. If any modern media goddess resembled those pagan deities it was Diana. Like them she was recognizably human. She was full of inconsistencies and frailties. Like them she was both loving and vengeful. And, like the most important goddesses of all, she was regarded as dangerous.

***

In prehistoric times, contemplation of the female body resulted in the fashioning of artefacts that historians refer to as Venuses or goddess figurines. Thousands of them have been unearthed from every continent. Some are delicate objects small enough to fit in the palm of the hand and they hold up their breasts in a pose not unlike that of a modern centrefold. Others are massive, with bulging bellies and monumental thighs. They have been discovered in domestic settings and in tombs and their significance has been the subject of all kinds of speculation.

One theory is that they were religious icons representing a great mother goddess who was revered as the prime creator of life; that they served to give graphic form to the magic of birth; and that their voluptuous contours were a tribute to the female body and its life-giving power. Another theory is that they represent slaves, concubines or wives and were placed in a man's tomb along with his other belongings, to accompany him on his journey into the afterlife.

Then there is the notion that they were simply prehistoric pornography. This is the school of thought – largely represented by men specializing in animal behaviour – which believes that women developed big breasts to attract men's attention rather than to feed their young. The assumption is that the figures were made by men and that, at a time when the human race was occupied with urgent life and death fears, men sat around in caves using their leisure time to dream up artificial aids to sexual stimulation.

It was in the mid-nineteenth century that the Venuses started being unearthed. Archaeology was flourishing and the codes of ancient languages being cracked, including the language of mythology and sacred faith.

At the heart of myth lies our perception of the awesome workings of nature, in all her complementary and contradictory power. We know about the uncertainty of life; we know that the spectre of death lurks alongside birth and that every sunlit figure has its shadow. Myths are a poetic account of these eternal truths. Like dreams, these tales of humans born from the heads of monsters and women with writhing snakes for hair describe what goes on at a subterranean level of consciousness.

Historians were intrigued by the similarity of creation stories in cultures thousands of miles apart, where no Chinese whisper can have penetrated. Many tell of a time before the human race was divided into two sexes. They describe the earth and everything on it as being created by an original androgynous being. When this being, with its combination of male and female attributes, grew too powerful it was separated in order to balance its power. From every continent come myths which describe a universe created by the coupling of earth and sky, sun and moon, and later by a god and goddess. These deities behave just like human beings, with the same jealousies and the same irrational behaviour and weaknesses.

Every culture has its tale of an earth mother from whose belly springs each new generation. This goddess has a companion who is weaker, smaller and younger than her. After impregnating her, his usefulness comes to an end and he dies, sometimes by her own hand – our first hint that this goddess has a dangerous side. Full of sorrow, she undertakes a journey to the underworld to find him. While she is gone the earth is barren. No fruit or flowers grow. Only when she brings him back to earth can nature bloom again. This re-emergence of life in spring was celebrated in the most important of all seasonal festivals, and we are still celebrating it today at Easter.

Since goddesses who created life were thought to possess a destructive side, it's easy to understand how women may have been held in awe as well as apprehension for their unpredictable power. For among her many names the great mother was known as the Dark One, Star of Lamentation, and around her there hovers profound ambivalence.

Fertility rituals, driven by dance and music, were designed to placate this all-devouring dark side and they have been found in nearly all surviving major religions. But in the mythic pattern there is no creation without sacrifice. As part of these rituals an animal was killed, dismembered and buried, the remains were burnt and the ashes scattered over the fields to fertilize the earth. Historians believe these rites became increasingly bloodthirsty and came to involve the sacrifice of a human male – a custom modified, over time, to castration.

A thousand years before the birth of Christ the goddess Cybele attracted a huge following in Anatolia (present-day Turkey). Known as the Lady of Wild Things, her cult was later taken to Rome, whose empire ruled Europe and the entire Middle East. Cybele was the goddess of caverns; she personified the earth in its primitive state and is often shown brandishing a whip. Legend tells that when her lover was unfaithful, she responded by turning him into a god of vegetation. As part of her rituals he was buried and his effigy tied to a tree. Three days later a light appeared in the tomb and he rose from the dead, bringing with him salvation and rebirth for all. In another version of the myth he voluntarily castrates himself, out of remorse for his infidelity.

Cybele was only one of the goddesses whose worship involved castration. Her priests are described dancing in the forest, flinging their heads back and forth as they worked themselves into a frenzy, when they slashed their bodies and sliced off their genitals. They changed sex in order to become the goddess and were afterwards referred to, in their priestly role, as 'she'.

From all over the world come myths equating woman with danger. Her greatest threat was seen as her emasculating power, most graphically expressed in the South American myth of the *vagina dentata*. This sharp-toothed opening was believed to chew up and destroy any penis intrepid enough to enter it.

India's Kali, the Black Mother, has her own way of dispatching her victims: she slices their heads off. Kali is portrayed with rolling, blood-red eyes, dancing on the body of her husband Shiva. Around her neck she wears a string of severed heads from her many male victims and in her hand she holds up the dripping head of her latest trophy.

It was Sigmund Freud who made a connection for the modern age between decapitation fantasies and castration, and every major religion has its version of the emasculating female. The Old Testament has Eve, the original temptress, who introduces man to sexual desire and causes him to be flung out of paradise. And it also has Salome, who danced for Herod in return for the head of a man. Salome is the dance world's most famous temptress, a *femme fatale* who enacts the sacrifice of manhood by using her sexual charms to satisfy a king's lascivious fantasies.

Freud was the first to spell out the neuroses which result from our deep-rooted anxieties about sex. He created a mythology which reflected early twentieth-century fears, and though some of his ideas are no longer fashionable, he was still the first to shine a light into the murkier corners of the human mind. Psychoanalysis was one of the twentieth century's most popular faiths and its symbols, borrowed from ancient mythology, include more than a passing reference to men's helplessness before the spectre of female sexuality.

Freud was writing at a time when the awe and fear of women – as well as the hatred which results from fear – had long since acquired a subtle twist. For, during the past two millennia, much of the human race has been living with the myth of a world made by a great god in the sky. He is a god who rules without a queen and creates without a queen, and this version of creation is just about as far away as we can get from everything we know about the natural world.

By the fifth century AD the hundreds of goddess cults which had flourished in the Mediterranean and the Middle East had been practically eradicated and women, who had once played a vital role in sacred faith, had been banned from serving at the religious ceremonies which took the place of paganism. The feminist writer Camille Paglia contends that this state of affairs came about after a perfectly reasonable rearguard action by men in revolt against women's power and the fearsome excesses of goddess worship.

Whatever the case, men clearly wanted to take back the power they had given over to women. And they realized they weren't going to regain it by cutting off their genitals and pretending to be women themselves. It wasn't enough to officiate as the high priests of goddess cults. It wasn't enough even to control those cults, which they came to do during the classical age in parts of the Middle East. Women had to be written out of the story altogether. The way forward lay in denying them any part in higher creation, as well as in religious ceremony itself. And in learning to control the natural world.

The history of the human race is largely the story of these endeavours and how the hopes and fears they engendered have shaped our world. We've come a long way from the original myth of an androgynous being who created the earth and everything on it; a world governed by balanced and complementary male and female power. And that is our tragedy.

***

Every major world faith has been, if not in theory, certainly in practice, hostile to women. Even Buddhism, which dispensed with gods and goddesses, came to exclude women and made its monks take a vow of celibacy. Religions come into being partly to justify human fears, and at some point in their development most major faiths have moved to outlaw sensual enjoyment. Today, when religious fundamentalists take power, one of the first things they do is to ban music and dance and cover women up. The separation of mind and body, the denial of the flesh for the sake of the spirit, are basic to the three apocalyptic male-centred faiths which all originated in the Middle East and now dominate world politics.

By the time monotheism began taking shape, men had figured out that they too played a part in human reproduction. With this knowledge came a diminished fear of nature and a lowered status for women. As a spoken and written language developed, dance – once our primary form of expression, and one which played a central part in sacred ritual – was replaced by abstract ideas.

Judaism, the first lasting monotheistic religion, was the faith of a tribal people living next to the most advanced of ancient civilizations. But it wasn't Egypt's traditional faith, with its hundreds of gods and goddesses, which may have proved influential to the Hebrews. It was a seventeen-year experiment with monotheism, under the turbulent reign of the pharaoh Akhnaton, who established a new faith dedicated to the worship of a single sky god. After his death he was branded a heretic and a madman, but his beliefs may have come out of Egypt with the exodus of the Hebrews.

Judaism, with its jealous, war-loving god, had a profound influence on the later religions of Christianity and Islam. It broke with the widespread tradition of religious ceremony involving music, dance, fragrance and a total involvement of the senses. It banned the worship of images and sought in every way to reduce sensual expression as part of sacred ritual. It replaced the use of colour with black and white and based its rituals on the novel idea of reading from a book of law. No previous religion had been based on the written word.

Its god was the first who had no visual image to represent him. He had no family, no companions, no human foibles and weaknesses, and he demanded total obedience to his laws on pain of everlasting damnation. His followers declared themselves chosen as upholders of the One Truth. Other religions were regarded as false, their followers inferior. Here was another 'first' scored by the Hebrews – the first example of religious intolerance, as historian Leonard Shlain comments:

> By their very nature polytheistic religions fostered tolerance. Piety did not lead ineluctably to religious hatred as it has so often in history. Although there were many bloody conflicts fought over land, women, booty, or to avenge perceived wrong, there were no religious wars in the ancient world before monotheism. One plausible explanation: monotheism does not mirror human society. Humans are first and foremost human animals. A deity who was alone, not by choice but because there were no other companions for Him, was a concept without parallel in human society.

But there's a price to pay for worshipping this abstract God. For, if everyone agrees that there is only one of him, and different groups perceive him in different ways, then whose god is the right one? This question, as Shlain comments, 'has goaded monotheists to wage war with an intensity and purpose never witnessed in polytheistic cultures'.

The most extraordinary concept of Judaism was that, despite the overwhelming evidence of nature's duality, creation was understood to be an exclusively male affair. Many of the strange concepts behind ancient mythology and early religion are equally amusing; but the fact that this idea continues to dominate world religion in the twenty-first century must make us wonder how far we've evolved, intellectually speaking, from our primitive past.

Not only did God create the world on his own, but women's part in human reproduction is portrayed in the Old Testament as being, at best, unreliable. It's significant that three of Judaism's founding fathers were married to women who failed to conceive. With God's permission Abraham, Isaac and Jacob all turned away from their old, barren wives and went to their servant-girls to found dynasties, confirming that it wasn't men's fault if their wives didn't become pregnant. So negative was woman's role in creation, according to the Hebrews' new faith, that it went to ludicrous lengths to deny it. In the Old Testament food, instead of springing from the fruitful earth, is made to rain down from heaven, the abode of the new sky god, in the form of manna.

Male-centred faiths allow women no part in their ceremonial. In the Christian Church the subject of female priests remains a highly contentious issue to this day. In synagogues and mosques women sit in a place apart and, in ultra-orthodox synagogues, they are concealed from view so that male worshippers won't be led astray by distracting thoughts about the female body.

Women were humbled in numerous ways by the male-centred religions of the Middle East. Their status was systematically downgraded and they were deprived of all kinds of rights, including that of owning property. Instead they were turned into property themselves. (The Hebrew word for wife – *beulah* – means one who is owned.)

Even a woman's talent for making herself and her home pleasing to the eye came under attack. In the *Book of Proverbs* men are warned to avoid women who perfume their beds with aromatic herbs and oils, and cautioned against those who announce their presence with glittering, tinkling jewellery.

Even now, ultra-orthodox branches of Judaism insist that a bride shave her head when she marries, and for the rest of her life she either wears a wig or else covers her bald head beneath a scarf. In myth and sacred faith, hair carries a potent sexual charge, and losing her hair can only serve to diminish a woman's confidence. As for sex, in ultra-orthodox versions of Judaism it became something to be engaged in purely for procreation; and to make sure no pleasure was involved it had to take place through a hole in the sheet.

In order to establish itself in the region Judaism (followed by Christianity and then Islam) changed the sex of the ancient goddesses and repressed their rituals. In Arabia black stone monoliths representing female deities were worshipped right up until the time of Muhammad.

The concept of religious sacrifice has never really disappeared though. The story of Christ himself is a version of ancient fertility myths: the sacrifice of a man in exchange for eternal life. Nor should we forget our wild whip lady Cybele and her eunuch priests, or the Virgin Mary's celibate clergy.

Though pagan goddess figures gradually faded from memory there is one who, intriguingly, remains: Sarah the Egyptian, a black madonna who is still worshipped in parts of Europe. In Spain her statue is paraded through the streets every year during Easter. Many of Europe's medieval churches once contained a statue of this enigmatic figure.

With male-centred religions came increased control of female sexuality, a move aimed at establishing paternity and property rights. For organized religion, sex is a necessary evil which has to be controlled in order to avoid social chaos and death. (The story of Adam and Eve is only one of many myths which reinforce the connection between sex and death that lies buried in our subconscious.) The belief lingered on that sexual conduct might cause harm by offending the gods, who would punish the community indiscriminately, the good along with the bad.

Four to five hundred years after the death of Christ a small number of Church Fathers entertained themselves by devising a catalogue of sexual sins. Driven by the desire for spiritual purity and closeness to God, they subdued their sexual desires by embracing celibacy and went on to justify the practice with theological argument. It was St Paul who started all the trouble. He warned men against having anything to do with women, who were likely to tempt them from the path of virtue, given half the chance.

Rules concerning sexual behaviour which are woven into monotheism spring from an extraordinary, exaggerated contempt and fear of the body. Christianity isn't alone in having bizarre sexual beliefs, but the Old

Testament does include something very curious, and it's to do with women dancing. The Song of Songs is a love duet between a man and woman, and it's strange to come across it amid the smoke and fire of the Bible. Carlos Suares has interpreted the Song of Songs according to the code of the kabbala, the mystical branch of Judaism. He discusses a verse towards the end, in which the man begs his veiled Shulamite to dance for him:

> *Your rounded thighs are like jewels,*
> *The work of a master hand.*
> *Your navel is a rounded bowl*
> *That never lacks mixed wine.*
> *Your belly is a heap of wheat*
> *Encircled with lilies.*

At first glance this doesn't suggest much in the way of movement. But when Suares looks at the translation of specific words a different picture emerges. The Hebrew *yerekh* means hips as well as thighs. Suares goes on to say that the usual translation of *hhalaeem* as 'jewels' isn't really accurate, for the root of this word is *hhal*, meaning to dance, writhe or tremble. So instead of 'Your rounded thighs are like jewels,' we have an image of curvaceous hips in motion. Another line examined by Suares is 'Earthly fire is active in your fertile body.' Here the woman describes herself as a keeper of vineyards, another symbol of fruitful production, and says she wants to show her desire for her lover by dancing for him as a prelude to sex.

Is this a song about a women's dance celebrating fertility, asks Suares? And if so, does it hark back to pagan rituals that Judaism either destroyed or else accepted after changing their meaning? For any incoming religion has to accommodate at least some of people's existing beliefs in order to gain a foothold. And when a new faith absorbs a myth which runs counter to its teachings it may well alter its meaning, even to the point of reversing it. This is what happened to many of the myths which were eventually absorbed into monotheism.

Whatever the case, the Song of Songs must remain the enigma of the Old Testament: an island of sunlit sensuality set in the raging sea of the scriptures.

***

At weddings in Egypt a professional dancer entertains the guests, then goes to have her photo taken with the bride and groom, who both place a hand on her belly. The ancient significance of her dancing is only a pale memory now, when this women's dance has long since evolved into more than a fertility rite. It has become the best-loved dance of the Middle East and no celebration is complete without it. Yet women who perform it in public transgress a basic Islamic code that women should not flout their bodies in front of male strangers.

Islam is no different from other male-centred faiths in making women carry the burden for men's uncontrollable urges with which they have failed to come to terms. Muslims say that the sensual aspect of existence is celebrated in Islam, that it's not separated off or hidden away. And indeed, the paradise of the Quran is a land of the most intense, exaggerated pleasures. But if we imagine Islam is a faith which celebrates sensual enjoyment for all, we are in for a disappointment. For when we read closely we discover that this paradise is designed to please only half the human race. It's maintained by female slaves who do the menial work and houris whose job is to satisfy male desire. When a man enters paradise he is given seventy-two of these houris, whose bodies are made of sweet-smelling musk and who bear his name in the form of a tattoo branded on their breast. Islam's most sacred writings say nothing about a woman's pleasure though, and there is no male equivalent of the houri provided to cater to female desires in paradise.

The word paradise means 'walled garden'. In this neat, tidy garden with its pathways and fountains and channels of water, nature is always in bloom. There are no seasons of drought, no time of hibernation for rest and renewal. Tree trunks are made of hard pearl and covered in precious stones. Everything has been stripped away which bears any resemblance to nature as we know it, red in tooth and claw. It's a place in which natural processes have been rejected and substituted with something perfectly glorious and perfectly artificial.

For thousands of years men of all faiths have been busy dreaming up ways of curbing the wildness of nature and replacing it with something they can control. But the illusion of having succeeded in the grand design of taming the wild is regularly shattered in the most violent way. Every storm and hurricane, every outbreak of a new, incurable disease or the re-emergence of an old one once thought eradicated is nature's savage reminder of her supremacy.

In the modern world everything is geared to hiding signs of grisly nature and our primitive origins. Everywhere attempts to control women continue. These attempts have been responsible for denying women education or any kind of public presence. They've been responsible for clitoridectomy, for shutting women away in nunneries and covering them in veils. As for the attempt to control female biology, it continues to yield interesting results. Thanks to the ingenuity of the human brain, we can now regulate conception, choose the sex of a child, pay someone else to carry an unborn foetus and plan the date, even the time, a baby will be born.

Despite all this, efforts to control female sexuality have yielded negligible results. Recent British surveys reveal that a surprisingly large number of men are bringing up children whom they mistakenly believe they have fathered. It must be frustrating for them that, despite their best efforts, women's sexuality continues to break out of even the most unlikely soil, like green shoots in spring.

***

Twenty years ago few people who lived far from the Indian village of Khajuraho knew about its temples. For many years they lay unnoticed by the outside world, strangled by weeds and abandoned to the weather. Today they are a popular tourist destination. Nestling in forests where tigers still prowl, only twenty out of the eighty-five temples thought to have been built between the ninth and twelfth centuries are still standing. Their facades are thickly covered with sculptures that it must have taken thousands of craftsmen to carve, and it's these which attract visitors from all over the world. People particularly come to see those which show men and women folded together in erotic bliss.

Christian explorers who hacked their way through the undergrowth to uncover the secrets hidden within the forest around Khajuraho professed to finding the erotic statues profoundly obscene. Over the years increasing interest in them has led to the recurring question of how the temples became what have been described as monuments to erotic delight. So well-known are they that, if you hadn't visited the site, you might think their facades were exclusively devoted to illustrating the *Kama Sutra*. But the temple walls chronicle all aspects of human activity, from men engaged in battle to temple dancers applying their make-up.

What the erotic carvings among this profusion of images demonstrate is acceptance of human sexuality. And in this respect Hinduism differs starkly from monotheism, which distrusts and fears the power of sex and offers denial of the flesh for the sake of the spirit. Hinduism is a faith which (despite being more puritan now than it once was) doesn't consider that sexual desire is something to be 'overcome'. It recognizes that without Shakti, the goddess of female energy, the god Shiva is nothing. Sexuality is accepted, with all its aspects of mystery, danger and ecstatic experience. The complementary nature of male and female and the beauty of the sensual world are reflected in the Hindu wedding ceremony in which bride and groom wear garlands of vivid orange and yellow blooms and say to each other, 'I am the melody, you are the words. You are the melody, I am the words.'

The belief that the physical and the spiritual need not necessarily be at war has never been more graphically illustrated than at Khajuraho. Its temples, it has been suggested, were built as centres of tantrism, a doctrine contained within Hinduism. In tantrism, release through sensual enjoyment is part of the soul's journey towards enlightenment. Religious worship is an exercise in beauty designed to awaken the senses, and this is illustrated perfectly by dance, which offers the beauty of the body as a source of delight. Khajuraho's sculptures of dancing priestesses have a joyous quality, their voluptuous curves twisting and turning as they lift their arms in languorous poses, a mysterious smile playing about their lips.

Over thousands of years and successive invasions a multi-layered culture developed in India. One of the most far-reaching came from a wave of Aryan warriors from central Asia, around 1500 BC. These war-mongering, patriarchal people spent a couple of centuries subduing most of the subcontinent and its subjects. Like any other conquerors they grafted onto Indian culture their own social and religious tenets, which became enshrined in India's cultural-cum-religious text, the *Rig Veda*. Parts of this book already existed prior to the Indo-Aryan invasion, and this early section describes Indian culture as an egalitarian one in which women enjoyed considerable power and status. By 300 BC, however, when a civil code (the Law of Manu) was added to the *Rig Veda*, a different type of sentiment towards women was in place: 'The source of dishonour is woman; the source of strife is woman; the source of earthly existence is woman; therefore avoid woman.'

If we think it strange that we are being encouraged to avoid the source and continuation of life, we must remember that Hinduism is based on the Law of Karma. Every religion asks what happens to us after we die. Some offer the carrot of eternal life in a heaven or paradise so exquisite that it rivals the joys of earthly existence. Hinduism, on the other hand, has come up with the answer that, rather than moving on to another, more glorious, life we come back in another form. This form depends on our karma: that is, on how good we've been during our most recent incarnation. Our eventual goal is to escape the cycle of repeated lifetimes and not come back at all. As for women, if they have obeyed their husbands and behaved well, they're offered the chance of coming back higher on the evolutionary chain ... as men.

By the time the Law of Manu was written many of women's early powers had been eroded. Later additions to the *Rig Veda* describe woman as an inferior being, 'an insignificant receptacle for the unilaterally effective male fluid ... a thing to be possessed'. The notion of women's independence no longer existed. Every woman had become subordinate to the men in her family, subject first to her father, then her husband and then, if he should die, her sons. Their permission had to be obtained for all kinds of activities.

By the third century BC suttee, the ritual suicide of a wife at her husband's funeral, was being enforced. This was rationalized as a necessary measure, which would avoid her becoming destitute; for widows were forbidden by law to remarry. The Greek historian Strabo, who travelled to India during this century, reported that priests justified suttee as being a kind of insurance against a wife poisoning her husband while he was alive, which must tell us something about conjugal relations at the time.

Many centuries later the storytelling art of Indian dance was reshaped to emphasize the social position of women. Classical dance evolved from the temple dancing of priestesses, brides of the gods who were known as *devadasis*. Their rise dates from around the ninth and tenth centuries AD, when many temples were being built in South India, some of them dedicated to the priestesses who danced within their grounds. *Devadasis*, many of whom began training in their childhood, served in the temples and performed at festivals involving the entire community. Some were offered to the temples as young girls by parents too poor to give them a dowry; others were married women unhappy with their husbands, or widows who, if they didn't throw themselves on their husband's funeral pyre, would be left destitute.

Devadasis handed down their dance to their daughters. They lived within the temple complex, which served as the heart of community life, and they had enormous freedom compared to other Indian women. They could read and write and own property; indeed, property was passed down through the female line, in contrast to Indian tradition. They took lovers from among the men who visited the temples to pay homage to the gods and who offered donations for the temple's upkeep and also, no doubt, to gain favour with the *devadasis*.

In the eleventh century the Muslims arrived in India and subjugated almost the entire continent. The Muslim practice of secluding women in separate quarters became part of everyday life in India, where it was known as purdah. The Mughal period had a dramatic effect on Indian art and culture, including its religious dancing, for, as Islamic influence increased, Hindu temples received less in the way of revenue and the *devadasis* were forced to find other ways of supporting themselves. So began the development of a secular tradition of dance at the Hindu court of Jaipur and the Muslim courts of Delhi and Agra. Many *devadasis* were taken into the palaces, where they provided entertainment and were also requisitioned into the harems of Hindu rajahs and Muslim rulers. Naturally enough, when they noticed that their patrons were more interested in them as women than performers, they realized they could use this to improve their status and began developing a more alluring style of dance.

The evolution of dancing from sacred rite to secular entertainment happened in other parts of East Asia too. In Japan dispossessed temple dancers were forced to find a living elsewhere. Some who failed to find court patronage became itinerant artists, offering unsolicited entertainment, much like street performers today. Among all the women trying to earn a living in the outside world there would have been many who were desperately poor, and also prostitutes, for whom dance became an added string to their bow. As it was only permitted to earn money from religious dancing, these women naturally claimed they had been attached to temples. So began a blurring between sacred and secular dance, and a blurring between the professions of dancer and prostitute which still exists today in some societies.

***

Of all the dangerous dancers who have come down to us through religion, the most notorious first appears in the New Testament and she's been popping up ever since, on stage and screen, in literature and art. There's only a brief mention of Salome in the Bible, yet an extraordinary number of associations surround the dance world's most famous *femme fatale*. Salome's dance isn't described in the Bible, but it's assumed to be an early form of striptease – although Middle Eastern women's dancing isn't about removing clothes, but about moving the hips and torso in subtle, alluring ways. There's nothing to indicate that Salome danced for a religious purpose, but there are many pointers which link her story to pagan sacrificial ritual.

According to the Gospels the prophet John the Baptist is found preaching in the wilderness, heralding the coming of the Son of God, who will save mankind from their sins. John is a political and religious trouble-maker and it isn't long before he's arrested and thrown into jail by Herod Antipas, who governs the area as part of the Roman Empire's desert lands. On Herod's birthday he asks Salome to dance for him. (In the story's incestuous twist, she happens to be both his stepdaughter and his niece.) He is so overcome by her dancing that he offers her the extraordinary gift of anything up to half his kingdom. Salome asks for the head of the Baptist, and though Herod is reluctant to kill a religious prophet with a large following, he agrees.

It's a curious tale. What does the Baptist mean to Salome, that she should want his death? In Oscar Wilde's play, he has her ask for the Baptist's head out of frustrated passion – as did all those who tackled the theme after Wilde. In his play Salome descends to the prison to tempt John, who ignores her entreaties and carries on preaching, in the way of mad religious prophets. A woman scorned, she wreaks her revenge by asking for his head on a plate – a nice touch, for a banquet.

As we've seen, Freud connected decapitation with castration stories. It reminds us of those pagan myths which describe the sacrifice of a male figure to fertilize the earth, and the castration rites long lost to memory. One of these is the story of the Babylonian love goddess Ishtar, who dresses in all her finery and goes down to the underworld to look for her dead lover. She has to pass through seven gates, and at each gate she removes one of her veils as the price of admission. At the seventh gate she takes off her last remaining veil, reveals her final mystery and is reunited with her lover. Only when she returns to earth with him does nature bloom again.

It seems that this myth of seasonal change is the origin of the best-known dance of all time. Salome is assumed to have performed a dance of seven veils. But unlike Ishtar, who gives up her veils in order to restore a man's life, Salome gives them up to bring about the death of a man. The Bible tale is one of sacrifice and emphasizes what was seen as the dark, destructive aspect of women's power, the evil magic of female sexuality.

Salome seldom appeared as a subject of Western art and literature until the late nineteenth century. Then, in the space of a few years, she became the most popular temptress of a period obsessed by the *femme fatale*. Amateur and professional dancers, actresses, even society hostesses all had a stab at portraying her. The most successful of all was Canadian dancer Maud Allan, who built her entire career around the tale. Her *Vision of Salome* was described in glowing terms by the press:

The pink pearls slip amorously about her bosom and throat as she moves, while the long strand of pearls that floats from the belt about her waist floats languorously apart from her smooth hips. The desire that flames from her eyes and bursts in hot flames from her scarlet mouth infects the very air with the madness of passion. Swaying like a witch with yearning hands and arms that plead, Miss Allan is such a delicious embodiment of lust that she might win forgiveness with the sins of such wonderful flesh. As Herod catches the fire, so Salome dances even as a Bacchante, twisting her body like a silver snake eager for its prey, panting hot with passion, the fires of her eyes scorching like a living furnace.

A dancer of considerable artistic pretensions, Allan introduced her *Vision of Salome* to the Viennese public in 1906. She publicized herself as a respectable artist whose work was drawn from biblical and classical sources. She created a personal mythology which she published in a (somewhat fictional) autobiography, but this approach proved a winner and her Salome met with huge success. At one performance twenty members of parliament were spotted in the audience and, such was her popularity, postcards and statuettes of her image sold by the thousand. It is a measure of her fame that, in time, she became the butt of comedians' jokes and was parodied by other music-hall performers, as well as becoming an early gay icon.

Allan was taken up by the British prime minister Herbert Asquith and his wife Margot (who replied famously to Jean Harlow's mispronounciation of her name, 'The "t" is silent, as in Harlow'). The Asquiths offered to pay the rent on Allan's Holford House apartment in London. This mansion, with its 150 rooms furnished with spindly-legged chairs, ceiling-high, gilt-framed mirrors and leopard-skin rugs, was a former residence of King George IV – a fitting setting for a dancer with grand ambitions.

In 1908 Allan celebrated her 250th performance of *The Vision of Salome*. So successful was the piece that she continued to rely on it as her principal creation over the following twelve years. In 1909, travelling to Birmingham for a single performance, she was met by 1,000 fans who stood waiting patiently to catch a glimpse of her at the stage door. Later on, hundreds of them bought platform tickets to wave her off on the train back to London. That same night she gave her usual show in London's West End, then rounded off the evening performing for the Earl and Countess of Dudley at a party attended by Edward VII and his wife. As Prince of Wales, Edward had been notorious for his amorous exploits, especially with dancers and actresses in Paris. The rumour that Allan had had an affair with the king only prompts the thought, who had not? But the gossip that she enjoyed lesbian as well as heterosexual relationships was more dangerous to her reputation.

In Britain there was not the same tolerance of sexual diversity as in France, and men in high places who indulged in 'vice', as it was known, lived in fear of discovery and blackmail. Lesbianism, unlike homosexuality, was not a criminal activity in Britain. (Popular history tells us that this was because when it was suggested to Queen Victoria that lesbianism should be criminalized, she refused to believe such a thing existed.) Homosexuality had been the cause of Oscar Wilde's downfall at the height of his fame and, by an uncanny twist of fate which linked him to Maud Allan through their exploration of Salome's story, lesbianism was to be responsible for the dancer's own fall from grace.

For a long time Allan could do no wrong. Such was the power of her carefully constructed myth, as well as her stage presence, that there were those in the audience who swore they had seen her dance naked, though this was never the case. Her Salome was calculated to be sensational, and the way in which she grasped the severed head of John the Baptist and kissed its bloodstained lips caused shudders of thrilling disgust to run through the audience. When a Hungarian count offered her 10,000 marks to dance in a lion's cage she cheated by substituting harmless little cubs. But the count honoured his debt, Allan donated the money to a hospital and he followed up by inviting her to give a performance at his palace.

An American guest present at the occasion reported on its shocking outcome. As a black servant carried in the head of the Baptist on a giant platter, the dancer bent down to its lips:

> Gently the severed head touched her wrists, and there shot through her a terrible tremor, a shivering of the soul. Upon her white flesh were the stains, dark crimson clots. It was blood. Her body rigid as though carved in marble, the dancer slowly forced her eyes to the face she held aloft. It was the face of a man not long since dead. As one from whom life passes very quickly, she crumpled to the floor. From her hands dropped the head. It rolled upon her breast and fell beside her, leaving upon her white body a crimson trail. So was the dancer Maud Allan taught that it is not well to jest with a noble of Hungary.

The substitution of a real severed head for a papier mâché model makes us wonder whether there may have been more to this Dracula-like scene than meets the eye. For Allan had a skeleton in the family cupboard, dating back to her youth in San Francisco.

As a medical student her brother Theo had suffered from what was then called 'brain fever' and was probably a kind of nervous breakdown. On 13 September 1895 the naked bodies of two women in their early twenties were found hidden away in the Baptist church attended by Maud Allan's family. One of them had been hacked to death and her breasts slashed, the other was laid out as if for a medical examination. The crime was compared to the contemporary serial slayings of Jack the Ripper in London. Discussion in medical journals and the popular press focused on the madness bred by the lowered moral tone of society, where the only outlet for people's neuroses was violence.

Theo had been acquainted with both murdered women. He was found guilty of the crime and sentenced to death. And, in a grisly foretaste of Maud's later career, it was reported that, following his execution, his mother hysterically kissed her dead son's lips.

The crime was widely reported in the press and it's possible that the Hungarian count's American wife knew of Maud's family secret. The suggestion has been made that she was paying him back for his interest in the dancer, and at the same time confronting her with past events in her history which may, by an interesting reversal, have influenced her most celebrated stage creation.

By 1915 Allan's career had begun to falter and she was reported living in a seedy part of Hollywood with her parents, making a film. Then, three years later, she was stopped in her tracks. Noel Billing was a British member of parliament who had set himself the task of unmasking homosexuals and lesbians. He believed they had played an important part in sabotaging the war effort, through the use of blackmail. As co-founder of the extreme right-wing Vigilante Society, he was dedicated to 'the promotion of purity in public life', to exposing corruption and vice in high places, and to bringing an end to the decadence which was seen as poisoning the fabric of social life. (He himself had a long-term mistress tucked away in the shadows.) Members of the society were part of a vigorous campaign against both Oscar Wilde's *Salome* and Strauss's opera of the same name.

Wilde's personal downfall was past history. Now it was the turn of Allan. Tainted in some people's eyes by having had lesbian lovers, as well as by displaying her body immodestly on-stage, she had built her career on the depiction of the most notorious dancing temptress of all time. On 16 February 1918 the society's journal, *The Vigilante*, mentioned Allan in a boxed paragraph headed 'The Cult of the Clitoris'. At that time very few people understood the meaning of the word, but using it in print was as great a taboo as the word 'fuck' still is (unbelievable as it may seem) 100 years later. Allan brought proceedings against Billing for criminal and obscene libel in an attempt to clear her name.

The Billing trial was an introduction, for the tabloid-reading public, to the details of lesbian activity. In *Wilde's Last Stand*, Philip Hoare writes:

> Three years later, in 1921, when an extension to the anti-homosexual laws was proposed to encompass lesbianism, it passed the Commons, but not the Lords, where Lord Desart reasoned, 'You are going to tell the whole world that there is such an offence, to bring it to the notice of women who have never heard of it, never thought of it, never dreamed of it. I think that is a very great mischief.'

Like the case of Oscar Wilde, the Billing case fascinated society at every level. A large part of the proceedings furnished a kind of re-run of Wilde's trial, by focusing on the 'immorality' of his play and its encouragement of 'unnatural vices' such as sadism and necrophilia. Allan could be accused of inciting audiences to both by biting the lips of the Baptist's severed head. When the verdict was passed on Billing (that he was 'not guilty' of having accused the dancer of being a lesbian), the crowd in the gallery jumped to their feet with wild applause and cheering.

Following her defeat, Allan became *persona non grata* in the eyes of London theatre managers. Her career spluttered on, with tours in obscure places, but she was never to regain her former popularity. Her assistant Doris Langley Moore wrote that, 'An atmosphere of supreme decorum surrounded her, the watchful decorum of one who is conscious of things to be lived down.' For many years Allan continued to live with her dog Perky in the decayed splendour of Holford House, surrounded by peeling walls, fallen plaster and shutters hanging off their hinges. She died in 1956 in impoverished obscurity in a Los Angeles convalescent home, the most notorious Salome of them all.

Sexual Imposters

The ideal woman can only be expressed by a male performer.
Yoshizawa Ayama

In 1985 I was asked to dance for the charity event *Fashion Aid* at London's Royal Albert Hall. My part was to shimmy down the catwalk as part of a designer's oriental collection. The atmosphere backstage was as sexually charged as at any rock concert. The models had nothing to do all day but look in the mirror and touch up their make-up; they leaned in the doorways of the subterranean dressing-rooms, chatting and flirting with passing men. Exotic birds in vivid plumage, they swaggered down the catwalk on six-inch spikes, throwing their hips from side to side. They oozed sexuality, yet there was something disquieting about them. Their legs were too long, their swollen silicone breasts too ample for their pared-down frames, and where they should have had fleshy hips and bottoms they had jutting bones.

Every culture has its own constantly changing image of the visually perfect woman. Down the years this ideal was first embodied by dancers, who were leaders of fashion and among the most widely copied women of their day. They and the actresses and models who came after them replaced the religious goddesses of antiquity in the popular imagination as revered, larger-than-life figures.

Performers were once revered for more than their physical appearance, but today's fashion models rely on provoking envy and desire for their bodies alone. Many refer to themselves as 'performers', and so they are. With their restructured bodies and extravagant clothes they belong in the world of female impersonation. A fashion model's body is an artefact moulded to suit the fantasies of dress designers. And today's designers prefer women who look like adolescent boys – which suggests a dislike, not to say a revulsion, for the natural female body.

There's no getting away from the fact that, historically, fashion has been dominated by men. They have held the purse strings and it's they who have dictated the ideals of female desirability. Throughout history women have bent over backwards to comply with other people's ideas about how they should look. Long before the twentieth century they were surgically remaking their bodies and torturing themselves in pursuit of fashion. Today the degree of surgical interference which even teenage girls are prepared to tolerate is rising at an alarming rate. But these operations are mild, compared to a form of self-torture to which women were subjected 1,000 years ago in China, a form of disfigurement which is said to have originated among dancers at the royal court.

***

In tenth-century China, affluent men considered the most sexually exciting part of a woman's body to be her feet. Dancers' feet were bandaged up in childhood so that they only grew to three or four inches. It's debatable whether dancers invented this form of self-mutilation themselves, for it maimed a part of the body which had to be strong and flexible for their work. We'll never know whether they were simply obeying the orders of their dancing masters when they agreed to have their feet bound; but we only have to look at the way classical ballerinas torture their feet to realize that masochism in pursuit of beauty is still intrinsic to the dance world.

In time foot-binding led to the art of dance becoming obsolete in China. Meanwhile the custom had caught on among the Chinese aristocracy and the aspiring middle class. Its purpose was to make a distinction between the big feet of poor girls and the delicate feet of those who didn't need to work. A woman with bound feet could neither work nor walk very far, and sometimes the only way she could move was to crawl along the floor. It was said that her tiny, bandaged feet aroused the protective (!) instincts of men, who were excited by her hobbling walk as well. Sex manuals listed the many positions in which sex could take place at the same time as allowing a man to fondle a woman's stunted stumps of feet. Parents knew they could sell their daughters as prostitutes at a higher price if they had deformed feet, and girls were praised for bearing the excruciating pain of binding, which resulted in broken bones for life. Even when this custom was abolished by the Manchu dynasty in the seventeenth century, women continued practising it secretly on their daughters. Right up to the 1930s tiny ornate shoes were still being made in China, not for dolls but for little girls.

Foot-binding was carried out in early childhood, retarding the foot's growth and deforming its bone structure. It reached a point where these dwarf feet were considered essential if a girl were to make a good marriage. Parents seeking a wife for their son asked about the size of a girl's feet first, rather than whether she was pretty or not.

The most alluring Chinese courtesans developed a swaying walk that was regarded as highly erotic, and imitating this walk became *de rigueur* for Chinese actors taking on female roles. (On the Chinese stage, as in most of Asia, women's roles were taken by men in drag.) As theatre historian A. C. Scott tells us, 'The mere sight of a popular actor of women's roles in the old days, one hand on swaying hip and flicking a coquettish handkerchief, was enough to bring down a delighted roar from the gallery.' Scott goes on to say that, when women were finally accepted on the Chinese stage as recently as the 1930s, 'they had to learn all the artful devices invented by men to simulate femininity on the stage, including the technique which enabled them to imitate walking on bound feet'.

The image of the Chinese actor *en travesti*, one hand on hip, the other waving a hanky as he totters across the stage, is a cliché of female impersonation. But how many of today's drag queens know how far back in time the model for this, their classic routine, originated?

***

The tradition of female impersonation arose because women were forbidden to perform in public. Today cross-dressing dancers of all kinds can be found all over the world. From the highly regarded Japanese *onnagata* to the male cabaret dancers of the Middle East and the despised *hijras* of India, men continue to enter the world of the opposite sex through dance.

No one knows how many *hijras* there are today in major Indian cities. Estimates suggest that there are between 50,000 and 2 million of these entertainers, who live in what has been described as a shadowy half-world of superstition and extortion. They go round in gangs, gatecrashing weddings and baby-naming ceremonies. Feared for their curses and their capacity to embarrass people, they are tolerated and reviled at the same time. A well-organized community, they are alert to every forthcoming local celebration. They turn up to murmur blessings and sprinkle rice even if they haven't been invited and, as often as not, they aren't at all welcome. Nine times out of ten they end up resorting to a variety of threats – such as lifting their skirts and displaying their mutilated genitals – until they're paid to go away. Not to pay them is to risk being cursed. They have been likened to a kind of small-time mafia. British journalist Peter Popham describes them as India's professional gatecrashers who go 'prancing into shops, dancing and clapping and threatening to expose themselves if they are not adequately bribed to go away. The whole thing is a baroquely extended oriental variant of door-to-door carol singing.'

Only a tiny minority of *hijras* are born eunuchs. The rest undergo castration, which may or may not be voluntary. Poor families may sell their young sons into the trade and good-looking boys are kidnapped and forcibly castrated. The operation is often performed in the most barbarous conditions and many boys die from infections caused by the mixture of cow dung and herbs applied to their wounds following the operation. For *hijras* this operation symbolizes rebirth, a kind of reincarnation, with the chance of a new life.

In 1977, when *hijras* were asked the reason for what they did, they replied that they were dedicated to the service of a goddess called Renuka. But the rocking hips and jumping bellies of today's *hijras* are probably a remote parody of the Indian temple dancing which, thousands of years ago, was performed by boys and natural eunuchs in the service of religion. It was in the eleventh century that boys began replacing priestesses who danced in front of religious effigies and acted as intermediaries between humans and the gods. Mixed troupes of entertainers were banned and over the next 5,000 years the females among them gradually disappeared.

This happened mainly as a result of the Muslim invasion of India and the consequent social segregation of men and women. In the lands conquered by Islam, women lived in separate quarters from men (known in India as *purdah*) and occupied themselves with domestic matters. The public domain was the domain of men, a place from which half the human race then vanished, or else appeared only when safely concealed behind veils. Hidden from the eyes of men, women – especially wealthy women – acquired a mystique which was to make them both more, and at the same time less, than human. No doubt their unavailability also had a profound effect on sexual habits in countries conquered by those Arabs who rode out of the desert and imposed their religion on India, Persia and the entire Middle East.

India was particularly influenced by Persian aesthetics for its version of Islam. And in Persia it was young men who epitomized ideal beauty. Though the word *hijra* is generally said to come from the Persian *hiz*, meaning effeminate, there are some scholars who suggest its origin is *hich*, meaning 'a person who is nowhere – a thing which has no place – no identity or personality of its own'. If so, it's a poignant reflection of the status of today's *hijra*s, who are regarded as even lower than India's despised untouchables.

***

From earliest times, most societies considered it unsuitable for a girl to be a public performer unless she was from the working class. In Shakespeare's England the theatre was no place for a woman. Apart from anything else, it was considered the height of immodesty for a woman to draw attention to herself in public. The Elizabethan age explored sexual ambiguity and androgyny is a common theme in Shakespeare, reflecting the contemporary fashion for cross-dressing. Women were seen wearing men's puffed-out breeches (known as hose), which revealed a good deal of leg; they wore men's high beaver hats and carried swords and daggers for good measure.

It was such a breach of decorum for a woman to carry a weapon that various observers put quill to parchment on the subject. One anonymous pamphleteer claimed that women who wore men's doublets left them unfastened in order to display their breasts; another moaned that these half-men, half-women were a great distraction in church. Conversely, men who wore long curled wigs and frizzed hair were attacked for looking effeminate, and young boys who took female parts on-stage were considered especially provocative. They were seen as encouraging wantonness and lust, and much ink was spilled on the subject of whether the theatre encouraged homoeroticism.

Only with the restoration of the monarchy in 1660 were women allowed to appear on the English stage. King Charles II reopened the theatres which had remained closed during the Civil War. He was used to seeing women on-stage at the court of his cousin, the French king, Louis XIV, and he wasn't interested in watching men in drag in his own country. (This English stage slang goes back to the middle of the seventeenth century, when 'flashing the drag' described a man putting on a woman's skirts, which dragged on the ground.) Charles issued a royal charter to the effect that, from now on, female roles must be taken by women to stop the 'scandalous and offensive' abuse of having boys stand in for the fair sex.

In England women would never again be banned from performing in public. But in other parts of the world women's roles as dancers and actors continued to be taken by men, and female impersonation developed into an art.

***

The template for the ideal woman has been studied and brought to a pitch of stage perfection by the *onnagata* of Japan. These men devote a lifetime to portraying the ideal woman in a form of theatre invented in Kyoto by a dancer at around the same time that Shakespeare was writing his dramas. Kyoto was the first Japanese city to host an official pleasure quarter. The neighbourhood was a magnet for women who flocked there to work in its tea houses, places which offered entertainment as well as refreshment. Some of the women had lost their husbands; others were unemployed priestesses; many were prostitutes for corrupt priests who sent them out all over the country to raise money for their temples.

The pleasure quarter was known as the 'floating world' or 'water business'. It was a place apart, a city within a city, where every kind of entertainment was strictly supervised. The bitter-sweet life lived by its inhabitants came, in time, to be described by the word *ukiyo*, a Buddhist term originally meaning the transience of all things. In the floating world people could forget their sorrow at the fleeting nature of life by indulging to the hilt in life's sensual pleasures.

But attempts to control this world (and sweep it under the carpet) by confining it to its own neighbourhood were doomed to failure, for it was simply the most glamorous and fashionable place to go. And, in Japan's strictly segregated society, it was the only place where the classes were free to mix. It had the best entertainment, the most gorgeous clothes, the wittiest conversation. Its most affluent customers were merchants, whose wealth derived partly from lending money to the ruling princes and *shogun* (who used to sneak into the floating world to enjoy themselves). Like tradesmen everywhere they were deeply despised by their social superiors. In Japan these superiors were just about everyone, except for 'non-people' who did the dirty work no one else would touch, and entertainers. Performers were of such low rank they didn't even figure in Japan's social hierarchy. Known as river-bed folk, they lived on dry river-beds and along the banks of towns, in areas unsuitable for permanent housing because of the dangers of flooding.

Entertainers have lived on the outskirts of every society. In the past they were popularly regarded as rogues and vagabonds, rather than gods and goddesses. And it's so long now since performers came only from the poorest communities that it's easy to overlook the fact that they were once widely despised and distrusted for their free and easy ways. From earliest times people have been able to escape the constrictions of class, sex and race by becoming entertainers. They've often been dependent on the aristocracy for their livelihood; and it's ironic that some who were born into the most miserable conditions were able to rise, through a combination of talent and charisma, to become a people's royalty.

Performers may have been idols in the popular imagination, but in many societies they had no civil rights. In Japan a strict code of behaviour was laid down to cover every aspect of their lives. They could be imprisoned for the infraction of numerous petty laws, including one which forbade them to marry or fraternize with those outside their own social class. They could only share houses with others in their profession and they had to live in the quarter where they worked. As in Shakespeare's England, there was a dress code governing the clothes they could wear, right down to the quality and colour of the cloth. Commoners weren't allowed to wear red or purple, only dark colours. But stripes were allowed, a cheerful exception which goes to show the quirky, not to say arbitrary, nature of such social constraints.

Merchants were slightly higher on the social ladder than performers. They weren't required to pay taxes, which would have given them rights; but from time to time their colossal wealth was confiscated on government whim. Rather than lose it all they set about squandering it in the floating world. They were looking for something new in the way of entertainment, something a bit more raffish and unstuffy than the aristocratic Noh theatre: they discovered it in the dances of a new kind of drama, christened kabuki (from *kabuku*, meaning to be wild or outrageous).

***

Kabuki was created by a woman called Okuni. For some time she had been wandering from place to place, offering her skills as a dancer. As it was only permitted to charge money for a public performance if it was for religious purposes, she naturally claimed that she was connected to a temple, though it's doubtful if this was really the case. One day, around 1603, she set up her performance platform on a dry river-bed just outside Kyoto and proceeded to entertain passers-by with a new kind of dance. Her combination of comic and erotic elements was so amusing that it didn't take long for word of this unusual new dancer to spread. Soon she was attracting huge crowds, in which there was a good deal of social mixing – a revolutionary phenomenon in Japan at the time.

The most popular part of her performance was when she appeared as a man, complete with moustache and sword. She strutted about in silk brocade trousers and animal-skin jacket, miming the chatting up of tea-house women and flirting with courtesans. She also dressed as a priest, sometimes Buddhist, sometimes Shinto. She even added a Christian holy man to her repertoire of male figures. It was probably the irreverent cheekiness of Okuni's impersonations which gave her an edge and she was soon attracting Japan's top-knotted samurai to her shows. She enlisted women to dance as men and men as women; and at the end the troupe invited the audience to dance along with them.

When kabuki was seen to be commercially attractive, men jumped on the bandwagon and recruited prostitutes to train in Okuni's style. After her death these women became even more blatant in mixing sexual soliciting with performing, and the authorities moved to confine kabuki to the outskirts of the city. This was probably as much to maintain public order as for reasons of morality, for there are many reports of fights breaking out between men vying for the favours of individual dancers.

In 1628 the first step was taken to ban women from performing in public, but the law was so difficult to enforce that it was only in 1647 that they disappeared entirely from the Japanese stage. Some of the women who lost their livelihood as dancers became teachers; others found positions in samurai households as private entertainers; and some moved into the world of prostitution.

With women banished from the stage young men took their place. Most of them were below the age of consent and turned out to be, if anything, even more available than the women. It's said that they became the prey of Buddhist priests, who had renounced the company of women but who could, with a clear conscience, make use of young men. In Japan homosexuality and heterosexuality were considered equally acceptable, though they were still regarded as a threat to social order. So in 1652 these all-male kabuki troupes were banned from the theatre, along with music and dance. Entertainment has been banned in many cultures when public order is thought to be in jeopardy. Yet though Japanese women weren't allowed to appear in public theatres, there was nothing to stop them becoming private entertainers in the tea houses of the floating world.

Times change, prohibition comes and goes, and in the late nineteenth century kabuki was eventually revived. Even today, though, female roles continue to be performed by men. It's the dream of every *onnagata* to play the most glamorous of all female types, the high-class courtesan, who wears the best costumes and has come to be seen as a nostalgic symbol of Japan's romantic past.

In the heyday of kabuki, the *onnagata* who took these roles were so popular that they became the model for fashionable women. Their hairstyles, clothes and mannerisms set the standard for all that was most elegant and feminine, and when the first geisha emerged, during the second half of the eighteenth century, it was these female impersonators whom they imitated. Curiously enough, the first geisha were men.

As for ordinary Japanese dancing girls, during the 1680s they became especially sought after for private parties by the merchants, samurai and princes. For poor families with many mouths to feed, training their daughters to dance, even at the age of six or seven, gave them a chance in life. With luck these dancing girls would attract patronage and a secure position at court. Artistic patronage went hand in hand with recruitment for the women's quarters. There the women combined the duel function of dancer and concubine, which brings us to the age-old connection between prostitution and entertainment.

***

Throughout Asia women were segregated from men in the interests of domestic propriety. This was the case in Hindu, Confucian and Muslim cultures alike. In tenth-century Japan noblewomen lived separately from men in windowless, unheated houses lit by oil lamps and tapers. It was a world of shadows, where they received male visitors from behind latticed screens and ventured out only in closed carriages.

For them marriage was an arranged affair designed to cement alliances between families. Marrying for love wasn't part of the equation. All over the world the role of a wife was to provide heirs and manage the household. A wife had her own sphere of influence in the home, where she was respected, but she wasn't expected to stray into the male domain of public life. Only entertainers did such a thing. An aristocratic wife didn't necessarily expect to have – or enjoy – a sexual relationship with her husband. Sex was for procreation, not recreation, and for a man it was something to be enjoyed with mistresses, concubines or courtesans. The entire world of pleasure had its place outside the family.

In the East this segregation gave way to the acceptance of a class of women who were trained in the performing arts and other social graces. They were taught to socialize with men in a way that wives were not, and in Japan they could be found only in the floating world. In its heyday, Kyoto's pleasure quarters housed some 50,000 registered prostitutes. Young girls who were sold into the business as children by their poverty-stricken parents were praised for having sacrificed themselves for the good of their families. They were bound to their owners much like slaves and weren't allowed to venture outside the quarter. Any social contact that young men had with members of the opposite sex was with these young girls and women.

Professional female entertainers, who may or may not have offered sexual services, were not regarded as 'fallen' women; they simply had their own allotted place in society. They fulfilled a function which has no modern Western equivalent and it allowed them a rather more varied life than their married sisters. Those at the top of the ladder were women of many talents. They provided amusement and educated conversation (indeed, in some cultures they were the only women who could read and write). They were trained in singing, dancing and reciting poetry and were skilled musicians. Unlike others of their sex they were free to move about in public, as long as they confined themselves to the walled city. Throughout history, their role – like that of mistresses, whether paid or otherwise – was to entertain and provide their male patrons with light relief from the cares of this world.

The many Japanese words for 'prostitute' reflect the different ranks of these women. In English the closest approximation to those who held a recognized place in society for their education and skill as entertainers is 'courtesan'. To be a patron of one of the most celebrated courtesans (who were few in number), a man had to be extremely rich – indeed, part of his reason for keeping one of these expensive and accomplished creatures was to demonstrate his wealth. Courtesans, of course, were free to turn down any man they didn't fancy and there are numerous stories, both factual and literary, of men who ruined themselves financially for the pleasure of keeping one of these women. They were seen primarily as entertainers rather than as women who sold sexual services and, indeed, the sexual aspect of their work was by no means the main part. The courtesan-dancers at the pinnacle of their profession often came from noble families who had fallen on hard times. They kept company with Japan's most powerful men, from statesmen to scholars, and led the fashion in dress and courtly manners.

Japan's many ranks of entertainer-prostitutes were known as floating women or play women. Somewhere among them were the *shirabyoshi*, or dancing girls, the precursors of the geisha. They were most popular when they dressed as men, just as Okuni had done, performing what were seen as erotic dances and songs.

Not every prostitute was connected with the stage. But even today there is a blurring of the two professions, and not just in Japan. In the Muslim world it's still generally assumed that dancers are, *ipso facto*, parading their bodies for hire; they have to rise to the very top of their profession to escape this assumption. It isn't surprising that prostitutes should have become synonymous in the public mind with dancers, whose allure lay in the way they moved and exhibited their bodies on the public stage. They belonged to a fairy-tale world of dreams and privilege; a world in which female entertainers, in some ways the lowest members of society, acquired the glamour and status of the highest citizens in the land.

***

Leonard C. Pronko is a great kabuki enthusiast. He writes, somewhat fancifully, that, whether the audience is aware of it or not, the *onnagata* 'stirs in the unconscious a dim memory of a time when human beings were both male and female, a time of natural androgyny and bisexuality'. He goes on to say that if a woman were to try and play a kabuki female role she would have to imitate the men 'who have so subtly and beautifully incarnated woman before her'.

Imitating the *onnagata* is what their successors in the entertainment world, the geisha, did. Lesley Downer lived for some years in Japan, studying the disappearing profession of the *karyukai*, the 'flower and willow world' of geisha. These women are the last in a long line of female entertainers who trace their origin back to the dancing girls of the twelfth century.

But the original geisha were men. One night in the late 1600s a group of male performers swanned into a courtesan's party and proved so entertaining, with their music, their witty banter and risqué talk, that they became a regular feature of these parties. Then in 1751 something rather shocking happened. Clients of one particular tea house were startled when a female geisha appeared at their private party. It took only a few years for other *onna* (female) geisha to appear. They decided to make music and dance their speciality and began calling themselves geisha, which means 'art-person'. Becoming highly skilled entertainers was a way of increasing their value and making sure they were in demand, and by 1780 they outnumbered their male colleagues. By the turn of the century they had entirely replaced them so that, by definition, geisha were now female.

Geisha were free from the restraints of other women who lived in the licensed areas. They could move between the walled city and the outside world quite freely, they could refuse customers if they wished, and brothel-keepers kept an eye open to make sure they didn't steal prostitutes' clients by offering to sleep with them. Their main role was to entertain, and they spent many hours eating and drinking with their clients at the tea house, where they sang, danced and made music.

An apprentice geisha, or *maiko* (literally, 'dancing girl'), might be as young as six or seven years old. She wore clogs with four-inch wooden heels to make herself look older and teetered around in them like a little doll, carefully holding her knees together. Her job was to pamper her client by subtly combining the personas of child-woman and mother. Needless to say, flattery was a vital skill for any ambitious geisha.

Downer writes that, in the past, geisha were the most independent women in Japanese society. They had enormous power compared to that of a wife, who was bound by all kinds of trifling limitations and some frankly absurd rules. One of these concerned the ways in which a man could obtain a divorce. There were seven, according to the marriage code laid down in the late nineteenth century: jealousy, sterility, adultery, disobedience to parents-in-law, theft, disease and – believe it or not – talking too much.

Being a geisha, says Downer, was the only way in which a woman could hope to take control of her own destiny. Geisha were women in a man's world, the popular heroines of kabuki dramas, and in due course they came to epitomize the most desired kind of femininity. In Victorian times, she says, geisha were queens of popular culture. This alternative society was considered so subversive that the *shogun* spent enormous energy in futile attempts to repress it, or at least keep it under control, and it wasn't unknown for writers who celebrated this culture to find themselves thrown in jail.

Geisha, on the other hand, seem to have evaded some of the restrictions imposed on others in their world. They managed this partly by making themselves as different from other women as they could. Not for them the fussy, over-embroidered layers of the kimono and the Christmas tree of hair decorations worn by every courtesan. Instead they favoured a plain kimono and it was considered especially chic, or *iki*, to wear over it a man's square-cut jacket with big sleeves, the kind of casual jacket an *onnagata* would fling on over his women's costume to go home in after he'd finished work. Nor did a geisha wear the traditional white-toed socks; she went barefoot in her wooden clogs, and the sight of her varnished toenails poking out from beneath her kimono was said to be the height of eroticism.

A geisha's make-up was especially distinctive. It derived from the *onnagata*'s expressionless theatre mask, which is a study in contrasts: glossy black sculpted hair surrounding a white face, covered in a thick layer of wax and rice powder; a vivid red slash of a mouth opening to reveal teeth blackened with powdered gall-nut and iron dissolved in vinegar.

52 Up until the late twentieth century in Japan, a pale complexion was universally regarded as beautiful and a sign of breeding. The faces of women who worked for a living, toiling outside in the fields, grew burnished under the sun. Only those who stayed indoors or shielded their faces under their parasols had pale skins. The make-up of the *onnagata* and geisha emphasizes this extreme pallor. In the past it was helped along by nightingale droppings, which women thought lightened their skin, and even white lead, which unfortunately made their flesh wrinkle and age prematurely and sometimes resulted in death. Downer speculates that geisha make-up dates from an era when these women:

> used to flit through the gloom of unlit tea houses, their magical mask-like faces glimpsed only in darkness or by flickering candlelight. Then it transmuted its wearers into shamanesses who could transport men into another world, a world of dreams.

She describes her first meeting with a 24-year-old modern-day geisha: 'I gasped when she opened her small mouth ... In the chalky white face with the blood-red lips, her teeth were painted black. It was macabre, like looking into a black hole.' Geisha outline their eye sockets in pink, with a spot of red in the middle of the cheeks. They paint their lips into a rosebud, shave their eyebrows and replace them with two grey dots high on the forehead. Their upper back and shoulders are also made up to startling effect, as Downer describes:

> When she turned she revealed a breathtaking expanse of exquisitely painted white back. I had not realized that the kimono was worn quite so shockingly low. It was like a *décolletage* in reverse, enormously erotic. At the nape of the neck, which Japanese men find especially sexy, was a titillating three-pronged fork of naked, unpainted flesh. She was not so much a woman as a walking work of art, a compilation of symbols and markers of eroticism, as far removed from a human being as a bonsai is from a natural tree.

The sight of white-powdered shoulders was enough to set the pulses racing, not to speak of the three-pronged tongue of bare flesh at the nape of the neck which is meant to conjure up thoughts of the vagina.

In Downer's book about life as a modern-day geisha, she describes a hairdresser sculpting a young woman's waist-length hair into a miniature landscape of hills and valleys dotted with all kinds of distractions. An extraordinary clutter of objects go into the hair: wads of pomade, handmade paper, a frame of lacquered wood, oil, string, yak hair, tinkling, dangling ornaments, flowers, pins and pearls, even sprigs of dried rice for fertility and luck. The hair is teased, knotted and oiled, folded this way and that and held in place so securely by red ribbons that it can last an entire week without a single hair escaping.

From having had their hair yanked and pulled into these elaborate styles, year in year out, geisha develop a little bald patch on the crown of the head. Needless to say, it isn't easy to sleep without ruining this confection; nor is it easy to relax, considering the fact that a wooden block is traditionally used as a pillow. Not surprisingly, some geisha prefer to wear wigs.

Today their world is dying out, though men still go to geisha to be indulged like naughty children. Descriptions of their parties suggest a scene reminiscent of the nursery, with the men throwing their food around and getting hopelessly drunk. And always at their side is the geisha, keeping the cups of saki filled, laughing at their jokes, flattering her clients as kings among men.

If the geisha world is on the way out, it's female emancipation and the desire for Western style and modernity that are killing it. Yet posters still welcome tourists to the city of Kyoto with images of these women, who took their style, make-up and dancing from the female impersonators of a bygone age.

***

One of today's most famous *onnagata* is Nakamuro Ganjiro 3rd, who is now in his seventies. 'The whole point', he says, 'is to idealize women, to make women who are more beautiful, more elegant than real women.' Descriptions of the ideal Japanese woman make for amusing reading. In a 1950s guide to kabuki, M. Miyaki writes:

> The women of Japan, as a rule, are lacking in dominant features. They are not therefore fitted for the kabuki, which requires strong

personality in its players ... Having been trained from childhood in the manners of the fair sex, the *onnagata* knows women from A to Z, even better than a woman knows herself.

Even geisha, he says, take second place to female impersonators: 'The *onnagata* has succeeded in representing on the stage a geisha even excelling that of real life in beauty of form and refinement of manners.'

The celebrated eighteenth-century actor Yoshizawa Ayame was one of the earliest *onnagata*. He lived at a time when it wasn't uncommon for those in his profession to dress and behave like women off-stage as well as on, and his words are quoted as the bible of female impersonation. He wrote that, if a woman were to appear in an *onnagata* role she could not hope to express the ideal female beauty; after all, he said, all she had was her individual physical characteristics and these could by no means satisfy the manmade ideal. He went on to add that a good *onnagata* should be like a woman in his daily life, even if he were married or had sired children. Ayame advocated maintaining this illusion in the dressing-room as well:

> When taking refreshment too, he should turn away, so that people cannot see him. To be alongside a *takiyaku* playing the lover's part and chew away at one's food without charm, and then go straight out on the stage and play a love scene with the same man will lead to failure on both sides; for the *takiyaku*'s heart will not in reality be ready to fall in love.

Miyaki offers us another reason why women aren't fitted for the rigours of the stage. Given that an *onnagata*'s wig weighs all of twenty-five pounds, he says, 'such a heavy burden would almost break the neck of a Japanese actress'. (One wonders how he accounts for the geisha's ability to bear the burden of her wig, which is just as heavy.)

A man wishing to become an *onnagata* spends years training in how to move while wearing his wig, high-heeled clogs and a kimono whose tubular skirt allows for little leg-room, not to mention its swaddling layers of underskirts. To dance as a woman, says Ganjiro, 'The backbone comes in. The legs are closer together, the hips are tilted, creating a particular angle to the shoulder. *Onnagata* practise walking 'like women' by holding a sheet of notepaper between their knees, which gives them a pigeon-toed shuffle. If the paper falls, their posture is incorrect. The fingers of both hands are held together and the elbows tucked in at the hips, where they remain motionless. (By contrast, male characters in kabuki hold their elbows away from the body and splay their fingers). It is a triumph of minimalism, a triumph of how to express the utmost while physically confined to the utmost.

China had a great influence on Japanese culture, though Japanese women didn't go as far as to bind their feet. Even so, they developed footwear and a style of dance whose tiny, shuffling steps had much in common with that of China. Ganjiro tells us that, compared to the male dances, which are pleasurable to do, dancing as a woman is painful: 'One must pose, with legs slightly bent and weight lowered, and all one's energy goes into the tortuous task of holding these difficult positions.'

Seeing an *onnagata* make his first move is as startling as watching a statue come to life: the delicacy of his gestures, the way he flicks the long train of his kimono out of the way, his tiny steps and little shuffling walk. He is like a porcelain doll, dipping at the knees and inclining his head, which wobbles from side to side beneath the weight of his wig. His high sing-song lament, issuing from a chest compressed by his tightly bound kimono, sounds like the cry of a strangled kitten.

The illustrious Mr Ganjiro does all this to perfection. He says he doesn't look to the women around him for inspiration. For they, after all, are less than perfect specimens of what it is to be a goddess in men's eyes. Only a man could, at the age of seventy, get away with appearing on-stage as the epitome of female loveliness. Any woman who tried it would be laughed to scorn.

***

Mae West wasn't much of an actress, but she was an inspired breaker of taboos, a street-smart gal who used her native wit to perform and write and generally incite. West mocked sex just as she mocked her own voluptuous body. In *I'm No Angel* she plays a dancer-cum-lion tamer in a carnival sideshow. Lazily swinging her hips she looks down at her entranced male audience and says, 'You get the picture, boys?' Then, swaggering off into the wings, she turns and mutters to them out of the side of her mouth, 'Suckers!'

Everything West did was done tongue-in-cheek. As critic William Bolitho noted, when she smiled that sideways smile of hers, audiences smiled with her. At a time when other women were bobbing their hair and binding their breasts to give themselves a flat-chested look, West had the fleshy contours of a nineteenth-century madame. She wasn't beautiful, according to the slimline standards of the day; but if she looked old-fashioned, what she put on the stage was way ahead of its time. The final, rather sad, evaluation of West is that she was a kind of female-female impersonator, and wicked rumour once had it that she was really a man in disguise.

West lived at a time when sexual stereotypes were being questioned. Turn-of-the-century medical treatises dwelt on the subject of sexual deviancy, and cross-dressing by men had started to be seen as a symptom of homosexuality. By the 1910s the flouting of sexual stereotypes came thick and fast. Middle-class flappers wore men's clothes and took up men's habits; they smoked and drank to excess and even sported monocles.

In the early twentieth century female impersonation was fashionable on both sides of the Atlantic. Back in the 1860s it had been a raunchy staple of low-class dives, but by the 1920s it was considered ideal family entertainment and was developed in vaudeville theatres with women and children as its target audience. Early twentieth-century drag acts billed themselves as 'female illusionists'. This placed them in the realm of magic, though it was a different kind to the circus-style magic of a conjurer or an escapologist like Houdini. The drag artist seemed to escape, apparently effortlessly, into the world of the opposite sex. In America the best-known female impersonator of the time, Julian Eltinge, had his own fan magazine, a cosmetics brand and even a theatre in Times Square named after him.

In her biography of Mae West, Marybeth Hamilton suggests that female impersonation was popular because it overturned the deeply held belief that men and women are fundamentally, inescapably different; that a chasm of thought, feeling and action divides the sexes. Men and women could no longer be seen as totally distinct species, different in the way they reasoned, spoke and showed their emotions. When West reflected this in her novels and stage shows she caused a scandal, and she was arrested more than once because of it.

Her play *Pleasure Man* challenged the assumption that drag artists were simply uniquely skilled transformationists. Instead she suggested that they were gay men engaged in expressing their hidden female side. West's camp bag of tricks – the preening and flouncing, the teasing, hand-on-hip *double entendres* and raised eyebrows – came from her gay friends on the New York scene. As Hamilton writes, 'She performed an impersonation at several removes: an authentic tough girl mimicking fairy impersonators mimicking the flamboyance of working-class women.' As a drag queen of sorts, West has become a gay icon surpassing all others.

Some commentators on sexual impersonation suggest that it exposes constricting roles imposed on the sexes by society; that its exaggerated gestures, costumes and attitudes serve to mock these arbitrary roles and show them up as a grotesque parody of natural behaviour. The writer Wayne Kostenbaum believes that highly artificial art forms hold a special appeal for people whose lives don't fit easily into the prevailing social order. (This is certainly true of both opera and ballet, which attract enthusiasts of camp performance styles by the drove.) What's interesting is that behind sexual impersonation lie completely different motives, depending on the sex of the performer. Historically, women have cross-dressed off-stage in order to assume male power and move about freely in public; and they have cross-dressed to dance on-stage for humorous purposes. Men too have cross-dressed to question sex roles, but they have used drag primarily to play out fantasies of femininity.

The longing to be revered as a dazzling, larger-than-life object lies beneath the exaggerated persona of drag queens. It's been remarked that they never tone down, always up – unlike women who appear in male dress. And today it isn't only through the transforming power of performance that men live out the fantasy of entering the world of the opposite sex. Increasingly, men who are uncomfortable with the sex they were born into are putting themselves under the surgeon's knife. Yet how many of those who claim they were born in the wrong body want the biological reality of being a true woman? What they are looking for, rather, is a glamorous external persona of femaleness. As Germaine Greer comments on men who seek a sex-change operation, 'None have ever begged for a uterus-and-ovaries transplant; if uterus-and-ovaries transplants were made mandatory for wannabe women they would disappear overnight.'

A performance *en travesti* may reduce the stress of having to act aggressively, if born a man, or passively, if a woman. It may call attention to our need now and then to escape and mock sexual stereotypes imposed by society. But it may equally serve to reinforce oppressive stereotypes of what it is to be and look female. For the overblown image of the drag queen can also be seen as a vicious, patronizing caricature which enables the performer to indulge in playing out stereotypes of femininity within the safety of a male body.

***

During periods of social unrest and change, women start putting on men's clothes. It happened after the French Revolution of 1789, when women wore military overcoats and jackets. And it happened after the First World War, when women bobbed their hair, dressed in men's suits and bound their breasts to give themselves a flat-chested look. If women have cross-dressed in everyday life to take on male power and freedoms, in performance they do it as a form of mockery.

Venus Saleh is an Iranian dancer who came to live in Britain as a young girl and has never been back to Iran. She's a natural performer. Dancing is how she expresses herself, especially her cheeky sense of humour, and it's how she maintains a link with Persian culture. At women-only parties which go on well into the early hours, the guests get up one by one to entertain each other. One of their dances, called *babakaram* ('tough guy'), is performed wearing a man's suit and hat. It's a cheeky parody of macho society that mocks the posturings of gangsters and tough guys towards women.

At a dance class one day, Venus entertained us all with this dance. She sauntered in, dressed in a man's jacket, shirt and trousers, hat perched at a rakish angle, and proceeded to eye each of us up in turn. She went over to one of the more voluptuous women and drew the shape of an enormous bottom in the air. She mimed weighing up this dancer's bosoms and tossed one over her shoulder. Indicating that she liked the look of another dancer, she framed her face with her hands and waggled each eyebrow independently. She slid her lower lip rapidly from left to right and pointed at her lips, as if to say, 'Look at these lips! They're hot – don't touch!' Then: 'Look at these hips: who can move their hips like me?' She rolled her hips and stuck out her bottom at us, and by the time she'd finished, people were almost hysterical with laughter.

Just as Middle Eastern women have cross-dressed in private to entertain each other, the public tradition of men dancing in drag is also widespread in Muslim culture. It used to be so common in the Arab world that travellers were often deceived by glamorous-looking dancers they encountered in the street. The nineteenth-century French writer Gérard de Nerval was enchanted by the sight of three women dancing in a cloud of dust and tobacco smoke. When he looked into the matter more closely though, he discovered the unmistakable signs of a week-old growth of beard on their chins: 'And just when I was going to fall madly in love with these mysterious creatures!'

To tell a familiar tale, the tradition of men in drag emerged when women were banned from dancing in public. In 1805 there were some 600 dancing boys in the coffee shops and squares of Istanbul. Most of them came from Greek, Armenian and Jewish communities. They were so popular they often caused riots, with members of the audience throwing tea glasses and getting into fights over their different merits. They imitated the hip swaying and shimmying of the women's dance and added variations all their own. One of these involved the dancer painting a comic face on his belly and working his muscles so that the face alternately smiled and frowned. In 1837 these boys were thought to be causing such a disturbance that they were outlawed by the sultan and many fled to Cairo.

Three years earlier dancing girls had been banned from the city by Egypt's ruler, Mohammed Ali. He sent them up the Nile to the village of Esna, which just happened to be his own favourite river retreat. Some of them stayed in Cairo, hiding out and working secretly, in fear of being discovered and flogged. Western travellers sought out these legendary entertainers, who were becoming as famous as the Pyramids and the Sphinx, but those who remained were hard to find. Travellers often ended up being entertained by boys instead. They wore embroidered jackets and baggy pantaloons, their long, braided hair covered in little gold coins, their eyes heavily outlined in kohl. They wore their trousers as low as they dared, at pubic level, secured with a shawl folded over several times to give themselves more shapely hips. In his travel notes the French novelist Flaubert records an afternoon entertainment by these boys:

> Expressionlessness of their faces under the streaks of rouge and sweat. The effect comes from the gravity of the face contrasted with the lascivious movements of the body; occasionally one or the other lies down flat on his back like a woman about to offer herself, and then suddenly leaps up with a bound ... Now and again,

during the dance, their impresario makes jokes and kisses Hasan on the belly. Hasan never for a moment stops watching himself in the mirror.

There are many early twentieth-century postcards of these boys, staring out at the camera with a cigarette between their teeth, and they look so like young girls that even the vendors of these cards often mistake their sex.

Men dancing as women – today this old, old story finds its most curious expression in the world of belly dancing. This nightclub act evolved in Cairo from the bold, sassy hip dancing with which women entertain each other. For thousands of years, throughout the Arab-Islamic world, where a kind of sexual apartheid has been the norm in public places, women have danced together in private to reinforce their sense of identity and to express their sensuality. Hip dancing was once practised throughout the world, and in ancient times had a part to play in fertility rites, but in time it died out in many countries. Ironically, it remained and became a subtle, complex dance in the Islamic Middle East, which has done everything in its power to exclude the public display of the female body and sensuality in general.

The cabaret version of this women's dance isolates its erotic power and serves it up to suit the expectations and tastes of consumers. And in the process it becomes an unconscious form of female impersonation. The belly-dance uniform – a sequinned two-piece outfit – the bare, vibrating flesh and bold pelvic movements scream 'woman' and 'sex' as loudly as any drag act.

Belly dancing developed back in the 1920s, at a time when the Cairo film industry was at its height. A feature film without dancing in it was almost unthinkable and most films included at least one extended nightclub scene, featuring dancing based on the format of the Hollywood musical. These movies made stars of the best-loved dancers of the day. In their turn they accepted the Orientalist fantasies of their culture and began drawing (half-heartedly, it must be said) on Western dance movements, adding to their routine whirls, twirls and wafting with veils. From then on their dance glittered and sparkled, from its diaphanous, rhinestone-covered two-piece costumes to its sparkly high-heeled shoes.

In clubs and restaurants today Middle Eastern men in drag perform this dance so convincingly that they may be halfway through their act before you realize it's a man up there on-stage. Others make no pretence of being women. At a Paris theatre I once found myself performing in the same show as one of them. From a hidden pocket in his voluminous trousers he produced a handful of glitter and threw it in the air. Wildly gyrating and rolling his belly, he took out a cardboard sword and balanced it on his head. Then he leant back and coyly fluttered his eyelashes at his largely female audience. His red harem pants, spangly bodice and sequinned hip belt contrasted sharply with my own unadorned costume. Afterwards, standing next to me in the wings, he glanced at my plain saffron-coloured dress and muttered with scarcely concealed disdain, 'I see you save money on sequins.'

Today such performers are popular not just in the Arab world but among Western women learning Arabic dance in the hundreds of oriental dance studios that have sprung up all over Europe and the United States since the 1980s. Just as men have been dancing as women for thousands of years, they've also been busy showing women how to be sexy on the dance floor. Word has got back to Cairo and other Middle Eastern cities that there's a lot of money to be made teaching Western women to flutter their eyelashes and wiggle their hips. In their own countries these men may have been shopkeepers or plumbers. Now, suddenly, they're dance experts. And since they come from countries where it's hard to make a living, who can blame them for taking advantage of a ready-made market? They quickly grasp the essentials of teaching and, more importantly, how to reinforce women's self-confidence with flattering attentions. It must be said that this isn't true of all Middle Eastern men teaching Arabic dance in the West; and there are plenty of women who also teach this cabaret style, with its standard routines and clichés of sexy glamour.

They aren't short of students. Many women are only too delighted to offer this image of themselves as obliging playmates, fingering their hair and leaning back in a slavish pose of pouting lips and fluttering eyelashes. A surprisingly large number are also keen to get up on-stage and become part-time performing dolls in their local restaurants.

The majority of cabaret dancers who strut their stuff in clubs and restaurants have little in common with the dance stars who rule the roost in Egypt and whose skill and magnificence make them riveting to watch. Coming out of a culture of sexual separation lends an intriguing aspect to their performance. Behind the dancer sits a line of dinner-jacketed musicians who look tiny in comparison to the goddess who stands with her back to them. They watch her movements like hawks, ready to provide the changes in rhythm and mood that her movements call for (and woe betide them if they don't give her what she wants!). These famous, fabulously wealthy dancers don't simper, they don't try to please – indeed, they often display a fine indifference to the ecstasies of their male audience, who join in the joke as they call out, 'Look how you make me suffer!' and other, no doubt less poetic, phrases. The best of them are women in their forties and fifties, with voluptuous bodies and a supreme confidence in their power. Sometimes they dance with a detached, expressionless look, sometimes it's with a twinkle in the eye, which hints at the fine joke they're having as Amazons of the erotic.

Going to see one of these dancers can result in a great night out, but being unexpectedly confronted by an inexperienced belly dancer is something else. In the intimate setting of a Western restaurant customers may be busy eating their supper and chatting away when suddenly up pops a dancer kitted out like a fairy on a Christmas tree, demanding their attention. There will always be customers who don't want a dancer sashaying up to their table and shaking her bosom in their soup. But a dancer up close can't be ignored. The British – with their well-known reserve – aren't quite sure how to respond to the sinuous, undulating movements and shimmying hips. With none of the physical distance which serves to diffuse its intensity there can be embarrassment, frozen smiles and shifty looks all round.

In Germany, where the popularity of Middle Eastern dance has led to thousands of women learning it, many restaurants now offer 'oriental' dancing. But customers are becoming weary of them. I remember passing a Munich restaurant that had a sign in the window enticing people in with the words, 'We do not have an oriental dancer.'

Marketing a ritual which once led somewhere and now leads nowhere has turned it into something bizarre. Removed from its cultural context and served up in a commercial setting, this dance has become a parody of itself. No more than a pale echo remains of a dance which, in ancient times, had significance as a fertility rite, celebrating female power. Meanwhile men who perform this dance in drag are becoming more and more popular. Camille Paglia writes that drag queens are a symbol of our sexual crisis: 'With geisha-like sophistication of gesture and costume the drag queen recreates the dreamlike artifice of culture that conceals the darker mysteries of biology.'

As we've seen, the phenomenon of men masquerading as women and seeking to take on their power has existed for thousands of years, and on every continent, and was originally connected with religious ritual. Paglia may or may not be correct in thinking it symbolizes sexual crisis; but if she is right, then this crisis is far from being merely an aspect of modern life. It goes all the way back to the days when men danced themselves into a trance and slashed off their genitals in order to become priests of the goddess figures of antiquity.

Revolution on the Dance Floor

A woman who has waltzed for fifteen minutes
is in the same condition
as a woman who has drunk champagne.
Havelock Ellis

Towards the end of the eighteenth century a great storm of change began brewing in Europe. In 1789 the French Revolution overturned the old order and sent shock waves across the continent. It was a call for social justice and personal freedom, and the spark of political revolt that it ignited soon spread far beyond the borders of France.

The revolution was people power on the move, and more than just politically, for it heralded the beginning of a new social mobility. The place the middle class and the aristocracy began mixing for the first time was the dance floor, where they engaged in a dance initially considered so scandalous that it was banned from 'respectable' gatherings. No one could have predicted that this lively, warm-blooded workers' dance would go whirling into upper-class ballrooms and become the toast of Europe. No one could have predicted that it would cause the biggest revolution in manners that high society had ever known.

Before the French Revolution the norms of European culture were dictated by the court of Versailles, with French spoken as a mark of refinement throughout the continent. The aristocracy took pains to distinguish themselves from the *hoi polloi* in even the smallest details of their everyday lives. Back in the seventeenth century they took to eating with a fork as well as a knife, and using individual plates instead of helping themselves from a communal dish. They also affected a new kind of speech, which included a coy refusal to refer to natural bodily functions or items of clothing that called to mind an intimate part of the body. It wasn't done, for instance, to refer to a man's breeches, or 'breeks' as they were known. Spontaneous behaviour, sensible clothes, anything which might link high society to the common herd, was discarded. Artificiality became the order of the day in speech and dress, and even in the way people moved on the dance floor.

People had once taken it for granted that their social status was divinely ordained. They dressed according to rank, following sumptuary laws which dictated the colours and types of fabric available to them. But with the dawn of capitalism in the eighteenth century all this changed. A spirit of acquisitiveness was in the air and it created a craving for fine clothes among even the poorest members of society. Clothes were valuable items which could be used to raise money in times of need. Thieves stole clothes trunks from the backs of coaches, they entered houses to steal clothes and even took them off washing lines. Historian Maureen Waller tells us that hangmen were known to strip the clothes off corpses to sell. She goes on to describe how men carried young lads through the streets concealed in a basket on their heads; from this vantage point the boys were well placed to lean out and snatch people's hats as they went along.

London became the hub of a trade in second-hand clothes. Even aristocratic women sold their cast-offs, and some passed them on to their maids. This democratization of dress led foreign visitors to comment that it was hard to tell the classes apart, so frequently did people succeed in dressing above their station. The nobility began decking themselves out in increasingly ostentatious ways. As with cars in the twentieth century, so with clothes in the eighteenth: the more space a person occupied through their dress and the more dazzling their clothes, the more important they thought themselves.

High fashion is a luxury which can only flourish in a wealthy society and it has always been used by the rich as a sign of social superiority. In the case of women's clothes, the three-dimensional dresses, hooped skirts, elaborate wigs, tottering heels and other fashions which have come and gone over the years served to show that anyone who dressed so extravagantly had no need to work. How could they have done, in such cumbersome clothing? Not only did wealthy women not demean themselves by working; they employed an army of servants to help them in and out of their clothes, which must have been quite a task, with all the fiddly hooks and bindings involved.

Fashion was dedicated to deceiving the eye and it's no coincidence that *trompe-l'oeil* painting was popular at the time. Gowns had trick sleeves and horsehair padding, and men and women alike wore long wigs with curls tumbling down their backs. Carriages were built high in order to accommodate these elaborate headpieces and the hats which perched on top of them, providing breeding places for all kinds of dirt and vermin.

The first illustrated fashion magazines were published in the 1770s and were distributed internationally. Some of these magazines appeared weekly and they show us how rapidly styles appeared and went out of favour. In the space of a few weeks, a woman's wardrobe could become entirely outmoded if she didn't keep her eyes open. Through its magazine *Le Cabinet des Modes*, Paris announced itself the fashion capital of the world (a situation which continues to the present day).

For an explanation of why women's dress has, historically, involved so many more layers than men's we have to go back to the Middle Ages. To the medieval mind the body was considered the home of the soul, with openings through which dirt, disease and evil spirits could gain entrance. Women's bodies were thought to be not nearly as well sealed as men's, and for this reason had to be swaddled in layers of fabric which were more difficult to penetrate. These extra layers served as both literal and moral protection, especially below the waist, with a girl's enormous skirts helping repel the advances of over-eager men.

Members of high society may have looked dazzling from the outside, but beneath the wide skirts and hooped petticoats, the white lace collars and cuffs, their bodies were so filthy they positively reeked. People believed it was a sign of cultural advancement not to need bathrooms, and well into the eighteenth century washing was still regarded askance. The only parts of the body exposed to view were the hands and face, but they seldom felt the refreshing touch of water. People simply put on clean clothes, and the more often they changed their clothes, the more refined they considered themselves to be.

Those who could afford it may have taken care to have their clothes laundered, but they weren't used to washing with any kind of regularity. For it was thought that water was harmful, that it opened the pores and let evil vapours enter the body and cause illness. Besides which, immersion in water was associated with undesirable pagan practices.

People covered up their dirt with make-up and their stench with perfume. Women used face powder containing white lead and arsenic, which led to many cases of poisoning, and those who were unlucky enough to carry the scars of syphilis hid them beneath black beauty spots or 'patches'. The scented lace handkerchief that a woman carried as a mark of elegance wasn't used for such an unseemly purpose as blowing her nose; instead she lifted it daintily and sniffed its perfume from time to time as a relief from the prevailing pong of unwashed bodies around her. More than one visitor from the East wrote home about the appalling stench at social gatherings of the nobility.

Steam baths had been introduced to England by soldiers returning from the Crusades in the Middle East. But in time they degenerated into places of low repute and fell into disuse. Towards the end of the seventeenth century there was an attempt to revive the old idea of steaming and some of the old London bagnios reopened. At first they were confined to men, with a women's day once a week; then they opened for mixing bathing. When this happened they soon became houses of assignation.

During this period the nobility began frequenting the Roman spas of Bath and Cheltenham. The sick went to sip and even immerse their bodies in the evil-smelling sulphurous water, which they believed had medicinal powers. In the evenings they amused themselves gambling and dancing in the assembly rooms, which were a new feature of social life. The assembly rooms were strictly for the use of the gentry. Clerks were refused entry, along with members of the retail trade, and there were certainly no theatrical types admitted. Despite this careful vetting system, 'riff-raff' and ladies of the town created a regular scandal by gatecrashing the masked balls which were held several nights a week and went on well into the early hours.

Around the large empty spaces reserved for dancing were smaller rooms for sitting out, taking refreshments and generally socializing. But the most important feature of assembly rooms was their wooden floors, some of them sprung, others made of boards or parquet. The polished surface of a wooden floor made it possible to dance faster and more smoothly than before. Now that dancers no longer had to lift their feet up to avoid stumbling over an uneven surface, they could move in a smooth, flowing pattern instead of leaping about, and this also made it easier to turn and spin.

That social dancing was fast becoming a craze throughout Europe is reflected in the number of spaces being set aside for it. By the end of the 1790s, 700 dance halls existed. In London people whirled about the open-air pleasure gardens of Vauxhall and Ranelagh. And for Londoners who didn't want to travel so far afield and had money to spare, a number of sumptuous new clubs with dance salons appeared in the fashionable West End to cater to the cream of society. The most famous of these was Almack's. The club opened in 1765, even though the finishing touches weren't quite complete, as the essayist Horace Walpole noted:

> In London the new assembly room at Almack's was opened the night before last, and they say it is very magnificent, but it was empty. Half the town is ill with colds, and many were afraid to go, as the house is scarcely built yet. Almack's advertised that it was built with hot bricks and boiling water – think what a rage there must be for public places, if this notice, instead of terrifying, could draw anybody thither. They tell me the ceilings were dripping with wet, but can you believe me when I assure you the Duke of Cumberland was there? Nay, he had a levee in the morning, and went to the opera before the Assembly! There is a vast flight of steps, and he was forced to rest two or three times. If he dies of it – and how should he not? – it will sound very silly when Hercules or Theseus ask him what he died of, to reply, 'I caught my death on a damp staircase at a new club room.'

Almack's became London's most exclusive club for snobbish reasons alone, and members of the *beau monde* went to extraordinary lengths to be invited to join. It was so exclusive that even the Duke of Wellington was turned away – once when he arrived after midnight, and once because he was wearing trousers instead of the fashionable knee-breeches. Foreign visitors like Prince Puckler-Muskau were astonished at the club's popularity, given its lack of entertainment, its bare rooms:

> where the most wretched refreshments were served; and a company into which, despite the immense difficulty in getting tickets, a great many nobodies had forced their way, and in which poor deportment and tasteless dress prevailed.

The club functioned chiefly as a marriage market for the cream of young debutantes, a place where they could be paraded by their mammas before London's most eligible bachelors. But spending an evening there proved so tedious for anyone interested in anything other than social climbing or finding a wife that the most attractive young men began looking elsewhere for their entertainment.

A historian of the Regency period, Venetia Murray, writes that more than one of Almack's patronesses cultivated an air of umblemished virtue while enjoying a racy past and, in many cases, current romantic intrigues as well. Metternich's mistress, Princess Lieven, commented on the discrepancy between the private and public lives of the English aristocracy, after attending a ball in the countryside. She noted that so many couples went wandering off into the bushes that, 'By the end of the dance almost the only people left in the ballroom were debutantes, chaperones and the host.'

For the nobility dancing was an important skill and a necessary social grace. For courtiers, daily dance lessons were essential as a way of bettering their position, and dancing masters could earn a good living instructing their masters on the niceties of how to move with elegance and grace. Manuals were produced instructing the nobility on deportment, and there are accounts of people who stumbled on a step or two and were disgraced at court. This was no joke because when they came back into favour, it was at a lower level and they had to start climbing the social ladder all over again.

Unlike the working class, who danced to let off steam, the aristocracy danced to show themselves off in their fine clothes, gliding, tripping and rising lightly on the toes. Dancing gave them a chance to parade their refined social manners as they bowed to their partners and to their audience of friends and family, and set off across the floor in a carefully choreographed set of steps and turns. In the ballroom there were always two sets of people, each as important as the other: those who danced and those who observed. The presence of onlookers not only gave a point to all that display, it also prevented dancing couples from becoming too intimate.

In its early days grand balls at Almack's were few and far between, even though the club boasted a splendid ballroom, complete with mirrored walls and gas lighting. But during the 'season' the club hosted a number of grand balls, where couples could be seen going through the stately measures of the most popular courtly dance of the time: the minuet.

The aristocracy have historically tended to appropriate working-class entertainment for their own amusement and they've often taken over their social dances. First though, they've taken care to prune them of their spontaneity and what was seen as their suggestive sexuality. The minuet (whose name comes from *menu*, meaning small) is a good example of this. Originally a French folk dance, it went romping along at a great lick. Toned down for the court, however, the minuet lost its gaiety and spirit of improvisation and become a dainty little dance with tiny steps interrupted by ceremonial bows. Couples danced the minuet holding their partners at arm's length, with only the fingertips touching as they turned outwards, the better to display their finery.

The minuet reflected the spirit of an age which was coming to an end in Europe; an age when everyone knew their place and no one broke the rules in public, whatever they might do in private. When the French Revolution came gusting in, flinging open the ballroom doors, it swept away the minuet and replaced it with a dance that was already making waves by cutting across class boundaries and which was to become the symbol of a new, democratic Europe.

***

When the waltz first appeared it was considered outrageously suggestive and was prohibited for its 'lascivious' music and 'voluptuous' movements. The word *walzen* comes from Old German and means to revolve or turn. A dancing embrace of wild, intoxicating spinning, its name was first heard around the middle of the eighteenth century. Like many popular dances which were to cause a scandal, the 'coarse and abandoned' waltz was born poor and went up in the world. It had its origins in sixteenth-century Middle European dances which involved couples whirling about in a close embrace. Warnings about this kind of dancing were sounded early on by clergymen criticizing young women who let themselves be grasped on any part of their body and who 'lusted' to be thrown into the air and twirled about. This kind of warning continued to be heard even when the waltz had become the most popular dance on the ballroom floor and been accepted by all classes of society.

The dance that gave birth to the waltz was known as 'roll-in-the-mire' or 'tumbledown', which gives us a good idea of what went on after the music ended. Performed in hobnail boots, it was a typical folk dance: boisterous and high-stepping, with couples spinning like dervishes. There was nothing new in social dances which involved turning or whirling. But in upper-class ballrooms a good deal of decorum was attached to this kind of dance, with pauses and bows to punctuate the turning. The waltz, unlike its predecessors, involved continual spinning and anyone who has tried it knows that whirling around the room with a partner soon produces a sense of euphoria.

The waltz was just plain wild. In 1793 the Earl of Banbury, serving in the Revolutionary Wars in Ghent, described the dance in a letter to his mother:

> The Valze is graceful and what I would call the Essence of Intrigue (you will forgive me Mother) ... In pairs, the lady's hands on the gentleman's shoulders, his round her waist, they turn continually round, each preserving the other from falling.

The waltz allowed young girls and men who barely knew each other to indulge in unheard-of physical intimacy as they set off across the floor, locked in a close embrace. This hold, which conveniently prevented them losing their balance and hurtling off into space, gave them a chance to press their bodies together and they were soon lost in their own private world. Even more scandalous was the way a man might hoick his partner's skirts up to avoid treading on them in their wild gallop round the room. And it wasn't unknown for him to place a hand on her breast in order to steer her across the floor. No wonder the waltz created a scandal. Manuals of polite behaviour warned:

> The waltz is a dance of quite too loose a character, and unmarried ladies should refrain from it altogether, both in public and private; very young ladies, however, may be allowed to waltz in private balls, if it is very seldom, and with persons of their acquaintance. It is indispensable for them to acquit themselves with dignity and modesty.

It was feared that a woman's weak powers of resistance would be so challenged by a man's touch that she would become feverish with desire.

Men persuaded themselves that women had such delicate constitutions, they were unable to handle the euphoria of too much physical activity. And it's true that later on, especially in the nineteenth century, women were known to faint from waltzing. But this was more than likely due to the imposition of tight corseting, which prevented them from breathing naturally.

> One might overlook [the waltz's] consequences, which cause the blood to race, and the disarray it causes in dress, yet I believe that as more cultured society, both in language, custom and dress as in all

pleasures, differs from the lower classes, it also ought to make its dance a little less accessible to those whose mind and manners are lacking the requisite grace. Because I consider that it is impossible to discern a degree of propriety in Waltzes ... I do believe it would not hurt to have a little less waltzing at balls.

The waltz was denounced for all kinds of reasons. A German pamphlet claimed that it caused illness and was a source of bodily and mental weakness. Pregnant women were especially discouraged from waltzing, but they took no notice, and some ballrooms had a room set aside in case their energetic dancing caused women to go into premature labour.

Lord Byron was appalled by the dance. He described the sight of his wife waltzing with another man as 'two cockchafers spitted on the same bodekin' and went on to write a poem warning of its dangers. Byron objected to what he called the 'lewd grasp and lawless contact' between strangers, as well as to the waltz's foreign origins. Most disgraceful of all, in his eyes, was the sight of young girls leaping around the floor in their thin muslin dresses; he thought it killed the air of mystery so vital to the female sex. His grumblings may seem strange, coming from a man regarded as mad, bad and dangerous to know. But perhaps Byron was more conservative than we think, for he also objected to mixed bathing, another contemporary habit.

Strong opinion about the waltz was expressed in books of etiquette as well as in the press:

> The character of this dance, its rapid turnings, the clasping of the dancers, their excited contact, and the too quick and too long continued succession of lively and agreeable emotions, produce, sometimes, in women of a very irritable constitution, syncopes, spasms and other accidents which should induce them to renounce it.

A letter to *The Times* in 1813 reveals that a duel was even fought over the dance, following a dispute in which one man praised it while his friend attacked its 'licentious consequences'. The scandalous waltz was reluctantly allowed onto the floor at Almack's in 1814. Its acceptance was responsible for reviving a fashion for morning dances, at which young girls (chaperoned, of course) could master their dance steps before sitting down to a late breakfast.

New dances don't appear out of nowhere, and rejection of the minuet served as a symbolic rejection of the old order. It also showed a turning away from fashions based on the artificial. Powdered wigs and cumbersome pannier skirts gave way to a more natural look. High-waisted muslin and cotton gowns after the style of ancient Greece became popular and were sometimes worn with no underwear except a flesh-coloured body-suit. Young girls who were looking for trouble damped down their skirts so that the fabric clung to their bodies even more revealingly. Unlike the wide skirts which prevented a woman's partner getting too close to her, these flowing gowns were perfect for the waltz. When the Prince Regent gave it his official sanction in 1817, this prompted another letter to *The Times*:

> We remarked with pain that the indecent foreign dance called the waltz was introduced (we believe for the first time) at the English court on Friday last. This is a circumstance which ought not to be passed over in silence. National morals depend on national habits: and it is quite sufficient to cast one's eyes on the voluptuous inter-twining of the limbs, and the close compressure of the bodies, in their dance, to conclude that it is indeed far removed from the modest reserve which has hitherto been considered distinctive of English females. So long as this obscene display was confined to prostitutes and adulteresses, we did not think it deserving of notice: but now it is attempted to be forced on the respectable classes of society by the evil example of their superiors, we feel it a duty to warn every parent against exposing his daughter to so fatal a contagion. We pay due deference to our superiors in rank, but we owe a higher duty to morality. We know not how it has happened (probably the work of some worthless and ignorant dancing master) that so indecent a dance has now for the first time been exhibited at the English court. But it is deserving of severe reprobation, and we trust it will never again be tolerated in any moral English society.

The royal nod to the waltz showed that, in England at any rate, there was no going back. But controversy over the dance continued to rumble on for years. Young girls were advised, in all the best books on social manners, not to dance with men they didn't know and only to take the floor with a man who had been formally introduced to them. By 1855 they were being given the more nebulous advice to waltz only with a man who was 'worthy of so close an intimacy'. A subtle hint was dropped that a man who understood and appreciated one girl wouldn't even want to waltz with another.

Behind all this advice lay the much-feared outcome of a girl having her senses dangerously awakened on the dance floor. The possible denouement of a night of waltzing is spelled out in graphic terms by T. A. Faulkner, a prominent opponent of the dance:

> But let us turn our attention again to the dancers, at two o'clock the next morning. This is the favourite waltz, and the last and most furious of the night, as well as the most disgusting. Let us notice, as an example, our fair friend once more.
>
> She is now in the vile embrace of the Apollo of the evening. Her head rests upon his shoulder, her face is upturned to his, her bare arm is almost around his neck, her partly nude swelling breast heaves tumultuously against his, face to face they whirl on, his limbs interwoven with hers, his strong right arm around her yielding form, he presses her to him until every curve in the contour of her body thrills with the amorous contact. Her eyes look into his, but she sees nothing; the soft music fills the room, but she hears it not; he bends her body to and fro, but she knows it not; his hot breath tainted with strong drink is on her hair and cheek, his lips almost touch her forehead, yet she does not shrink; his eyes, gleaming with a fierce, intolerable lust, gloat over her, yet she does not quail. She is filled with the rapture of sin in its intensity; her spirit is inflamed with passion and lust is gratified in thought. With a last low wail the music ceases, and the dance for the night is ended, but not the evil work of the night.

If the waltz allowed a woman to play with fire by pressing her body close to a strange man, she had other means of signalling her interest in him. All she had to do was use her handkerchief, fan, even her gloves, to communicate her interest. Everything from 'I desire your acquaintance' to 'I wish to be rid of you' (twisting the hanky in the left hand, or biting the tips of the gloves) could be communicated. A woman who sat calmly smoothing her gloves was telling her suitor, 'I am displeased.' Opening her fan in front of him meant, 'You are cruel'; holding its handle to her lips, 'Kiss me.' And the parasols that women carried even when no sun was shining could be equally eloquent. Twirling the parasol signified, 'Be careful; we are being watched.' If today's

film directors were familiar with those old manuals on the language of
flirtation, there might well be a good deal less twirling of parasols and
opening and shutting of fans in period dramas.

76

***

The French Revolution was followed by reaction, revolt and the long-drawn-
out Napoleonic Wars. Between 1792 and 1814 Austria went to war no less
than five times, and after twenty-two years of conflict people were battle-
weary and ready to let their hair down. In 1815 the Congress of Vienna met
to broker peace and it was there that the waltz first attracted attention.
When one of the delegates was asked how negotiations were proceeding,
back came the legendary reply, 'Le Congrès ne marche pas – il danse.'
(Congress isn't working – it's dancing!) Every night there were balls for up to
10,000 people. When the Austrian chancellor Metternich took to the floor in
the new dance, Britain's foreign secretary Lord Castlereagh, not to be
outdone, hired a dancing master to show him the ropes. Rumour had it that
when his wife was unable to partner him, he practised with a chair.

Most delegates at the Congress of Vienna represented the old order. They
were more interested in damping down revolutionary movements within
their own borders, especially in the growing cities, than in fighting among
themselves around the table. At the congress the old aristocrats were obliged
to mix with the new bourgeoisie, which had its own social and political
agenda. The fact that the classes were mixing on the ballroom floor for the
first time, and in a dance which broke all the rules, was a portent of things
to come.

Delegates and their entourages from the congress took the waltz home
with them and in Europe's capitals there began a passion for dancing. The
nobility practised in the morning behind the high walls of their mansions,
and one countess recorded that, every night, during the season, there were
two or three balls. In winter, she wrote, she could go dancing for sixty-three
nights in succession and not be home before dawn.

In some European cities the waltz wasn't just disapproved of, it was
banned for a time – and France was loudest in its disapproval. French
domination of the European cultural scene was especially galling to the
Austrians, whose vast empire included Hungary, Czechoslovakia, parts of

present-day Germany and Poland and the whole of northern Italy. Vienna was the first truly cosmopolitan modern capital and we can imagine how France's cultural pre-eminence must have annoyed the Austrians. The waltz, for all its early hobnail-boots clumsiness, had one thing to recommend it: it was a home-grown product, not French, and perhaps this was one reason why it was embraced so fervently in Austria.

The woods surrounding Vienna were famous for their taverns. Even the poorest alehouse provided entertainment and had a small dance floor. Travelling musicians were rarely short of work. They played at weddings and during meal times and for an hour or so afterwards in the taverns, in return for a carafe of wine and a bowl of goulash. Unlike the French, Austrians weren't allowed to take to the streets to celebrate. They were forced to go indoors if they wanted to dance, and here was a problem: to waltz freely requires space.

Vienna's well-loved hostelries became outdated because they were too small to cater to this requirement. As a result new dance halls were established, like the Apollo Palace, which could accommodate up to 3,000 waltzing couples in its thirty-six salons. Rooms were even set aside for pregnant women who preferred dancing in private rather than mingling with the crowd. So great was people's passion for the waltz that, every night, a quarter of the Viennese population went out dancing.

During the thirty years following the Congress of Vienna sporadic outbursts of rebellion continued to rumble on in Europe. These short-lived revolts were suppressed without too much trouble and the Austrian government wasn't the first to use dance to keep people's minds off politics. It was quick to encourage the establishment of new dance halls where people could let off steam in a harmless way.

One legacy of the French Revolution was the belief that the arts, and culture in general, should be available to everyone, not only the rich. It was the age of Romanticism, a movement which rejected the classical virtues of balance and restraint and in their place introduced dynamism, demonic energy and passionate unrest.

Johann Strauss the elder was the embodiment of Romanticism, right down to the way he conducted his orchestra:

> Strauss was wont to give the signs of expression to his orchestra by all manner of extreme motions of his body. Whenever a sudden loud emphasis was required he flung his arms wide, previously crossed

upon his breast. To indicate a soft passage he bent down, the lower the quieter the volume he wanted. Then, when a crescendo came he would raise himself by degrees, and at the beginning of a forte, would spring bolt upright!

Looking on at this spectacle, the young Wagner was shocked at how each waltz seemed to summon up some demon in 'these curious people, the Viennese. The shudders of sheer pleasure in the audience, and the frenzied enthusiasm for the magic of the music master struck me as frightening.' On a visit to the dance-crazy capital, Chopin echoed Wagner's observation with the comment, 'The audience is so overwhelmed it doesn't know what to do with itself.' The moment when Strauss raised his baton to signal the start of a new waltz was described by one foreign journalist as 'a moment of worship'. Berlioz, on the other hand, was more thoughtful:

> The Austrians have elevated ballroom dancing into an art, as far above the conventional Parisian variety as Strauss waltzes and his orchestra are superior to the polkas and hack fiddlers of our entertainments. And there stands Strauss, directing his splendid orchestra, and sometimes the dancers step forward to applaud.

Serious music, music to sit and listen to, was a thing of the past. What people required was music they could dance to, and Strauss's light-hearted melodies matched perfectly the spirit of the age. Innkeepers and ballroom managers joined forces to mount vast open-air festivities complete with firework displays, which brought the parks and rolling landscapes alive as couples ventured out into the open air to dance the night away. One of Strauss's contemporaries wrote that, were he a despot, he would shower gold on the composer's head for helping divert the population from more serious concerns. And the public couldn't get enough of him. At his concerts women were known to burst into tears and faint.

When Strauss left the city to go on tour in 1837, the heavy touring coaches were stuck in the narrow streets for over an hour because of the crowds of women who gathered to see him off. By his mid-twenties he was at the height of his success. But many years later, when his son the younger Johann embarked on a musical career, his father was so jealous he hired a group of *claqueurs* to disrupt his son's debut concert. *Claqueurs* were professional hecklers, hired to jeer and howl people off stage. This time they didn't succeed, and Johann went on to become even more popular than his father. He too had women swooning, and more than one husband reportedly sent out seconds to demand a duel. The demand by fans for locks of his hair was so great that he once cut the hair off a black Newfoundland dog and sent it out as his own.

It was said that the speed-crazy Viennese waltzed on flat feet, throwing themselves from side to side. The French, on the other hand, waltzed on their toes. As they were later to do with the tango – another shocking, imported dance – they strove to give the waltz a more refined courtly air. Gustave Boullay was one who lamented the demise of a more decorous style of social dancing. In the middle of the nineteenth century he wrote nostalgically about the pre-waltz dance scene in France:

> Under the First Empire, and I even believe since the First Republic, the waltz was the result of international wars, brought to us from Germany, but it only penetrated to the aristocracy after a long wait in the antechamber before it was allowed into the salon. From the beginning one saw that there was, in this intimacy between the dancer and his partner, something too familiar, and one felt that this was not suitable for us. In France one thinks more than one acts.

There will always be those for whom the past is a golden age. But dances are thrown up by the tide of history; and whatever the inspiration for the waltz, it went on to become the most popular of all nineteenth-century dances, cutting through the entire spectrum of society.

***

In America, which at that time took its fashions from England, the rage for waltzing was just as strong as in Europe. The *Boston Weekly* magazine published a lighthearted poem on the subject, beginning:

> *They rise, they twirl, they swing, they fly,*
> *Puffing, blowing, jostling, squeezing,*
> *Very odd but very pleasing!*

Reasons of health were used to buttress arguments against social dancing. It was alleged that 'women of refinement' weren't strong enough for the rigorous waltz and that it caused abortions. And though one would expect the idle rich to be healthier than those who toiled for a living, there may have been something in this; for neither fashion nor social habit allowed women any more exercise than the occasional gentle walk. Dancing for hours in the humid air of ill-ventilated ballrooms and sitting in damp, low-cut gowns may well have caused them to develop chills. Women's tight bodices and even tighter corsets caused breathlessness, and many accounts describe their bosoms rising and falling as they gasped for breath.

At the end of a ball some hosts made it a custom to offer everyone a bowl of hot soup before they went home, but women still had to venture out into the biting early morning air with only a flimsy cloak to protect them. 'Every dancer knows that after a night spent in the ballroom it takes two or three days for the system to recover its wonted elasticity and spirits,' warned one anti-dance campaigner.

The dance floor was a dangerous place for more oblique reasons. For it was where strangers met and talked for the first time; the place where they went to be swept off their feet:

> He presses [his partner] close to his breast and they glide over the floor together as if the two were but one. When she raises her eyes, timidly at first, to that handsome but deceitful face, now so close to her own, the look that is in his eyes as they meet hers, seems to burn into her very soul. A strange, sweet thrill shakes her very being and leaves her weak and powerless and obliged to depend for support upon the arm which is pressing her to himself in such a suggestive manner, but the sensation is a pleasant one and grows to be the very essence of her life.
>
> She grows more bold, and from being able to return shy glances at first, is soon able to meet more daring ones until, with heart beating against heart, hand clasped in hand, and eyes looking burning words which lips dare not speak, the waltz becomes one long, sweet and purely sensual pleasure …

In 1796 an article in the *Philadelphia Minerva* expressed a sense of horror that young girls were being sent to dance lessons even before they could read and write: 'Versatility of mind, hatred for study, or sober reflection, are the inseparable companions of dancing schools.' In some places dance schools were banned. Despite the criticism of these places, some parents were more than happy to pay over the odds to have their daughters lose their less ladylike habits:

> Some girls have a trick of jiggling their bodies (I am obliged to coin a word to describe it); they shake all over, as if they were hung on spiral wires, like geese in a Dutch toy shop; than which nothing can be more ungraceful . . . Some do it only on entering a room, others do it every time they are introduced to anybody, and whenever they begin to talk to anyone. It must have originated in embarrassment, and a desire to do something without knowing exactly what; and being adopted by some popular belle, it became, at one time, a fashion in New York, and spread thence to other cities.

Mothers reasoned that if dance lessons could rid their daughters of these clumsy mannerisms and teach them grace and elegance, then what could be wrong with them?

It's interesting to contrast the comments made for and against dancing by the sexes. Women in favour tended to confine themselves to matter-of-fact comments such as, 'Dance confers grace and dignity of carriage upon the female sex [and] invigorates the constitution ... Nature gives us limbs, and art teaches us to use them.' Men who objected to dancing, on the other hand, tried to influence their readers by tapping into their fears. American journalist Ambrose Bierce charged that the waltz wasn't only suggestive, it was 'an open and shameless gratification of sexual desire and a cooler of burning lust'. The odd thing about Bierce's comment is that he was writing in an age when many men were seeking to persuade women that they didn't have a strong sex drive.

Bierce wasn't alone in concluding that dancing is a substitute for sex. Even today there are writers who believe that the principal reason for dancing is to relieve sexual urges. However, nowadays no one would go as far as to agree with Bierce that, 'The dancing hall is the nursery of the Divorce court, the training ship of prostitution, the graduating school of infamy.'

The anti-dance lobby was dominated by Christians of various denominations. Predominantly male, they quoted God as if he were an actual person they'd sat across a table from and discussed the matter with personally. From the Middle Ages onwards theologians had criticized any activity that might lead us into temptation. Dancing between men and women was high on the list, in that it profaned the Sabbath and led to consorting with the devil. (One only had to think of the harm done by that wicked temptress Salome.) Evangelists promised that those who became converted to the higher cause of religion would be delivered from the craving for frivolous pursuits. Self-denial and purity were the supreme virtues. People who had money to throw away, they said, should use it to help the poor rather than indulge in throwing balls, which involved the vast expense of food, drink, new clothes and who knew what else in the way of self-indulgence and cost.

An abiding fear (and one which lasted well into the first half of the twentieth century) was that dancing encouraged people to disobey the commandment against adultery. All those bodies locked together, spinning across the dance floor in harmony and grace, was explosive stuff. Besides which, lust could be stimulated by any one of the senses, not only touch and sight. The seductive sound of music, the scent of a woman's perfume, the heady effects of alcohol were all a source of temptation. (Despite this, manuals on etiquette prescribed champagne as the correct drink at society dances.) Baptist evangelist William Evander Penn blamed women's 'semi-nude' fashions for exciting men's lower passions and sending 'hundreds of thousands of men, women and girls to premature graves, felons' cells, and to an endless hell.' According to one lobbyist, dance was 'an actual realization of a certain physical ecstasy which should at least be indulged in private ... The privileges of matrimony relieve the necessity for the dance.'

As we've seen, most protests against the waltz were concerned with its effect on women. The mantle of temptation was draped alluringly around female shoulders, yet women were at the same time regarded as being helpless dupes of male passion. It's certainly true that, circling the floor in a formal embrace, a woman could learn a great deal about her partner in terms of physical compatibility. Whereas one man might make dancing enjoyable, another could make it an ordeal. If a man bullied his partner round the floor or handled her insensitively, she had a pretty good idea of his physical sensitivity in other departments.

Presbyterian minister Sylvester F. Scovel was on to a losing wicket, though, when he suggested that women should simply stop enjoying themselves and refuse to dance. Another bit of wishful thinking was that dancing occurred less as human beings moved upwards in society, elevating themselves through education and a more refined sense of morality. The truth was that as the nineteenth century got into its stride the waltz, as the most popular dance of the era, helped liberate middle-class women from the increasing constraints imposed on them.

During the latter years of the century, patterns of socializing were evolving in a fascinating way. The public places set aside for social dancing gave women freedom to venture out of the house and get some exercise into the bargain. It all began with the development of the first grand department stores in Britain and the US. These 'palaces of women', as they were known, became the perfect meeting-place for those who wanted to go out unchaperoned without fearing for their reputations. For there was only a certain kind of woman who wandered the streets and sat in cafés on her own.

The great high-street emporia offered women a respectable place to meet and pampered them with comfy sofas and cups of tea. It soon became a habit for women to spend the entire day there. The trouble was, they were happy to potter around and chat to their friends, without bothering to buy anything. Store assistants (mainly male in the early days) learnt to 'spot the jays', but there wasn't much they could do about them, given that the women's custom was vital to a shop's success.

In the end managers hit on a solution. They opened restaurants, cleverly situated on either the top floor or the roof, so that customers had to make their way through the store's entire range of tempting merchandise to reach them. It wasn't long before these restaurants provided entertainment in the form of live music, and the next natural development was the tea dance. Little by little, shopping, eating, drinking, dancing and live entertainment were coming together under one roof.

***

The waltz made history by enclosing men and women in an embrace. It was always a dance about romance, about meeting someone across a crowded room and forming a magical partnership. And there are all kinds of theories as to what it represented, including the notion that its turning and spinning symbolized the movement of the planets. One writer even suggests that it was an unconscious salute to the newly invented steam engine and its rolling movement. Johann Strauss echoed this idea in the *Railway Waltz*, a piece dedicated to the engine which resounds with hissing and puffing and the clatter of coaches.

It was the steam engine which began the process of conversion from a rural to a mainly urban economy, a momentous invention which marked the beginning of the industrial age. In every sense life was exploding with invention. Never had so many areas of experience been revolutionized in so short a time. Various historians have suggested that the waltz expressed the new speed of travel and the rapid rate of change in nineteenth-century society. Whatever the case, it dominated the century and only began to decline in popularity as the 1800s drew to a close.

The most evocative description of the waltz and its sensual intoxication appears in Gustave Flaubert's most famous novel, *Madame Bovary*, published in 1856. It tells the story of a provincial doctor's wife who is filled with romantic longings and the desperate need to do more than sit around sewing a fine seam. Emma Bovary's frustrated desire to break out of a life which engages few of her senses eventually results in a series of doomed love affairs.

Her downfall begins when her husband takes her to a ball. There she dances with a man who will jolt her out of the numbing boredom of her life. Flaubert builds up the mounting excitement and sensual rapture of the event. He describes the heady perfumes, the magical glow of lantern light, the air made stifling from the exertions of the dancers. The women sit, bare-armed and resplendent in their glittering jewellery, fluttering their fans and hiding their faces behind nosegays of flowers.

To this scene, tense with the promise of intimacy, comes a glimmer of danger. For there in the ballroom doorway linger the male guests, their sleek, pomaded hair falling over their foreheads as they watch the women dance in their rustling gowns. Flaubert presents these young aristocrats as determined hunters. Behind their nonchalant glances, he writes, lurks 'the peculiar brutality developed by dominance in not over-exacting activities such as exercise strength and flatter vanity – the handling of thoroughbreds and the pursuit of wanton women'. The first bars of music strike up. Smiles appear on the faces of the guests and their eyes light up in anticipation:

> Emma's heart beat a little faster when, her partner holding her by the tips of her fingers, she took her place in line and waited for the sweep of the fiddler's bow to start them off ... Emma's nervousness soon vanished, and away she went, swaying to the rhythm of the orchestra, gently nodding her head as she glided forward. A smile rose to her lips at certain subtleties from the violin, playing solo. When the rest of the instruments were silent, you could hear the

gold coins clinking on the baize tables in the next room. Then they all joined in again, the cornet blew a rousing blast, the dancers picked up the time, skirts swelled out and brushed together, hands were caught and released, eyes that lowered before you came back again to fix themselves on yours.

At three o'clock in the morning the waltzing begins. Emma doesn't know how to waltz, but the Viscount, to whom she has just been introduced, offers to teach her, and away they go:

> They started slowly, then got faster. They turned, and everything turned round them – the lamps and chairs, the panelling, the parquet floor, like a disk on a pivot. As they swept past a door, Emma's skirt swirled out against her partner's trousers. Their legs intertwined. He looked down at her and she looked up at him; a numb feeling came over her ... Then they were off again, and the Viscount whirled her away still faster, till they were out of sight at the end of the gallery. She was panting for breath, she nearly fell, for an instant she leaned her head on his chest. Still turning, but more gently, he brought her back to her seat. She sank back against the wall and covered her eyes with her hands.

Flaubert's account of sensual seduction on the ballroom floor reflects, better than any other, the allure of a dance which is all about losing the self, letting go and giving way to the senses. When the novel appeared he was prosecuted for causing an outrage to public morals. It was thought that his book cast a slur on the character of the French and ridiculed them in the eyes of the world. The very idea that such women existed ...! Women who piled up debts, made secret rendezvous with their lovers, deceived their husbands! No matter that Emma Bovary came to a sorry end, gulping down arsenic – a warning in itself, we may think, to other young women tempted to follow in her footsteps.

Flaubert loathed provincial life and in *Madame Bovary* he set out to paint a scathing portrait of the bourgeoisie. He was writing at a time when the middle classes were busy establishing an ultra-respectable image. They'd begun their economic rise in the eighteenth century, amassing fortunes from the growth of commerce, the rising value of land and – in Britain and America – the slave trade. The Industrial Revolution enabled them to consolidate their new status and power. These *nouveau riche* businessmen spent their money on mansions and fashion; and those whose life wasn't centred on the church occupied their leisure time enjoying themselves, which resulted in the rapid growth of entertainment.

In order to be taken seriously, men abandoned their former dashing clothes and kitted themselves out in sober colours. It would be a long time before they were again seen in colourful clothes; in fact, not until the 1960s. From now on, fashion was strictly women's business, and as the century progressed middle-class women allowed themselves to be turned into a decorative luxury.

Having previously been an upper-class foible, fashion became a preoccupation of the bourgeoisie. A woman's clothes served to advertise her husband's wealth, just as her impeccable behaviour was expected to reflect his moral rigour. Woman was cast in the role of household goddess, an icon of empty-headed virtue. Her moral purity was intended to cleanse her husband of his sins and draw a veil over the grubby business of how he'd come by his money. It cleansed him of the taint of business and factory life and at the same time, with women carrying the burden of goodness and virtue, freed him to indulge in all the vices.

Men have long made women responsible for keeping them on the straight and narrow by setting an example of saintly self-denial. Yet ever since Eve and the apple, men have known that women are just as frail, just as vulnerable to temptation as they are. So this saintly purity had to be helped along by a little control. One way of controlling women's tendency to transgress was to literally restrict their bodies. By the 1850s the female body beneath the waist resembled an igloo, a massive base within which the contours of legs and hips could only be imagined. Voluminous skirts and petticoats and horsehair padding took up so much space they provided a barrier against intimate contact. These confections, which were sometimes thirty feet in circumference, were so heavy it was impossible to drag their weight along.

When the crinoline was revived as a fashion around the middle of the century it came as an enormous relief to women, for it gave them some leg-room and enabled them to move about more freely. Described as 'the first application of the steam age to women's dress', the crinoline kept the steel industry busy and eliminated at a stroke the need for horsehair padding. Supported by fragile hoops of steel, skirts became ever wider, requiring hundreds of yards of material. As the crinoline weighed little, skirts could become wider without being heavier, and they created a wonderfully suggestive effect, swinging to and fro and lifting ever so slightly to reveal a woman's ankles as she whirled round the dance floor. These huge skirts were ridiculed by the dress reform movement, which became active in the last quarter of the century. Meanwhile the 'any colour as long as it's black' fashion for men was receiving its share of scorn:

> Who that ever sits in the gallery of a crowded ballroom, looking down on the whirling dancers below, is not struck with the ridiculous incongruity in their dress, as they glide in close couples over the floor? The ladies, huge and cylindrical in masses of vaporous tulle, while the poor little men, black as ebony and straight as clothes-pins, pirouette in bold relief against their unsubstantial edges with an anxious look, as if they felt that at any moment a sudden gust might puff them off into the air, or drag them out beyond their bearings … But, unlike clothes-pins, the men are not wooden-headed; for, when the music strikes up a quadrille, they show marvellous dexterity in piloting themselves through the vaporous lanes and around their huge partners; and no one of them treads on the lowest, outlying ruffle of the tarlatan mists through which they pick their way. When the music stops with a long scrape from the violin, they are always found bowing in their right places, though they have had to circumnavigate great circles in their devious voyage.

The crinoline was something of a fire hazard and there were women who died after being engulfed in flames when they stood too close to an open fire. Wearing a crinoline, though, was nowhere near as dangerous as wearing another item of female underwear which had its heyday in the nineteenth century.

**

No item of Western dress has given rise to more debate, nor been so fiercely defended on one hand and reviled on the other, as the corset. Between the 1860s and 1900, it was the most widely and persistently advertised of all consumer items. Ads for corsets were placed in the popular press, in dance programmes, religious magazines and even trade union journals.

In the eighteenth century gorgeously decorated, brightly coloured corsets were worn by men, women and children alike as top garments. By the 1900s they had become an item of underwear for women only. And though occasional ads for men's corsets could still be found, they had practically vanished by the mid-nineteenth century, when they were ridiculed as effeminate. During the 1870s the corset once again became an outer garment – and a highly erotic one. It threw into relief the bosom and pelvis; it lifted the breasts, hollowed the lower back and pushed the bottom down. To achieve a smooth, tapering effect, someone had the bright idea that the bulky lines of the ribcage should be hidden.

Corsets became *de rigueur*, not just for those with money to spare, and any woman who failed to get herself trussed up in one was criticized for it. 'The fact is that the woman who affects loose garments is lazy and violates all the rules of good dressing,' wrote a certain Dr Hunt in 1882, adding for good measure, 'Nature demands that women should have small waists.'

If early nineteenth-century fashion favoured the ethereal ballerina type, by the 1890s the buxom chorus girl was all the rage; but though this model gloried in a voluptuous bosom and beefy thighs, she was still expected to have a minuscule waist. No genteel woman wanted to have the coarse, thick-waisted body of a washerwoman who spent her time leaning over the tubs. So vital was a wasp-waist for fashion slaves that some were even willing to remove a couple of ribs in order to achieve this. Believe it or not, in those days a thirteen-inch waist was considered a mark of breeding. Not only that: the waist's natural oval shape wasn't good enough. It had to be a perfect circle, something which could only be acquired through the constant pressure of tight lacing.

The corset created a rigid torso and condemned women to a degree of discomfort and pain which, in time, resulted in all kinds of ailments. Before steel took over, the corset's basic structure was made of leather and whalebone. The most extreme version had bones, or 'stays', extending all the way down the thighs and closing in a kind of chastity belt between the legs. This type of corset was impossible to sit down in, and French novelist Colette tells us that it obliged one actress of her acquaintance to remain standing throughout the evening, even during the intervals. Relaxing in an armchair was impossible. Women could only perch lightly on the edge of upright chairs and they sat through long journeys, meals and evenings at the theatre in varying degrees of discomfort.

The continual pressure exerted on the body's inner organs was responsible for displacing the lower ribs, the liver and even the uterus. A woman's ribs were pushed up, out of the way, to help pull in her waist; and so effectively did a corset's pressure numb the flesh that, even when one of its steel bones snapped or turned inwards, pressing into the skin, a woman often felt no pain. Only when she undressed did she realize what had happened. Sometimes, as she removed her corset, she discovered that her flesh had been pierced by broken stays, leaving her underwear stained with blood.

During the eighteenth century, designing, making and fitting corsets was an exclusively male preserve. In the early 1800s women began infiltrating what was becoming a very lucrative business. In her history of the corset, *Bound to Please,* Leigh Summers shows how, when women began designing corsets themselves, their innovations were largely to do with making them less painful. By contrast, she writes, male designers seem to have been more concerned with reinforcing their strength and making them even more restrictive.

David Price, who has written a history of the cancan, maintains that corsets were unlikely to cause any harm when worn properly. His imagination moves into overdrive as he continues, 'For some women, tight lacing may have been a method of providing sexual thrills.' There's no doubt that a prisoner gets used to her prison after a while, but Price is clearly one of those men who believe women enjoy and even invite pain. He goes on to make the extraordinary statement, 'It is true that corseted ladies were unable to breathe deeply, which, in general, did not matter, as middle- and upper-class women were expected to be idle and dependent.' Being idle and dependent is one thing. Fainting because you are unable to breathe properly, suffering palpitations, having your liver sliced into by broken whalebone stays, suffering miscarriages and displaced wombs is something else.

Nor is Price correct in his airy assumption that only the wealthy wore corsets. By the late 1840s they were freely available to working women. Some of their upper-class sisters weren't too pleased at this state of affairs. One wrote that a well-fitting corset could be had for so little money that 'even one's maidservants [could] walk into any corset-makers and buy a figure, fit for a lady of the highest respectability, for a mere trifle'.

The challenge to middle-class distinction thrown up by working women even provoked comment in the press. *Woman* was one of the magazines to pour scorn on the 'silly anaemic maidservant or stage-struck barmaid' who tried 'to reduce her podgy frame'. For a working woman, having the fashionable, genteel shape bestowed by a corset helped her 'improve' herself and offered her the chance to attract a man above her class. Nor did being corseted prevent her doing the kind of work which involved leaning forwards or sideways, for she could always loosen her suitably named 'stays'. Or else she could choose one of the many different designs – sometimes called 'jumps' – which had a looser fit and allowed sufficient mobility for menial work.

Poor women acquired their corsets in a variety of ways. From the 1830s pattern books became available, containing detailed information on how to make them. Wealthy women tended to hand down their old corsets to their maids, even if they still had plenty of wear in them. Later on the invention of the sewing machine and the growth of industrialization made it easier and cheaper to obtain them ready-made. By a simple process of transference, physical constraint was thought to have an effect on the mind. It calmed a woman's naturally wayward thoughts, just as tight lacing hid the sight of unruly, wobbling flesh. In this way a corseted woman came to be regarded as being both physically and morally disciplined.

In order to justify the imposition of the corset on women still further, there arose the concept that the female, unlike the male, torso was an imperfect design that needed 'support' in order to remain upright. More than one early feminist commented dryly that, if women's bodies were so unevolved that they needed to be corseted in order not to collapse, God must be a hopeless failure in terms of his design skills. Was it really the case that the Almighty had made man fit for all life's requirements and woman unable to hold herself erect by her own unaided efforts? As Lady Harberton, founder of the American Dress Reform Society, commented, 'No creature has yet appeared on this earth which as a species requires a mechanical support for its own body.'

Aside from being strapped into rigid underwear, a woman's petticoats and knickers gave her up to fourteen bindings around her waist. As the century progressed, fashion latched onto the idea of boned jackets for women, providing yet a further layer of entrapment. Meanwhile sleeves became so narrow that it was impossible to lift the arms very high. When the *Atlantic* steamer foundered in high seas all the men on board managed to climb up the masts out of danger, to await rescue. But not a single woman survived, for none of them were able to lift their arms above their shoulders. Every effort was made to help them, recalled one survivor, but 'They could not climb ... and so we were forced to leave them to their fate.'

It wasn't only tightly set sleeves that hampered a woman's movement. Trailing bustles were attached to the skirt from thigh to lower calf by means of tapes tied behind the legs (this helped prevent a 'masculine' stride). One wonders how women avoided going stark staring mad from the restrictions imposed on them by their clothes. At exactly the same time, Leigh Summers notes, men's clothes were being redesigned to make them more comfortable!

There were corsets for every situation, from prison life to pregnancy and exercise. Nor were women released at night; they were encouraged to wear a corset in bed to maintain their new shape. There were even corsets with air holes designed for hot climates, and it must have required an iron will for Englishwomen who accompanied their husbands to India and the Far East to carry on trussing themselves up like chickens for the spit. Luckily, whatever other alien customs were imposed on the subjects of the British Empire, tight lacing wasn't one of them. Contemporary press accounts show that non-Western women regarded corsets with a combination of amusement and contempt.

One of the most pernicious aspects of the fashion for corsets is that they were imposed on the growing bodies of children, some from the age of three. Women were told that children's corsets 'protected the hips and abdomen, gently braced the spine and encouraged breast development'. In *Period Piece, a Memoir of a Victorian Childhood*, Gwen Raverat recalls that when her thirteen-year-old sister was put into corsets she 'ran round and round the nursery screaming with rage'. Raverat rebelled more quietly by running away and removing them. When she was discovered there was a row and she was forced to put them back on. 'To me they were instruments of torture,' she says. 'They prevented me from breathing, and dug deep holes into my softer parts on every side. I am sure no hair shirt could have been worse to me.'

In an age when pregnancy was considered a repugnant sight, corsets enabled women to disguise their condition. Pregnant women were advised to keep out of sight, stay away from balls and other social activities and remain in a reclining position as much as possible. The fact that wearing a corset hid their pregnancy gave them a few extra weeks of relative freedom to attend social events before going into *purdah*. But we can only imagine the discomfort they endured, and evidence suggests that corsets were responsible for many a miscarriage.

It has also been suggested that women laced themselves extra tightly in a deliberate attempt to induce an abortion. In this way, an unwanted baby, if stillborn, could be quietly disposed of without it being known that a woman was pregnant in the first place. It is the case that the birth rate fell drastically among the middle classes during the second half of the nineteenth century (a time of increasingly harsh penalties for abortion). But those who claimed that it was the waltz which caused miscarriages were barking up the wrong tree. Summers suggests that tightly laced corsets may well have contributed to the falling birth rate.

The social life of middle-class women became heavily circumscribed during Victorian times. The theatre was considered a dangerous place of moral laxity and was pronounced out of bounds if a ballet were included on the bill, for this would involve the vulgar display of legs and lightly clad female bodies. The ballroom alone was available to middle-class women as a legitimate outlet for their energies, and they made the most of it and danced with a vengeance. Pregnant women, their condition safely concealed beneath their billowing skirts, continued waltzing, and if they fainted it was more than likely due to their inability to draw breath beneath their tight lacing. Besides, fainting was considered one of the normal hazards of belonging to a poorly evolved sex who couldn't even hold their backs straight without the aid of a mechanical device.

The convenient assumption was made that not only was the female body poorly designed, but God in his infinite wisdom had created girls dull-witted. Incapable of thought or serious cultural achievement, why waste time and money educating them? Girls were discouraged from reading, which was thought to cause illness when indulged in to excess. According to an 1838 edition of the *Ladies Companion*, those who craved education were in danger of becoming 'semi-women or mental hermaphrodites'. It was also feared that books would introduce women to sinful ideas, ones that they weren't constitutionally strong enough to deal with.

Some men abhorred this infantilizing of women. 'Out of laziness and corruption', wrote French poet Jules Laforgue, 'we have created a being set apart, unknown, having no arm other than her sex ... adoring or hating but not a candid friend ... an eternal little slave.' In *Madame Bovary* Flaubert describes the numbing frustration of this kind of life for a woman of even the most limited imagination. (Flaubert's friend, the literary critic Sainte-Beuve, wrote to a female friend, discouraging her from reading the novel, 'It is too crude for most women, and would offend you.')

Doomed to ignorance of most activities outside the domestic circle, middle-class women had little to contribute to the conversation, and after dinner they trotted off obediently to their own drawing-room. There they could talk about frivolous matters, leaving the men free to discuss meaningful topics (or so it was assumed) while enjoying a smoke – another pastime discouraged among the fair sex.

This enervating scenario would be enough to sap anyone's vitality and it was hard for middle-class women, who had previously helped in the family business and played an active part in economic life, to be stripped of meaningful work and left high and dry. Since it was not they who held the purse strings, most of them had no choice but to try and live up to the new role allotted them. Gradually they allowed their activities to be curtailed. They stayed at home, bent over their watercolours and concentrated on harmless, not too taxing pastimes such as organizing the servants.

Early nineteenth-century portraits depict women as flower children, lost in fields of grass and corn, as though growing out of the earth itself. There they stand, holding a single rose up to their lips, with garlands in their hair and blossoms adorning their tiny, perfectly circular waists. So complete was their identification with nature that women were thought to be ruled entirely by their bodies. The notion that they were totally lacking in grey matter went right across the social spectrum. The literature of the time is full of descriptions of women as dumb, bestial creatures driven by primitive urges.

Man was the tree, woman its flowers and fruits, and as the century progressed she began to wither on its branches. If ever a group needed to rebel it was middle-class women. But their rebellion wasn't to erupt for many years. It was working women who were the first to show their claws and kick their legs in the air, and it happened on the dance floor.

Forbidden Fruit

It was a sexually predatory ritual, open to all comers,
in which most women went knickerless,
flashing glimpses of their genitals to the men,
challenging them to thrust and enter.
Rupert Christiansen

The 1830s was one of those times of upheaval in Europe when people's ideas about themselves and their place in the world were being redefined. While scientific and evolutionary thought was throwing up challenging new ideas about the nature of human existence, the Industrial Revolution was changing the landscape at an alarming rate.

Just as the Industrial Revolution consolidated the status and power of the new middle class, it also drastically altered the lives of working people. In England it brought them swarming into the expanding cities and created a gigantic shift in their way of life. With the move to cities and the division of labour in factories, women were faced with a choice of evils: they could either work for long hours in factories or they could work as laundresses, servants or dressmakers. But factory conditions were nothing short of barbarous and none of the available choices paid well.

Right up until the early twentieth century there was no legal weekly day of rest; nor was there sick pay or holiday leave, paid or otherwise. In the free-for-all, sink-or-swim capitalist economy, job security was non-existent. Life was what you made it and lone women who managed to carve out a living for themselves as independent operators often fared best economically.

Though industrialization came later to France than England, people in both countries still toiled for low wages in the service industries. In Paris girls began work at the age of seven, delivering washing. As fourteen-year-olds they worked ten hours a day at the tubs for the sum of two francs. A dressmaker on piece-work might earn as little as a franc a day, a chambermaid forty francs a month. Being an artist's model, on the other hand, paid a good deal more – certainly exceeding the wages paid by sweatshops where women toiled for a pittance in dirty, ill-lit, poorly ventilated conditions.

In time, an enormous number of women in Paris and in Western Europe's other newly rich cities would turn to prostitution to supplement their meagre wages. For others the best bet, financially speaking, was to become entertainers. In the public estimation the two jobs were practically synonymous.

Political events have a profound influence on art and entertainment and it was in the turbulent 1830s, as revolutions flared across Europe, that the embryonic cancan appeared. Under France's new liberal regime everyday life changed little for the poor, who carried on working as normal and letting off steam at the end of the day in dance halls, *bals musettes* and bars. But the political upheavals of the period left a spirit of revolt in the air, which came to be personified by the cancan. Never had there been such a wild dance, and when it was reported that cancan dancers threw their skirts over their heads to display their frilly underwear, the middle and upper classes flocked to see it.

In 1832 the cancan was presented at the Variétés Theatre in Paris as a surprise piece of programming for the annual masked Carnival Ball. It didn't take long before everyone was joining in the new dance and the police stepped in to call a halt to the fun. One of those who witnessed the dance on this occasion was scandalized:

> When one sees with what gestures and movements of the body the masked men approach the masked women, press close to them, and actually throw them backwards and forwards between themselves to the accompaniment of continual acclamation and laughter and ribald jokes, one can only be filled with disgust ... The beat of the music is hastened, the dancers' movements become more rapid, more animated, more aggressive, and finally the *contredanse* evolves into a great gallop, in which the dancers form into double pairs, four in a row, and gallop madly round the floor ... One finally sees masked women, like ecstatic maenads, with flushed cheeks,

breathlessly heaving breasts, parched lips and half-undone, flying hair, careering round the room, less on their feet than being dragged along bodily, until with the last chord they collapse breathlessly on the nearest seat.

The word cancan comes from the Old French *caquehan*, meaning 'gossip' or 'scandal', a perfect description of the dance. It began as an exuberant romp and climaxed in a forward bend, a flinging up of petticoats and a saucy display of bottoms. *En route* to this startling denouement came high kicks during which, with a nimble sweep of the foot, female dancers divested high-class gents of their hats in a ritual decapitation. From being a mixed-sex social romp it was appropriated by women, and even today it symbolizes the carefree sensuality of Parisian life.

It's been said that the cancan wasn't really a dance at all, more a frame of mind. But as *cancaneuse* Rigolboche wrote in her memoirs, 'It is above all a dance of liberty.' It's certainly a dance with attitude. And the best-known *cancaneuses* weren't necessarily the prettiest, unlike nineteenth-century ballerinas, who were engaged primarily for their looks and less for their ability to dance.

A rebellious high kick was part of the cancan right from the start. Originally done by men, it wasn't long before women began imitating their partners and flinging their legs into the air as well. The main reason the cancan was notorious was because it was impossible to execute these high kicks unless women lifted their skirts and showed not just their legs but their underwear too. This was at a time when knickers were not commonly worn. Women had far too much material rustling around their legs, with all those skirts and underskirts and petticoats, to welcome any further encumbrance. When they did start wearing knickers it was in the shape of long, flimsy see-through tubes open at the crotch for convenience. A famous *cancaneuse* from the early period, Nini-la-Belle-en-Cuisse (Nini with the Beautiful Thighs), acquired her nickname after walking on her hands the entire length of the dance floor, showing everyone that she wasn't wearing any knickers. Legend has it that a watching policeman was so overcome by the sight that he cried out, '*Cré Dié! Les belles cuisses!*' (Dear God! What beautiful thighs!) and forgot to arrest her.

That the cancan was invariably danced without knickers is something of a myth. It's certainly true that, once the dance acquired status as a performance piece, and once women started wearing long knickers as a routine item of clothing, dancers took care to make their underwear so attractive that displaying it became a main feature of the dance.

The early cancan was performed by couples in groups of four. It owed something to the polka, which also appeared, to considerable scandal, in 1830. 'To dance the polka men and women must have hearts that beat high and strong. Tell me how you do the polka and I will tell you how you love,' wrote one dance teacher of the time. The Vicomte de Saint-Laurent, in his *Observations on Modern Dancing*, went further:

> For many the polka would seem to be but the prelude to whoring, for they visit their mistresses immediately after the ball. And even those who do not go so far are stimulated by the intimate rhythmic bodily contacts of the dance into sexual fantasies involving their partners.

The polka ended in a boisterous gallop from one end of the floor to the other, and soon cancan dancers were incorporating this gallop into their dance, each group of four mingling, crossing and parting before launching into a wild dash across the room. The cancan also used the same exuberant 2/4 beat as the polka, a beat which leaves no space for pausing and taking a breath, but drives relentlessly onward.

The cancan was first seen in the Montparnasse district of Paris at the Grande Chaumière dance hall. Sailors, students, porters from the food markets, dressmakers and washerwomen gathered here and at similar establishments after the day's work. Later on in the evening came a more well-heeled clientele.

At that time the dance was known as the *polka-piquée* or *chahut*, meaning 'noisy uproar'. According to one theory it was imported by sailors who had picked it up in Algiers; but this is unlikely, for its movements have nothing in common with North African dance. Nor is it true, as some have suggested, that the cancan was just wild, anarchic improvisation. It was – and is – a tough dance and *cancaneuses* had to be strong. Manipulating the skirts, a piece of display harking back to the Andalusian fandango, was easy enough, but other movements demanded great skill and energy. One of these was the *porte d'armes*, a step often sketched by the artist Toulouse-Lautrec. In this the dancer performs a high kick, catches her ankle in her hand at its highest point and holds it there while spinning rapidly on her supporting foot.

The cancan became a feature of dance halls and *bals dansants* at the Paris Opéra which went on, with non-stop music and dancing, into the early hours. The best *cancaneuses* were offered free entry on condition that they entertain the crowd, who cheered and egged them on in their wild improvisations. The Creole dancer Finette was skilled at knocking off men's top hats with her foot and once won 1,500 francs for doing so at the Opéra Ball. She was one of the first to execute the *grand écart*, a wild, bold move that involved leaping into the splits from a jump. The daring of this move, as well as the skill of the *porte d'armes*, was described by many an observer:

> One of the women suddenly sprang into the air and then came down to the ground with both legs at right angles to her body. A shout of laughter hailed this exploit, and a dozen hands were held out to help her from the ground; but disdaining all such aid she sprang lightly to her feet, and both she and her companions took their places for the final effort. Deliberately gathering up their long skirts, they threw them over their shoulders and thus left themselves unencumbered and exposed to the public view from their waists to their feet … The brown-haired girl has closed her eyes, and has gathered her drapery under her arms. She sees nothing of the scene around her, but hears only the music and the applause. She is pale and panting, but she keeps on and on in the wild dance, until her strength is utterly exhausted.

Rigolboche wrote that when she danced she was afflicted by a kind of madness, for the music stirred her up like champagne. Among her clients she boasted the Duc de Gramont-Caderousse, who one day dared her to walk naked across the Boulevard des Italiens as far as the Café Anglais. No doubt the duke also bribed the police to turn a blind eye, for no one turned up to bring her promenade to a halt. Rigolboche was careful not to fritter away her money, unlike many female performers of her day, who managed to raise themselves from poverty to great riches in the music halls of Paris. When they had it they spent it and lived for the moment.

It was best not to think of the future, for there were two great shadows looming in the background of nineteenth-century life: the twin scourges of tuberculosis (then known as consumption) and syphilis, for which there was no cure at the time. Many who lived riotous lives in the *beau monde* shared a sense of fatalism and didn't count on making old bones. Rigolboche was more fortunate than others. She may have over-indulged in cigars and alcohol – particularly the notorious absinthe – but the worst that happened to her was that she finally put on too much weight to continue working as a dancer. As *Le Figaro* reported:

> The diva has returned in an anatomical condition that gives no cause for worry about her health, but which must hinder her very much when she raises her leg to its customary height. So much the better for our noses!

In 1840 the Bal Mabille opened its doors:

> The mad, bad, merry music would strike up and a set formed, the men challenging the soles of their shoes and planting their high silk hats on the back of their head, the ladies coyly examining the condition of their skirts. The foreigners and country visitors and *gobe-mouches* [bumpkins] would gather round forming a wall six or seven feet, leaving a space of ten to fifteen feet for the dancers. Bang! And the dancers would commence their wild gyrations, the men slinging their limbs about as if they did not belong to them, the women frisking their draperies in time to the music, and posturing while revealing a liberal display of lower limbs. Faster and faster the pace would grow, the women more madly energetic, their postures more hideously indecorous, until the final bars of the tune would be wound up in a series of acrobatic movements that would call down the vivas of the excited and amused spectators.

Middle-class observers found they could live vicariously for a few hours through the uninhibited sensuality of the cancan and enjoy the kind of behaviour which was a far cry from the polite socializing and artificial manners of bourgeois life. Meanwhile, the riotous abandon of the dancers themselves, as they flung up their skirts to show their frothy underwear, must have given rise to many shivers of delight.

In time-honoured tradition, the wealthy fed from the vitality of the workers and took pleasure in watching them entertain themselves. However much they may have enjoyed slumming it in dance halls, though, they had no desire to be more than spectators of proletarian abandon. The cancan was simply too wild for bourgeois women, and was always to remain a working-class dance.

Cancaneuses broke more than just the rules of showing their legs. When La Reine Pomaré appeared at the Opéra Ball wearing men's dress it was considered outrageous. She was ahead of her time in cross-dressing, a custom that would later become popular at these events. Men and women lived in different worlds and the blurring of sexual divisions was initially considered daring. Women were expected to dress like women and behave like women and they were forbidden by law to go about in public in men's clothes. There were a number of practical reasons why dressing *en travesti* was attractive to women. For one thing, it was a way of escaping unwanted sexual advances. Besides, suits were comfortable and easy to move about in, compared to women's dress. They were also less expensive.

The crinoline which re-emerged as a fashion in the nineteenth century had an unexpected – and highly erotic – effect in motion. Its light steel hoops swung and swayed from side to side in the most exaggerated way and it took skill to move about in it without a woman revealing her underwear. If she wasn't careful and made a sudden movement – especially when sitting down – the entire contraption was liable to shoot into the air. Walking in high winds, even just going upstairs, she could easily reveal her ankles, knees, even her thighs. It was because of this that women took to wearing short boots. They discarded their comfortable ballerina slippers and hooked and laced themselves into these little black leather items which, inevitably, became fetish objects and created an erotic focus in the ankle. At the same time, women took advantage of the fact that their legs might inadvertently be displayed by wearing coloured stockings and petticoats.

It was the crinoline which ultimately made it necessary to wear knickers. Initially women were reluctant to wear them, for long lace-trimmed drawers were a popular item of underwear among prostitutes, who turned them into a sexually inviting item. These long knickers naturally drew attention to a woman's legs – whose existence was denied by all those layers of skirts and petticoats; but women soon realized they had to wear something to counteract the immodesty of the crinoline.

A change in fashion that was used to great effect in the cancan (indeed, it became one of its best-known aspects) was the evolution of gorgeous underwear which was far too beautiful to be hidden. Hand-embroidered garments of silk and fine satin were threaded with coloured ribbons and decorated with lace. Originally lace was only used for the hem, which might inadvertently be revealed. But little by little, flounces of lace began creeping up the petticoat as far as the waist.

This new fancy underwear was a feast for the eye. Amateur *cancaneuses* who worked as laundresses borrowed petticoats that their clients had left for cleaning and made a great display of them during the dance. We can imagine how they must have enjoyed flaunting this underwear, which they couldn't possibly have afforded themselves and whose owners were certainly unaware had been 'borrowed' for a rackety night out!

Those frothy petticoats and embroidered corsets were clearly meant to be displayed. Yet many middle-class men would not have seen a woman's underwear at close quarters. Their wives dressed and undressed in a separate room, assisted by their maids, and only emerged into the bedroom in their nightgowns. So seeing the cancan dancers' snowy white petticoats and black stockings held up by garters must have provided quite a *frisson* of excitement. Here was the secret world of women; it was all on display and – who knows – perhaps even available. So excited were they at the sight that men sometimes strayed too close to the dancers to get a better look:

> One of the spectators venturing to thrust his face too close, the younger girl suddenly threw up her leg and with her foot sent his hat rolling into the circle amidst the yells and laughter of the lookers-on, and without pausing a moment went hopping round the circle with her foot higher than her head.

In August 1869 outrage at the turn that social dancing and, by implication, social life was taking was graphically expressed outside the Paris Opéra, where a specially commissioned sculpture by Jean-Baptiste Carpeaux had been erected in the front courtyard. It showed a lightly draped woman with her arms uplifted in ecstasy, a self-absorbed smile on her lips. Around her cavorted a group of naked women with hands linked and similar smiles of knowing enjoyment on their faces. Unlike the statues of classical Greece, which show the human body as either stationary or in decorous motion, this group looked as if it was having a good old romp. This wasn't the stately measure of Greek dance (as it was imagined), the 'silent assembly' of Plutarch. It was the bawdy dancing of the Bal Mabille and the Grande Chaumière. These were nineteenth-century working women letting their hair down, and if the sculpture didn't go so far as to show them cocking a leg in sexual invitation, what it did suggest was the anarchic spirit of women on the loose.

Soon after the sculpture was unveiled, a big bottle of black ink was thrown over it, spattering the thighs of the central dancing figure. In *Tales of the New Babylon*, Rupert Christiansen charts the unfolding of events after this initial act, which gave rise to a spate of copy-cat ink throwing. The rumour grew that sculptors had instigated these events themselves in order to draw attention to their work, and it wasn't long before the railways set up special day trips to view the damage. Supporters of Carpeaux took up a vigil around his sculpture and demonstrated with anti-establishment slogans. The debate grew heated: on one side stood those who supported artistic freedom, on the other the defenders of public decency. Letters appeared in the press decrying the new spirit of vulgarity in the arts. One cartoon shows an old man lecturing his wife, who stands hypnotized by the sculpture, 'Don't stare like that, it only encourages them!'

Carpeaux' sculpture brought to mind the wild shenanigans of the dance halls. The humour which characterized the scandal shows to what extent the cancan was already accepted as part of the social scene. By now it had spread far beyond its boundaries, and in Russia two cancan dancers were even escorted out of the country on the orders of the tsar. At London's Alhambra music hall a 'Roast Beef and Plum Pudding' version was performed by a dancer known as Wiry Sal or Sarah the Kicker. Her antics caused the theatre to lose its licence in what was only one of many complaints against the dance in England. Almost from the start, the cancan was regarded as shocking by respectable society. As for the women who performed it, we can imagine how they were secretly admired for their daring.

***

Having invented the rules which put them at the top of the social ladder, the upper classes have always broken them with impunity, unlike those people scrabbling up the rungs, seeking to find a foothold. But being at the top encourages complacency. By the second half of the nineteenth century, the aristocracy's power had slipped away through its own inertia. From now on it would be left behind by the bustling energy of bourgeois entrepreneurs whose factories and grand department stores created the first consumer society. During this period the economic structure of Europe and the United States underwent a radical transformation. Vast personal fortunes were built up in trade and manufacturing, with the *nouveaux riches* using their wealth to play the stock market and invest in all kinds of ambitious new schemes.

One such venture was the remodelling of central Paris by Baron Haussmann, whose wide boulevards replaced the narrow, winding streets where it had been easy to throw up the barricades in times of unrest. Along these broad new thoroughfares men with money to spend sallied forth, looking for distraction. Leaving their wives at home on their pedestals, they fled from the dull-witted household nuns they had created, whose energy had been sapped by enforced inactivity. Having fashioned a prison for their wives and created conditions ensuring everyone's sexual frustration, these men were out in search of fun. They found it in dance halls, where women behaved with a freedom that was an aphrodisiac in itself.

Even artists, who were used to seeing models strip off in front of them, were enraptured by the sight of working women strolling along the boulevards in the early evening light, linking arms with their beaux. Armand Sylvestre recalls sitting outside on a cafe terrace with Degas, Manet and Zola:

> How many times did we not sit there and, in ecstasy, watch the wonderful women who, during the warm summer evenings, their workday past, with a flower touching their lips, and often with a lover on their arm, would return home along that street, bareheaded and with a beautiful glow of liberation in their eyes! ... [Never] did I ever see a more delicious procession of gorgeous women in the full unfolding of their youth and health.

Artists and students lived up in Montmartre, which at that time was outside the city centre and was still sufficiently rural for Parisians to be able to fill their lungs with fresh air from the surrounding fields. *Le haut* (upper) Montmartre was the intellectuals' quarter, while *le bas* (lower) Montmartre housed dance halls and mean streets where it wasn't advisable to venture alone at night if you had too much money in your pocket. Dance halls flourished around the Place Blanche alongside cafe-concerts, which were a forerunner of cabarets. In these smoke-filled dens, solo artists stood up and entertained audiences with only a piano as their accompaniment. Poets and singers did the rounds of the tables, offering their verses to the noisy crowd.

The most famous of the cafe-concerts was the Elysée Montmartre. It was shabby and cheap, a low-down dive described as having a smutty look. At l'Ely, a police inspector known by the dancers as Le Père Pudeur (Father Modesty) was given the enjoyable job of checking their underwear for decency. One of the best-known cancan dancers, Jane Avril, didn't enjoy working there, for she said the women danced crudely and had a shameless air:

> The dancers kicked up a dark thick dust and the girls of the promenade were ugly and dirty and sat themselves next to the fops in the room in such a manner that there was no mistaking their profession.

She refused payment for her performances because, she said, 'There is less pleasure in it if you get paid.'

In Montmartre you could find pantomime, circus acts, freak shows and clowns. Then in 1867 came the first Universal Exposition. Its most popular attraction was the villages presenting 'ethnic' music and dance. From then on, giant trade and cultural exhibitions would be held in Paris every eleven years until 1900. The 1889 Paris Expo had a special significance, being the centenary of the French Revolution, and it was marked by the building of Monsieur Eiffel's tower. (Originally intended as a temporary structure, the Eiffel Tower was initially hated by Parisians, who considered it a blot on the landscape of their newly beautified city.)

From the entertainment point of view, 1889 was significant for another reason. In September that year an establishment described by its proprietors as 'the first palace of women' opened its doors to the public. A contemporary press report on the opening of the Moulin Rouge commented:

> Remember the name of this new dance hall in the Place Blanche – you've not heard the last of it. Last night the whole of Paris was there to celebrate the opening, and the show was not only on the stage but also in the audience.

Listing the royal personages and well-known artists in the audience, the report went on to say:

> Picture carriage parties arriving from the chic districts of Neuilly and Passy, hobnobbing happily with natives from lower Montmartre and Rochechouart, cloth-capped roughs and young women with

unkempt hair, knotted in a bun ... Never have we seen an audience enjoy itself so much. The scene was indescribable: you had to be there to believe it! When, supported by the brass section, the dancers invaded the hall, whirling and kicking their legs up in a frenzied rhythm, a thrill of pleasure ran through the company.

The Moulin Rouge's proprietors, Joseph Oller and Charles Zidler, were far from modest in their claims for this new establishment. They promised it would be the most magnificent of all the temples of music and dancing in Paris; and they had secured the perfect site for it in fashionable Montmartre, where *le tout Paris* already went slumming for its entertainment. The red windmill perched rakishly above the entrance showed a miller and his wife peeking out of the windows. As the illuminated sails began to turn, the two figures exchanged kisses – a symbol, if ever there was one, of the activity with which the Moulin Rouge would forever be associated.

In the summer tables and chairs were laid out in the immense garden, in the middle of which stood a small platform for staging ballet, dwarfed by a giant elephant. Men paid one franc to enter and climb the spiral staircase (women weren't allowed in). There, in the belly of the elephant, they found a small platform on which an Arab dancer proceeded to entertain them.

The Moulin welcomed everyone, regardless of how much money they had to spend. The poor strolled up early for a coffee, the wealthy arrived in their carriages much later on, after dining with their own class. Entertainment went on well after the end of the official programme, as Zidler encouraged *cancaneuses* to experiment with their steps and coax customers onto the floor with them. There was laughter and singing and the popping of champagne corks, as top hats were knocked to the ground and garters were turned into armbands.

The most famous dancer at the Moulin Rouge was La Goulue. In her autobiography, *La Chanson de ma Vie* (The Song of My Life), the singer Yvette Guilbert remembers her from their music-hall heyday:

> La Goulue, in black silk stockings, with one foot shod in black satin held in outstretched hand, made the sixty yards of lace in her petticoats swirl and showed her drawers, with a heart coquettishly embroidered right in the middle of her little behind, when she bowed her impertinent acknowledgements. Knots of pink ribbon at her knees, an adorable froth of lace falling to her dainty ankles, now

disclosed, now concealed her beautiful legs, nimble, adept, alluring. The dancer sent her partner's hat flying with a neat little kick, then executed a split, her body erect, her slim torso sheathed in a blouse of sky-blue satin, her black satin skirt spread like an umbrella five yards in circumference.

Journalist Georges Montorgueil was not so flattering about La Goulue, however. He described her as having:

> a wilful, vicious and flushed baby face, a nose with quivering, impatient nostrils, a nose of one sniffing after love, nostrils dilating with the male odour of chestnut trees and the enervating bouquet of brandy glasses, a mouth gluttonous and sensual, a look shameless and provoking, the milk-white bosom freely escaping from the corsage.

La Goulue was known to appear bare-breasted at the Moulin Rouge and she often posed nude for photographers. The general consensus was that she was loud and coarse, and she relished her vulgar reputation. Neither conventionally pretty nor glamorous, she was shrewd enough to devise an image for herself which didn't depend on the fleeting nature of youth and beauty. Her nickname, which means 'The Glutton', says it all. Montorgeuil goes on to describe her style of dancing as 'brutal, blunt, without feminine grace, almost bestial'. Other, equally unflattering portraits exist of La Goulue. Jean Lorrain called her 'a great fishwife, a repugnant mound of flesh'. A male dancer at the Moulin Rouge, Edmond Heuzé, commented, 'For me, she represents excess, seizure of possession, the release of the passions, savagery. She has the blood of the revolutionary.'

Yvette Guilbert described La Goulue's chignon, 'piled high on top of her head like a helmet, [which] sprang from a single strand tightly twisted at the nape of her neck, so that it would not fall down when she danced'. Immortalized by Toulouse-Lautrec's posters for the Moulin Rouge, La Goulue's hairstyle, as well as the coloured ribbon she wore round her neck, were adopted as a fashionable style by working girls living as far away as New York.

La Goulue was born in 1866 near Paris to a washerwoman and educated by nuns. Her rebellious streak was evident from an early age, for it is said that she arrived at her First Communion wearing ballet shoes ('borrowed' from a trapeze artist, who had sent them to her mother for cleaning) and a tutu, which incensed the priest. She started out working in the laundry, which gave her further opportunity to show off rich women's fancy underwear in the dance halls. Legend has it that her mother once reprimanded her for keeping late hours, warning her to think of her reputation. 'My reputation?', La Goulue is said to have replied. 'If you go to the Île St Ouen you'll find it there, provided it has shown a little patience.'

When La Goulue's talent was spotted she soon made her reputation at the Moulin Rouge. Everything about her was considered outrageous, including her preference for female lovers. She referred light-heartedly to her fellow dancers as 'a bunch of tarts' and then went on to live with one of them, La Môme Fromage (the Cheese Kid). She delighted in being cheeky to the upper crust who came to watch her flaunting her underwear. When she caught sight of the Prince of Wales at the Moulin one night, she demanded that he pay for her champagne – and thanked him by lifting her leg in the air and showing him her crotch.

Montorgueil described how La Goulue tried, by every available means, to reveal her body. She allowed as much thigh as possible to show between her garters and the legs of her transparent knickers:

> She observes the fascination this provokes, gradually stirring it up through movements each more risqué than the last, and encouraging healthy curiosity to stretch to frantic searching, making the most of the effects of shadows in the pink areas glimpsed through gaps in the lace.

La Goulue earned 800 francs a month, not including the money she made on foreign tours and giving private appearances for visiting royalty. She played up to her fame for all it was worth, posing for dance tableaux bare-breasted, arriving at rehearsals with a little goat on a lead and creating arguments in the best prima donna fashion.

But at the height of her fame she made a big mistake. Fabulously wealthy as well as fabulously conceited, La Goulue believed people would flock to see her whatever she did. Declaring that she was bored with the cancan, she left the Moulin, set herself up in a fairground booth and decided to specialize in Arabic dance, which was known in France as *la danse du ventre*. The public failed to flock to see her, for the truth was that La Goulue was at her best at the Moulin Rouge. The spirit of the cancan with its wild, flaunting rudeness suited her talent far better than the more restrained nature of Arabic dance. Without the racket of the dance hall she was nothing. Too late she realized she had made a catastrophic mistake. Too proud to go back, she began drinking, sold her jewellery and added lion taming to her programme in a desperate attempt to attract customers. But her animals were mangy old beasts with as much fight in them as pussy cats, which caused even more scorn to be heaped on her head.

In one of her 'Letters from Paris' for the *New Yorker*, Janet Flanner charted the end of La Goulue's career:

> A month ago she reappeared: fat, old and dancing drunkenly in a few feet of a remarkable documentary film about the rag-pickers of Paris – called, after their neighbourhood of wagon shanties, *The Zone* ... Her last interview was given to the weekly *Vu*. After the first glass of brandy of the interview she took out a cracked mirror; after the third glass she recalled her cab-driving father. After the fourth she remembered the Grand Duke Alexis and, on the promise of a box of face powder, even remembered her son, who had died in a gambling den. A few weeks later her rag-picker friends took her to the city clinic, where she too died, murmuring as if declining a last and eternal invitation, 'I do not want to go to hell.'

La Goulue survived into her sixties. By the cruellest stroke of fate, she ended up selling matches outside the Moulin Rouge, where she had made her name.

***

In the 1870s a new kind of establishment appeared in Paris, a French version of the English music hall. The most famous was the Folies Bergère. An innovation of the Folies was a promenade at the back of the stalls, where customers could stroll about during the show. Inevitably, the promenade attracted women parading themselves for hire.

The Folies presented one of the best-known courtesan-dancers of the age, Caroline Otero, a Spanish dancer originally from Andalusia. Hughes Leroux wrote of her, 'She has the whole of the Orient between her legs.' Otero lived in a sumptuous apartment near the Bois de Boulogne that had been given to her by a duke in payment for a champagne dinner. Among the many possessions she amassed during her career was an island in the Pacific, bought for her by the Emperor of Japan. Otero reduced some of her admirers to ruin but, by the end of her life, the huge fortune that she had won during the days of her great glory had vanished. Some men were said to have committed suicide over her and several duels were fought on her behalf. She even fought a duel herself once, with an actress who had poked fun at her.

Caroline Otero grew up with a passion for dancing. As a child she remembered her mother slipping a set of castanets on her fingers and showing her the gypsy dances of Andalusia. By all accounts Caroline was a stunning beauty and by the age of twelve looked much older than her years. She lost no time in finding a young boy to initiate her in the pleasures of sex and, young as she was, persuaded him to take her to a cafe-concert, where she asked to dance for the owners. Their customers were so entranced they offered her a payment of two pesetas a night (double the normal fee) to dance for them. Years later, performing at the Folies at the height of her fame, her fee was 35,000 francs a month. The day after her Parisian debut, *Le Figaro* described the sensation Otero caused there:

> We had seen quite a few things in Paris, but we had to wait until She came to see this: a woman with Andalusian eyes, of which the poet speaks, blood-red lips, a magnificent head of wavy, raven black hair, rearing up and throwing her head like a young thoroughbred. The gyrations of her hips and legs drive the public crazy. She is loaded with jewels like an idol: diamonds, rubies and emeralds whose sparkle dazzles the audience. Her bosom is more covered with jewels than a Chief of Protocol's chest is with medals and crosses; they are in her hair, on her shoulders, arms, wrists, hands and legs, and dangle from her ears and, when she ends her dance, the boards continue to glitter as if a crystal chandelier had been pulverized on them. And she is watched over by two guards who protect her millions.

There are many stories about Otero and her priceless collection of jewellery. One of the best concerns a time when she and the singer Yvette Guilbert were appearing on the same bill. As neither was willing to give up top billing, it was arranged that they should take it in turns. One night, when it was

Guilbert's turn to close the show, Otero's fabulous pearl choker broke in the middle of her act and the pearls scattered and went rolling all over the stage. Proceedings came to a halt while they were being gathered up and by the time the curtain rose on Guilbert, the public had grown fractious. She was greeted with desultory applause, and in the middle of her first song, the lack of interest made her pause. Walking down to the footlights she pretended to pick up an overlooked pearl and with a wicked glint in her eye bit it, then gulped it down. The audience was delighted.

The novelist Colette worked in music halls in her early thirties and came to know Otero well. In her memoir, *My Apprenticeships,* she left a portrait of the dancer who was referred to in the press as 'the most scandalous person since Helen of Troy'. Colette describes afternoons spent playing bezique at Otero's apartment. Men were excluded from these afternoons, where the dancer sat around carelessly in her underwear, her dressing-gown falling open to reveal jewels nestling in her bosom. She played cards with fierce concentration, a glass of anisette on one side, an ashtray on the other and, having finished the game, tucked into a gargantuan feast:

> I have always enjoyed food, but what was my appetite compared to Lina's? Her queenliness melted, and a gentle bliss, an air of happy innocence took its place. Her teeth, her eyes, her glossy lips shone like a girl's. There are few beautiful women who can guzzle without loss of prestige. Lina did not push away her plate until she had emptied it four, five times. A little strawberry water-ice, a cup of coffee, and up she sprang, fastening a pair of castanets to her thumbs ... Until two in the morning Caroline Otero would dance and sing – for her own enjoyment, she cared little for ours. From a handsome forty she became a lively seventeen. The bath wrap tossed aside, she danced in her petticoat, which was of brocaded silk with a flounce five metres round, the only garment essential to Spanish dancing. Soaked with sweat, her fine lawn chemise clung to her loins. Her moist skin gave off a delicate scent, a dusky scent, predominantly of sandalwood, that was more subtle than herself. There was nothing base in her violent and wholly selfish pleasure; it was born of a true passion for rhythm and music. She would snatch up her sauce-stained table napkin and wipe herself vigorously, face, neck and damp armpits, then dance again, sing again, 'Ziz one? Do you know it?' Her feet were not very light but her face, tilted

backwards over her shoulders, the muscles of her hips rippling above the powerful loins, the savage, swaying furrow of her naked back, could defy the harshest glare. A body that had defied sickness, ill-usage and the passage of time.

Otero lived on into her nineties. She was still known, even then, as 'the Andalusian volcano' with a reputation as a *croquesse de diamants* (chewer of diamonds). By the end of her life she had squandered her great fortune and was living on a pension in a small hotel in Nice. Something of a recluse, she turned down frequent requests to meet visitors and journalists; but on her ninetieth birthday she agreed to talk to one of them about her past. She told him:

> I was very beautiful indeed. Everyone knows that. But I was not just beautiful, I was a great artist. If you could have seen me in *Carmen*. And how I could dance! I danced in a way that you could never understand.

***

Female dancers have enjoyed a freedom impossible to other women in many cultures; indeed, this was a principal reason for entering the profession. It offered them escape from a destiny otherwise dependent on class, sex and race. Like others who live on the outskirts of society, they have been more careless of its rules than other women, who had more to lose than they did.

Colette was already well known for her writing when she began a second career on the stage. She lived in the *beau monde*, but she too found escape from its constraints when she embarked on a stage career after divorcing her first husband. 'Monsieur' Willy, as she called him, was in his early thirties when he married the sixteen-year-old country girl with floor-length chestnut hair and brought her to Paris. Willy was a *roué* who began taking mistresses almost from the first day of their marriage. Looking back, Colette wondered whether she had married Willy from a desire to have a more dangerous life than she could have enjoyed as a respectable, provincial middle-class girl. But for a long time she hesitated to break out of her safe, compromised existence as Monsieur Willy's betrayed wife. Becoming a performer was such a daring move that in the end she had to be pushed, and it was her ex-husband who pushed her. Shortly after their separation and her stage debut Willy joked, 'Everyone has broken with Colette except me.'

Colette discovered that performing offered her independence and self-respect and she took to it with relish. Her stage career was only one aspect of a life marked by minor scandals. She was someone who created a rumpus without deliberately setting out to do so. Kissing her female lover on-stage created one storm; appearing bare-breasted at the Folies created another. Many years later, having divorced her second husband, she was to create an even bigger scandal by having an affair with her stepson.

Colette's subtle, languorous writing style celebrates sensuality in all its guises: the smell of steam rising off a hotpot, the feel of silk and velvet, the sleek fur of cats, all are present in her supple prose. So too are the glorious sights and sounds of music-hall life around the *fin de siècle*, when Paris was the pleasure-loving capital of Europe. Many of Colette's heroines use their sexuality to survive. But they are far from being dumb animals who bow their heads beneath the male yoke. With their bracing, difficult lives in the outside world, these female adventurers present a contrast to those women who sit wilting in their pink boudoirs, waiting for men to come and rescue them and give their life meaning.

Colette's experience on the road provided vivid material for her early masterpiece *The Vagabond*, which paints a portrait of performing life from the inside. The heroine is a divorcee like Colette herself. Dancing at a society party she spies acquaintances with whom she used to socialize during her marriage, including one of her ex-husband's mistresses:

> Round the sides and at the back there is a dark row of men, standing. Packed closely together they crane forward with that curiosity, that cynical courtesy which men of the world display towards a woman who is considered *déclassée*, the woman whose fingertips one used to kiss in her drawing-room and who now dances half-naked on a platform.

If her first marriage robbed Colette of her self-respect, it also gave her some valuable connections. As the wife of a journalist she was well acquainted with high society. She had experienced its hypocrisy at first hand and was only too aware that, though the cream of Parisian society might invite her to entertain in their grand houses, they still regarded her as little more than a servant.

Like many female dancers before and since, the dream of performing was, for Colette, a dream of escape. On-stage she didn't have to pretend, she could revel in her body, she could express her wildness, and in the camaraderie of touring life she could become a member of the casual family of performers. As a born outsider this was where Colette fitted in. At the Folies her boss Paul Derval remembers her keeping a pile of notebooks in her dressing-room. In between going on-stage she would scribble away endlessly, making notes for her short stories and novellas.

By the time Colette was writing, women who, for centuries, had exerted their most powerful influence in the domestic sphere had come to play a prominent role in public life as entertainers. There was enormous fascination with female performers, especially dancers, and in Colette's Paris they were everywhere: ballet girls at the Opéra, actresses at the Comédie Française, music-hall performers, society entertainers. Among these (mainly working-class) women was a small band of dancers like Colette, from further up the social ladder and who, by the closing years of the century, were in revolt against the constraints of bourgeois life.

Orientalism was in vogue and it was quite the thing to have so-called 'Egyptian' turns as a party entertainment. As Colette herself commented, a dance in the Egyptian style meant playing with gossamer veils, it meant a dance in the nude, laden with a heavy chain-mail of costume jewellery. Unnerved by the close proximity of so many people from her past, her heroine realizes she must pull herself together:

> I have recovered myself and forget nothing. Do these people really exist, I ask myself? No, they don't. The only real things are dancing, light, freedom and music. Nothing is real except making rhythm of one's thoughts and translating it into beautiful gestures. Is not the mere swaying of my back, free from any constraint, an insult to those bodies cramped in their long corsets, and enfeebled by a fashion which insists that they should be thin?

During the late nineteenth century fashion became increasingly extravagant as it changed to throw different parts of the female body into relief. Below the waist women were swathed in a plethora of skirts and petticoats. For a while skirts grew shorter, with the outer layers draped and folded to reveal a tempting flash of multicoloured underskirts. This sea of skirts with its bows and lace trimmings obscured the natural shape of the body. Horsehair bustles came in, and at one point they stuck out at a ninety-degree angle. They were replaced by a flexible wire cage which could be folded up when a woman sat down, but by the 1890s these cages had disappeared and in their place long skirts came back into vogue, skirts which sometimes trailed two feet behind the wearer.

Jean Cocteau describes Caroline Otero and a friend sitting lunching together one day: 'It was no small affair,' he says, and goes on to list the breastplates and shackles, the shoulder pads, thigh pieces and gauntlets, the aptly named chokers and numerous other pieces of armour with which they bristled:

> These sacred scarabs armed with asparagus holders, these soldiers of pleasure who were harnessed and caparisoned early in the morning by robust maids, seemed incapable, sat stiffly opposite their hosts . . . Confronted with one of these beauties, any of our modern gigolos would take to his heels . . . The idea of undressing one of these ladies was an expensive undertaking, which was better arranged in advance, like moving house, and before we can picture them in the midst of a chaos of underwear, hair and scattered limbs, we must intensify our powers of imagination.

The fashionable woman was moulded by her corset into an S-curve, with a shelf of bosom, a padded, protruding bottom and a wasp-waist. The music-hall entertainer Polaire was envied for managing to pull her waist into an incredible fifteen inches and for a few years she was advertised as having the smallest waist in the world. The effort in maintaining it seems to have given her a fierce temper. After meeting her at the Palais de Glace, Jean Cocteau wrote, 'She was as violent as a Yiddish insult and stood poised at the edge of the rink like a fit of hysterics.'

A dress reform movement began in the 1850s, but it was only towards the end of the century that it began gathering momentum. When designers did release women's bodies from the corset's iron grip, it was largely due to the influence and fame of Isadora Duncan, the most revolutionary dancer of them all.

***

A disturbing phenomenon arose during the final decades of the nineteenth century, a phenomenon which today has spread like wildfire through every section of society. For it was during this period that affluent women began starving themselves. In her biography of Colette, Judith Thurman comments that the novelist – who delighted in food as she delighted in all pleasures of the flesh – is probably the first writer to describe an anorexic in her memoir, *The Pure and the Impure*. Colette herself was appalled by the fashion for dieting and took pains to over-emphasize her own sturdy contours by describing herself as 'a pleasant little cob pony of a person'.

Alongside a growing fashion for slimness something even more sinister was happening. By the turn of the century many otherwise intelligent women were coming to stifle their physical and mental vitality and accept a life of passive self-negation. This life-denying process resulted in their falling prey to all kinds of nebulous ailments whose origins lay in the psyche. A generation of 'natural' female invalids grew up, suffering from this type of disease, which was seen as a mark of breeding. In his fascinating study of Victorian art, *Idols of Perversity*, Bram Dijkstra charts the nineteenth-century cult of the natural female invalid.

A romantic eroticism became attached to the image of dying women and was seized on by writers such as Edgar Allan Poe, who described them as 'unquestionably the most poetical topic in the world'. When the British writer Lady Amberly arrived in Boston, she commented that she had never seen so many pretty girls all in one place at one time, adding cheerfully, 'They all look so sick!'

The controlling idea of illness as a mark of female beauty was balanced by the notion that there was something masculine and unnatural about women who showed physical vigour through engaging in such energetic pursuits as dancing and sport. Muscularity was connected with being lower class, even criminal, certainly a throwback to our primitive past, and independence was considered even more unfeminine.

A growing number of women began resisting these ideas. They advocated gymnastics, bicycle riding and other kinds of exercise to build up strength, together with diets designed for gaining weight. Battle lines were drawn up, challenging the notion that true femininity lay in being pale, thin and liable to keel over at the least puff of wind.

American feminist Abba Goold Woolson criticized those middle-class women who, rather than being saddened by illness welcomed it, and even discussed their ailments with relish. Woolson pointed out that American women had formerly enjoyed the outdoor life; that their vigour and bravery was part of America's pioneering history. They had crossed a continent with their families and endured all kinds of hardships and dangers *en route* to making a better life for themselves, yet it was these same women who now abandoned physical pastimes, and when they did venture out into the open air they tottered along on high heels and shielded themselves from the sun beneath their parasols. Woolson railed at society for trying to crush out of women 'every trace of healthy instincts and vigorous life, and to reduce them to the condition of the enfeebled young ladies that meet us on every side, who are all modelled after one wretched pattern'. Voices were raised, stating that the fashion for illness constituted a national crisis: 'An appearance of incapability has come to be looked upon as a mark of good breeding ... a definite object to strive for among many classes of women.'

Meanwhile the same thing was happening in Britain. Mrs E. Lynn Linton wrote:

> Less and less every year are the nerves and muscles, the restless activities of arms and legs, exercised and made to purvey new vigour to the life. The body is allowed to grow stagnant. The life of the woman, even as mere animal, becomes poor and morbid and artificial.

In lives unlived, the drama of illness rendered women more interesting; it excused their acceptance of a frustrated existence. And it was easy enough for them to make themselves look ill. Tight lacing helped along the pale, ailing look and there was always powder and rouge at hand to create the Gothic look. Some women even traced blue veins onto their dead white forehead and throat. The dancer Lola Montez wrote, 'Many a time have I seen a gentleman shrink from a brilliant lady as though it was a death's head he was compelled to kiss.' Lead, mercury and arsenic were all ingredients of make-up and were also used for dyeing fabric. In her memoirs, the courtesan Liane de Pougy recalls the time she appeared in the same show as the performer Blanche d'Arvilly:

> She filled a costume made of virulent green wool. It was a hot night, her dance was energetic – and she was found unconscious in her dressing-room, her tongue black, half-poisoned by the arsenic in all that green, mixed with her sweat.

Blanche d'Arvilly may not have known she was dressed in a poisonous garment, but women who ate tiny quantities of arsenic in order to achieve the Gothic look knew very well that arsenic was lethal. And if we're surprised at this casual disregard for their own safety, we have only to think of today's legion of women who voluntarily paralyse their facial muscles with the virus Botox, in the vain belief that having a few less wrinkles will radically transform their lives for the better.

Drinking vinegar was another nineteenth-century habit which some women indulged in, in the belief that it would give them a fashionable pallor and help them lose weight by acting as a laxative. The editor of *Bow Bells* magazine in England tried to dissuade its young readers from the habit by urging them, 'Be boldly fat ... If nature intended you to be ruddy and rotund, accept it with a laughing grace which will captivate more hearts than all the paleness of a circulating library.'

In the novels of Henry James, which centre on the lives of women, the author criticizes the modern speech and manners of American women for lacking true femininity. He prefers the social graces of their European sisters, who display 'definite conceptions of duty, activity, influence; of a possible grace, of a possible sweetness, a possible power to soothe, to please, and above all to exemplify'.

James's sister Alice was plagued by unspecified ailments during her brief life, ailments which may well have been brought on by her attempt to fit the mould of virtuous passivity. She described her body as 'a sick carcass' and wrote in her diary, 'How sick one gets of being good. How much I should respect myself if I could burst out and make everyone wretched for twenty four-hours.' But she couldn't bring herself to do so, and slowly she slipped away and died.

For death is the logical outcome of women turning themselves into invalids. Death is the ultimate sacrifice. The French actress Sarah Bernhardt capitalized on the fashion for dead women by buying herself a coffin and taking it on tour with her. She even had herself photographed in it, with her hands crossed demurely over her chest. The daughter of a courtesan, in her youth she was painfully thin and coughed up blood. Her doctor told her that she had only a few years to live, but Bernhardt was a survivor. After conquering tuberculosis she entered the acting profession, where she transformed herself into so formidable a creature that, even in her seventies and with a wooden leg, she was still treading the boards.

By some cruel chance, tuberculosis gave its victims a beautiful translucent skin and the inner glow of the half-starved. They died pale, thin and ethereal, like the doomed heroines of the Romantic ballet. So it came about that some women, desperate for the undernourished tubercular look which showed they were as good as gold, took up the slow suicide of self-starvation. Here, in women's failed urge to revolt, we find the seeds of anorexia nervosa.

Unlike the genuinely poor little underpaid dressmakers whose health and ability to eat well wasn't a matter of choice, some affluent women deliberately turned themselves into undernourished invalids. Those who fell victim to consumption, and who consumed so little themselves in the way of food or experience, were eaten up from inside. It must have been terrifying for a woman suffering from the disease to take her lace-trimmed white handkerchief from her mouth and see on it the vivid red stain of a body rejecting its very essence.

It was this pale, fragile being with her thirteen-inch waist held in a vice-like grip by her corset, this creature as insubstantial as a shadow, who was idolized by artists. She was a far cry from the energetic *cancaneuse*, who had to be strong and robust to dance as she did. But no poet dedicated delicate sentiments to women who danced the cancan.

***

When Augustus Gardner wrote that the physical condition of Western women was noticeably deteriorating he wasn't imagining it. Towards the end of the nineteenth century this state of affairs was being challenged, however. One American magazine article entitled 'What to Teach Our Daughters' offered girls ten pieces of advice for a happy life: among them was that tight lacing was 'uncomely as well as injurious to health'. Some reformers believed dress reform was an even more urgent issue than gaining the vote and, given what we now know, they may well have been right.

On both sides of the Atlantic the raised voices of dress reformers, women doctors and feminists began to rattle those who had a vested interest in controlling women. Among them were the corset-makers, who had a hugely profitable business to defend. They were challenged by Orson Fowler, who maintained that the true cause of death in some women who died of consumption was tight lacing; it was, he said, a slow suicide by strangling their inner organs and rendering them incapable of functioning properly. Desperate at the prospect of diminishing sales, corset-makers designed garments to accommodate the new breed of woman who had intellectual aspirations and liked to go bicycling. Ads started to feature images of corseted women gazing inquiringly into the distance, a pair of reading glasses perched on their noses. There were even corsets with air holes in, for playing sport.

As we've seen, one effect of tight lacing was that it prevented women from fully drawing breath. This made any form of exercise, including dancing, a bit of a problem. Nineteenth-century literature includes numerous accounts of women fainting prettily into the arms of their dance partners. These lucky men had the chance to display their strength and sensitivity as they lifted up their darlings and tenderly deposited them on the nearest sofa.

There is something enormously erotic in descriptions of these young women, flushed with exertion and gasping for breath. Their inability to cope with the exertions of the waltz more than satisfied the stereotype of the frail, ailing female, while at the same time awakening men's sexual desire. Sexologists wrote enthusiastically about the allure of conspicuously heaving breasts in their whalebone stays. Anti-dance lobbyists like the Rev. Dr S. Vernon, who feared the eroticism unleashed on the ballroom floor, wrote of 'the beating hearts brought into close contact, the warm breath against the hot cheek, the electric currents flowing from hand to hand and eye to eye'. Anyone might think he was encouraging people to go dancing, rather than the opposite.

Among the ills caused by corsets, one of the most serious was the displacement of the uterus. Harriet Beecher Stowe, who suffered a prolapsed womb herself, wrote of the increasing number of gynaecological complaints among married and single women alike. (It was previously assumed that the condition was caused by a woman having given birth too many times.) Doctors placed all manner of mechanical devices in the vagina to correct this problem, and there are reports of some who took the opportunity to sexually molest their patients at the same time.

Corset designers, never slow to miss a sales opportunity, weighed in with their remedy for alleviating the worst symptoms of prolapsed uterus. This was the 'passive exercise' corset (!), which allowed electric shocks to pass through the body. Here was a really novel idea: exercise could be obtained without any activity at all and women could safely carry on being 'done to' rather than doing something active themselves to help cure their condition.

However, the voices suggesting that corsets might be responsible for the alarming rise in uterine displacement were few and far between. Doctors kept quiet for a very simple reason, as Leigh Summers explains in *Bound to Please*. She cites the second half of the nineteenth century as a crucial period in the development of gynaecology and obstetrics. Damage to the uterus gave doctors a great opportunity to examine that most intimate – and mysterious – part of a woman's body. Many doctors knew this damage was caused by the constant pressure and pain caused by corsets, but they were loath to tell women their problems would be solved if they would only throw these garments away.

Curing problems of the uterus would have robbed specialists of their livelihood and limited their research possibilities (and hence their possible prestige). Most male doctors simply advised patients to remove their stays temporarily and go for a lie-down. At the same time, within the limited circulation of medical journals, the corset's suspected ill effects on the body were described in detail. As Dr Anna Galbraith commented, it was a vicious circle with the corset at the centre as the 'chief support' of gynaecologists.

***

In the nineteenth century sex was a dark reef whose hidden dangers stirred deep beneath the surface of the waters. Never had there been so many writers eager to plumb the depths of human (especially female) sexuality. Middle-class women weren't expected to enjoy sex – indeed, to show enjoyment was to expose themselves to the suspicion of being degenerate; but they were expected to endure it in order to produce children. The great Russian novelist Leo Tolstoy considered that women who chose to give birth were akin to saints. But, he went on, 'Every woman, however she may call herself and however refined she may be, who refrains from childbirth without refraining from sexual relations is a whore.'

In 1854 Auguste Comte, the father of sociology, proposed artificial insemination as a way of continuing the human race while keeping women in an eternally virginal state:

The highest species of production would no longer be at the mercy of a capricious and unruly instinct, the proper restraint of which has hitherto been the chief stumbling block in the way of human discipline.

So women were to be relieved of the 'chore' of sex – which they might just happen to enjoy. For the belief that respectable women didn't like sex was balanced by a sneaking desire that they were capable of physical pleasure. After all, women were defined by their physicality. Their apparently insatiable urge to throw their bodies around on the dance floor was evidence of a primitive, undeveloped nature ('The child and the savage are very fond of dancing'). Hysteria, a newly defined female malady with sexual origins, became linked to the female love of dancing. In the words of Havelock Ellis:

> One reason why women love dancing is because it enables them to give harmonious and legitimate emotional expression to this neuro-muscular irritability which might otherwise escape in more explosive forms.

One of these 'explosive' outlets was masturbation, suspected of being rife among women and seen as an evil habit which was harmful to the health. In both Britain and the US cases of clitoridectomy were reported as a way of dealing with it. This operation was pioneered in the 1860s by the English physician Isaac Baker-Brown, who thought it useful for mental as well as sexual diseases. Among the scores of women on whom he operated in his London clinic were a handful whose madness lay in wanting a divorce. He returned each of them to their husbands much subdued. The American Cornflakes king J. D. Kellogg was one of those who advocated clitoridectomy, believing it an effective cure for masturbation. He thought it even more efficacious when accompanied by bland food such as ... a big bowl of his breakfast cereal. Some social commentators, however, feared that by lessening female sexual desire, clitoridectomy would make women dangerously independent of men.

The suspicion that women did experience sexual desire was echoed in the belief in 'nymphomania', a curious word still in use back in the liberated 1960s. Its male equivalent – 'sex maniac' – has a comical tone and nowhere near the same pejorative associations. In his book, *Woman*, published in 1904, American gynaecologist Bernard Talmey wrote, 'At the mere sight of any man the nymphomaniac woman gets into such a state of excitement that without any tactile manipulation whatever, she may experience real orgasm.' One wonders whether this conclusion was based on his own experiments.

Making women the weak victims of passionate urges was a convenient way for men to use hidden fears about their own nature to justify the control of female sexuality. Indeed, men's writing on the subject generally tells us more about their own desires than anything else. Men sallied forth into the night, seeking out women as much unlike their tidy wives as possible. Those available to them were working girls who had to choose between back-breaking toil in factory sweatshops, an animal existence in terrible conditions for next to no pay, and selling their bodies for sex. It isn't surprising that many of them opted for the latter.

The second half of the nineteenth century saw the phenomenal spread of prostitution in Europe's rapidly expanding cities. It has been estimated that, in London, one in ten women were involved in the sex trade and in Paris an 1869 police report revealed 30,000 registered prostitutes. (This didn't include the vast number who worked part-time to supplement their inadequate wages.) By the turn of the century Paris had approximately 100,000 whores serving the needs of a population totalling just under three million. One reason why the trade flourished was that rural labourers who had swarmed into the newly industrialized city couldn't afford to marry. By 1900, though, the trade in women's bodies had come to satisfy what was seen as the Parisian's insatiable hedonism.

Never had the sight of prostitutes been so common or so taken for granted in public life. There was even a guide for male tourists printed in 1871 – *Paris By Night* – which listed different classes of whores. At the top were the dazzling high-class courtesans known variously as *grandes cocottes*, *grandes horizontales*, *amazones* and *filles de marbre*. Being able to keep one of these women gave a man a certain cachet, even though the end result might be financial ruin. At the bottom of the heap were the little *grisettes*, who also made their living from taking in washing, and the army of truly wretched whores whose miserable existence has been described by contemporary writers in lubricious detail. There was also a thriving trade in child prostitutes, with what would have been, in any age, a phenomenal sum of money paid for a virgin.

Most middle- and upper-class men were acquainted with some aspect of this *demi-monde*, while society women were brought into indirect contact with courtesans at social functions, as well as through the world of fashion. For part of these women's currency was to look spectacular. They were daring enough to experiment with their dress and in doing so they became leaders of fashion. Their clothes were often more splendid than those of the married women whom they challenged directly for a man's wealth and protection. As the French writer Maxime Du Camp complained, 'One does not know nowadays if it is honest women who are dressed like whores, or whores who are dressed like honest women.'

Courtesans gave their name to the Belle Epoque, the final decades of the nineteenth century, when Paris appeared to go mad, engaged in the headlong pursuit of pleasure and oblivion after the Franco-Prussian War of 1870, which had left France humiliated. These courtesans were the film stars of their day and some of them used the stage to advertise their charms to prospective clients. Middle-class women had a limited education and were largely ignorant of the outside world. They couldn't compete, either as companions or as conversationalists, with these glossy, confident icons of extravagance.

The most celebrated courtesans were few in number, but they were unassailable. In their salons, artists and writers rubbed shoulders with bankers and royalty. The Prince of Wales (later Edward VII) supped hungrily from their bowls and was often seen in the dressing-room of the popular *cancaneuse* Hortense Schneider. Caroline Otero remembered him in her memoirs: 'It often happened that the Prince of Wales sent for me to dance before him after supper at Voisin's, Durand's or the Café Anglais.' He would pick up a napkin and draw a clock on it, indicating the hour when he wanted to visit her at her apartment, before sending it across via the *maître d'hôtel*. According to Otero, the prince wasn't known for his generosity and was more likely to present his mistresses with a brace of pheasants than jewellery. But he was generous with Otero and bought her a hunting lodge just outside Paris, in order to visit her more discreetly. Remembering one of her rivals, she wrote, 'La Goulue's dancing specially amused him and we often went in a party to applaud her in her famous *danse du grand écart* at the Jardin de Paris.' Towards the end of her career Otero adopted an Algerian boy, a refugee of the First World War, and christened him Edouard in memory of the prince.

Queen Victoria's son was not the only member of royalty to keep an account with several dancers, whose services he offered to friends. France's Emperor Louis Napoleon (who kept a room backstage at the Opéra for his private use) was another. On one occasion he welcomed the King of Piedmont to Paris as his guest. The king paid a visit to the Opéra and was

infuriated when a ballerina whom he fancied demanded payment of fifty
louis d'or. No doubt he thought the honour of his interest was payment
enough. But working girls cannot live on air alone and Louis Napoleon
smoothed the waters by telling the dancer to charge it to his account.

***

An extraordinary amount of hilarious nonsense about female sexuality was
spouted in the nineteenth century. There was the convenient belief, for
example, that women chose to become prostitutes out of nymphomaniac
tendencies. German sexologist H. Lippert wrote that the long-term practice
of their profession made prostitutes' eyes acquire:

> a piercing, rolling expression; they are somewhat unduly prominent
> in consequence of the continued tension of the ocular muscles, since
> the eyes are principally employed to spy out and attract clients ...
> The mouth, in continuous activity either in eating or kissing, is
> conspicuous ... The hair of the head is often scanty – in fact, a good
> many become actually bald.

Otto Weininger's book *Sex and Character* (written at the age of twenty-three
and published in 1903) includes many pithy little sayings, of which 'The
longer the hair, the smaller the brain' is typical. Weininger assembled various
hand-me-down ideas into a 'scientific' system (science was the new god then)
that won him an enormous popular readership. He convinced himself that
women were dominated by sex, unlike men, who could take it or leave it.
With a careless disregard for the law of supply and demand, he wrote that
prostitution was as natural to women's nature as motherhood, but that it
wasn't natural to men's, despite the equally hard nature of working men's
lives. He ignored the possibility that, had respectable women been able to
stroll about at all hours in search of men to relieve their sexual frustration,
they might well have done so. But only loose, abandoned women were on the
streets after dark. Those who theoretically possessed the money and freedom
to loiter in theatre foyers propositioning men were at home, doing their
embroidery. According to Weininger it followed that, as sex was the only
part of a man's life that a woman understood, it was also the only way she

could reach him and drag him down to her primitive level of existence. Even Freud wasn't above contributing to this nonsense when he wrote that, because of the immodesty of their work, female performers had a natural aptitude for prostitution.

There's a long connection between prostitution and the theatre. And it wasn't only along the *promenoir* of the Folies Bergère or on the dance floor of the Moulin Rouge that the trade in women was conducted. It thrived, too, at up-market establishments like the Opéra. There, *grandes cocottes* displayed their charms along the balcony and in the boxes, which were designed to face onto the auditorium. Those with box seats could be seen down to the level of their breasts, and if a women's *décolletage* were low and her shoulders bare, it looked as if she were sitting there naked. The Opéra was cynically dubbed 'the most exclusive brothel in town'. It was where society's elite went on the prowl, with ballerinas and fashionable courtesans as its prey.

For the hunters, as well as the hunted, there was a hazard lying in wait, for the dark reef of sexuality was made especially treacherous by the threat of syphilis. Venereal disease was, unsurprisingly, blamed on prostitution. In France prostitutes were supervised under the brothel system, where inmates were obliged to undergo a regular medical inspection. These establishments had been set up partly to contain the spread of syphilis, and it seems to have worked to some extent, for incidence of the disease was far less there than in England, where the profession was unregulated. However, many whores operated outside the brothel system, including those who worked part-time in the profession.

In both fiction and the 'non-fiction' of sexologists, whores were identified with everything filthy and loathsome. The city of Paris was the proud possessor of a brand-new sewage system (which was advertised as a tourist attraction) and many writers compared the service it provided with that provided by whores. The man in charge of the sewers, Dr Parent-Duchâtelet, condemned this enormous swathe of women in a truly chilling comment: 'Prostitutes are as inevitable in a great conurbation as sewers, cesspits and refuse dumps. The conduct of the authorities should be the same with regard to each.'

Certain influential French writers, including Emile Zola and Alexandre Dumas *fils*, even blamed prostitutes for the fall of the Second Empire in 1870. In the case of Dumas, his condemnation seems rather churlish. It was a prostitute, after all, who provided the raw material for the book which brought him fame, and it is the only book for which he is remembered today. *La Dame aux Camélias* is based on his brief affair with the courtesan Marie Duplessis. Known as 'La Divine', she was noted for wearing white camellias tucked in her corsage, except on five days every month when she signalled her unavailability by switching to red flowers instead. She was seen dancing the cancan at the Bal Mabille in the 1840s and died, coughing up blood, at the age of twenty-three. On hearing of her death, Dumas hastened to her apartment and, entering her bedroom, found it empty save for the trellis where her untended flowers had already turned black. A fund was raised to care for her grave, but most of the money subsequently went on erasing the signatures of unhappy admirers who scribbled their names on her tomb.

Consumptive mistresses like Marie Duplessis were considered intensely desirable. The symptoms of tuberculosis were thought to be similar to those of sexual appetite, and one of the booklets advertising Parisian prostitutes listed those who possessed the added attraction of being tubercular. For a man who liked to live dangerously, having sex with a woman dying of consumption provided an added *frisson* at the thought that he too might become infected.

The suspicion that a woman had a contagious illness was no reason not to consort with her, even if this happened to be syphilis or smallpox. In his diary, playwright Frank Wedekind records taking home a dancer who may well have been in the early stages of either illness:

> She begins to dance a cancan and climbs on my shoulders, and, heavy as she is, I carry her round the room. She's enough to make one's mouth water, and, unusually for me, I'm pretty much in love with her. We get stuck into each other, she inflicts a number of love bites on me, and in spite of my false teeth I manage to leave a suggestion of the same on her thigh. When we get into bed she draws the curtains as close as she can. She does this on account of the glandular scars beneath her chin, which have got noticeably larger. Whether they are open sores I can't tell. I act as if I didn't notice them. Exceptionally, I find I'm more potent than otherwise.

The suspicion of having contracted syphilis even acted as an aphrodisiac. For some men, having lived in dread of the disease, it was a relief to know that the die was cast and they cheerfully set about spreading their infection. In the spring of 1877 the writer Guy de Maupassant learnt that he had finally contracted syphilis. He recorded the fact in a letter to his friend Robert Pinchon:

> I've got the pox. At last! The real version, not the wretched clap – no, no, the true pox, the one Francis I died of. The pox majestic and straightforward, elegant syphilis … and I'm damned proud of it, and I despise the bourgeoisie. Alleluia, I've got the pox! That means I'm no longer afraid of catching it, so I screw the street whores and those who prowl the highways. After doing it I tell them, 'I've got the pox.' They're scared. As for me, I just laugh …

In his novel *Bel Ami*, Maupassant's hero Duroy goes to the Folies with his society mistress, Madame de Marelle. He has previously enjoyed the services of one of the *promenoir* ladies, Rachel, and when he spots her there he is horrified and decides to ignore her. As he sits nervously awaiting possible ructions, his companion stares at the *promenoir* women. Like others of her class she is fascinated by this strange breed of women and she scarcely bothers to look at the stage:

> She wanted to touch them, to feel their clothes, their faces, their hair, to discover what those creatures were made of. 'There's a stout dark woman', she said suddenly, 'who keeps looking at us. I thought just now that she was going to speak to us. Did you see her?'

But Duroy has already ignored Rachel, who now greets him in a low voice, winking conspiratorially. Madame de Marelle continues looking at Rachel, who approaches Duroy directly and once again says hallo. This time he does not even turn round to acknowledge her:

> 'Well,' she continued, 'have you suddenly become deaf since last Thursday?'
> He made no reply and affected an air of disdain, as if he would not compromise himself by as much as one word with a baggage like that.
> She burst out into angry laughter. 'You're dumb, are you? Has Madame there bitten out your tongue?'
> With a furious gesture and in an exasperated voice he broke out: 'Who gave you permission to speak to me? Get out of this box or I'll have you arrested.'

The divine Isadora Duncan pictured in 1912, in the days of her great glory. (Photo: Otto, Paris.)

The scandalous waltz allowed partners an unprecedented physical intimacy as they whirled round the ballroom.

In the cancan women revealed their legs and underwear to strangers.

Early 20th-century dancing boys performed *en travesti* in North Africa and the Middle East, and were often mistaken by tourists for girls.

African-American dancing during the Roaring Twenties.

Dancing tango in a Buenos Aires dance hall in the 1990s. (Photo: Andrew Oldroyd.)

Ballet-dancing dolls made of wax and cloth by Lotte Pritzel.

Wendy Buonaventura and Company explore humorous aspects of Middle Eastern dance in *Mimi La Sardine*. (Photo: Nick Spollin.)

Then with flaming eyes and heaving bosom she screamed: 'So that's it, is it? You silly mug! If you carry on with a woman, the least you can do is say, "How do you do?" to her. Because you happen to be with someone else today isn't a reason for cutting me. If you had only made a sign when I passed you just now, I'd have left you alone. But you meant to give yourself airs. You wait, I'll pay you out. What, you can't even say good evening to me when I meet you … '

She would have kept it up, but Madame de Marelle had opened the door of the box, and was escaping through the crowd, frantically looking for the exit.

Courtesans understood the wisdom of discretion; they knew that to make such a scene would ultimately rebound on them, and this fictional incident is a reflection of their rage. Sometimes, paying back an insult from men who made use of them yet were terrified of discovery was just too hard to resist. And if whores revenged themselves on customers via a dose of syphilis, it only served to confirm the growing fear of them as tainted, poisonous creatures. At the same time, of course, they were irresistibly alluring.

From the middle of the century a powerful new stereotype of women – and not only whores – began taking shape. Woman as angel of death is a popular figure in late nineteenth-century art and literature. Zola's novel *Nana* is the tale of a *grande horizontale* who ruins every man who comes within her orbit. In his preliminary notes for the book, Zola describes its subject as 'a whole society hurling itself at the cunt'. Nana is described as a golden fly, born and bred on a dung heap, a performer who performs badly, who can neither sing nor dance. But at her debut, the sight of her body, clad in the filmiest of draperies, fills the theatre with a deadly hush:

> There was no applause. Nobody laughed any more. The men's faces were tense and serious, their nostrils narrowed, their mouths prickly and parched. A wind seemed to have passed over the audience, a soft wind laden with hidden menace. All of a sudden, in the good-natured child the woman stood revealed, a disturbing woman with all the impulsive madness of her sex, opening the gates of the unknown world of desire. Nana was still smiling, but with the deadly smile of the man-eater.

Her goal is revenge on men, the revenge of the poor on the rich, and for such a woman Zola reserves the most horrifying of deaths. Nana dies of the pox at the height of her powers. She is described as a suppurating mound of putrefying flesh lying on her deathbed:

> It was as if the poison she had picked up in the gutters, from the carcasses left there by the roadside, that ferment with which she had poisoned a whole people, had now risen to her face and rotted it.

Slumbering in the male subconscious lurked the ancient image of the *vagina dentata*. In his journal, Edmund de Goncourt records a dream of being at a smart party where he recognizes an actress among the guests:

> She was draped in a scarf, and I noticed only that she was completely naked when she hopped onto the table . . . She started to dance, and while she was dancing took steps that showed her private parts armed with the most terrible jaws one could imagine, opening and closing, exposing a set of teeth.

The *femme fatale* existed side by side with the symbol of woman as goddess. Visitors to the 1889 Paris Exposition were greeted by La Parisienne, a twenty-foot-high beauty in a flowing gown and fur cape, balancing on a golden ball. Placing women on a pedestal was an ideal way of controlling them. But the heyday of the voluptuous, wasp-waisted Aphrodite was on the wane. Hard on her heels came a more threatening type of woman. She chopped off her hair and wore comfortable, mannish clothes. She agitated for basic rights that men took for granted, including an education; and she demanded honourable work and the control of her own money.

The first glimmer of women's revolt at their subservience created something of a panic. In France men sought to assert their collective masculinity by trying to undercut women's efforts at emancipation. (As Judith Thurman points out, the French *affranchisseur* translates tellingly as both emancipator and castrator of cattle.) Edward Berenson commented, 'If the French woman could become a real woman once again ... submissive, obedient, emotional, unthreatening sexually or otherwise, Frenchmen would necessarily regain the virility believed to characterize the Napoleonic age.'

All kinds of trifling restrictions were placed in women's path. Cross-dressing was forbidden by law, except on stage, and when Colette danced at a masked ball in Nice with another woman she was stopped by a bouncer. Tapping her on the shoulder he cautioned the couple, 'Separate, if you please, ladies. It's forbidden here for women to dance with each other.' In the desperate bid for new, ever more extreme, pleasures which characterized *fin-de-siècle* life, lesbianism among the leisured classes was the most up-to-the-minute thing. It had long been a fact of life among prostitutes or 'gay ladies', as they were known. In the popular imagination there was both fascination and horror of the flourishing gay (in the modern sense) scene; and it became linked to a palpable misogyny in the arts.

Just as lesbians and New Women represented a novel kind of threat to the established order, so did the fashion for recreational drugs. Among the Decadents, opium dens were in vogue, while morphine and ether were the chic drugs of oblivion. The tourist age had begun and travellers to the Middle East brought back with them a taste for hashish. It was especially popular among artists for its expansive, mind-altering properties. They smoked it in tall, bubbling narghiles while reclining on low divans covered in Persian carpets. Artists' studios and grand mansions alike had alcoves furnished with oriental rugs, brassware and potted palms, and it was quite the thing to throw parties on an oriental theme with the host and hostess all decked out in turbans, brocaded jackets and baggy pantaloons.

At these parties guests were sometimes treated to an oriental turn. Arabic dance had been introduced to Europe and America via the great *expositions* and the work of writers and travellers. The Western version consisted of wafting around with veils and indeed, even when people witnessed the more earthy reality, either on their travels or at the great exhibitions, they preferred their own version. Society women who entertained their guests with an oriental fantasy, and even performers like Colette, who included an Egyptian dance in her repertoire, chose not to roll and shake their hips in true Middle Eastern style.

In Paris, where a sixth of the population went to a theatre or music hall at least once a week, female entertainers provided a prime topic of conversation. Adored for their dazzling glamour, feared as bestial creatures and dark angels of death, women's unsettling power was epitomized, *par excellence*, by the dancing temptress, whose vibrant, animal energy was thought to reveal her sexually voracious nature.

The nineteenth century had every variety of this stereotype: the wild *cancaneuse*, the dark gypsy and the oriental dancer. Each of these expressed what was considered dangerous female energy, but the Arab dancer was the most disturbing. Her chief representative was that archetypal temptress Salome, who demanded the head of a man in return for her dancing. The story of Salome started to capture the imagination of artists during the 1870s. Flaubert drew on his Egyptian experiences to describe her dance in the short story *Herodias*:

> Her poses suggested sighs, and her whole body was so languid that one could not tell whether she were mourning for a god or expiring in his embrace. With her eyes half-closed she twisted her body backwards and forwards, making her belly rise and fall and her breasts quiver, while her face remained expressionless.

Salome appears in paintings of the time in a variety of guises: doe-eyed innocent staring out at the spectator with her finger in her mouth; ferocious vampire in transparent veils seized by bloodlust; and female beast, head thrown back in transports of abandon. She is shown cradling the severed head of John the Baptist, fondling it, even drinking its blood. The hero of J. K. Huysmans' novella *A Rebours* spends hours contemplating Gustave Moreau's paintings of the biblical seductress. He ponders over 'the disquieting delirium of the dancer, the subtle grandeur of the murderess'. For him Salome is more than a mere dancing girl:

> who exhorts a cry of lust and concupiscence from an old man by the lascivious contortions of her body, who breaks the will, masters the mind of a king by the spectacle of her quivering bosoms, heaving belly and tossing thighs; she was now revealed in a sense as the symbolic incarnation of world-old Vice, the goddess of immortal Hysteria, the Curse of Beauty supreme above all other beauties by the cataleptic spasm that stirs her flesh and steels her muscles – a monstrous Beast of the Apocalypse, indifferent, irresponsible, insensible, poisoning, like Helen of Troy of the old Classic fables, all who come near her, all who see her, all who touch her.

Colette included Salome in her repertoire of dancing temptresses, and so did Mata Hari, who came to people's attention as an oriental dancer and was shot by the firing squad for her alleged espionage activities. (Whenever anyone criticized Mata Hari after her death, Caroline Otero would reprimand them, 'Let her alone. They've killed her. Don't talk about it any more.')

The turn-of-the-century Salome fever hints at particular stirrings in the female subconscious. It may have reflected only women's obscure urge to rebel against their place in society, but that urge was as instinctive and powerful as the one that had prompted Parisian working girls to kick their legs in the air seventy years earlier. Both rebellions were articulated through the language that men believed best revealed women's essential nature: the language of dance.

Hidden behind the mask of Salome, it seems that women were expressing their rebellion against male domination. Acting out in public her cruel revenge, they revelled in a sexual power which they knew terrified men. Women from all social backgrounds rushed to get in on the act. Amateur dancers, music-hall artists, serious performers, society hostesses – all were keen to play out the fantasy of the biblical temptress.

In an age of rampant misogyny, women may be excused for wanting revenge on all that male fear and loathing. And perhaps those scores of Salomes had a great laugh to themselves as they stood in the magic beam of the footlights, crowing over their victims' severed heads. They went one better than cancan dancers, who only knocked the hats, rather than the heads, off the powerful men who came to ogle them. Who knows? Perhaps they provided a kind of catharsis for all those middle-class women who, though they didn't dare get up on-stage themselves, were beginning to rattle their chains as the century drew to a close.

Twentieth-Century Goddess

She rode the wave of the revolt against Puritanism;
she rode it, and with her fame
and Dionysian raptures drove it on.
She was – perhaps it is simplest to say –
the crest of the wave, an event not only in art,
but in the history of life.
Max Eastman

When he was a struggling young writer, Balzac used to cheer himself up by visiting the newly opened cemetery of Père Lachaise in Paris. 'And while I wander about in search of the dead,' he wrote, 'all I see are the living.' Père Lachaise was the final destination of Chopin, Colette, Oscar Wilde, Jim Morrison, Balzac himself and countless other celebrated artists. In the wall of the crematorium, in a plain grey box engraved simply with her name, lie the ashes of Isadora Duncan. The time I saw it, someone had left a cheap red plastic rose beneath the box; an ironic tribute considering that Isadora was a woman who, all her life, spoke out against artificiality and ugliness.

In the next row down are another two stone boxes, each bearing a single word: 'Deirdre' and 'Patrick'. These were her children – 'the best of my life' she called them – who drowned in Paris in a freak accident when their car stalled on a bridge and rolled into the Seine. Isadora never recovered from their death, and in a strange reworking of fate, she too was to die in a car accident.

Isadora was only forty-nine when she died in 1927, but her life had been an epic adventure. During her heyday thousands of people saw her dance and were spellbound by the force of her personality and her dramatic gifts.

She lived in both capitalist America and communist Russia; and she lived through revolutions and the first wave of the women's movement. To the narrow-minded, her dancing and her apparent nudity on-stage were scandalous. At the end of her life, out of fashion as a dancer and bowed down by debt, she was also considered scandalous for her private life. She inspired numerous stories among her contemporaries about her extravagant lifestyle, like this one from the American journalist Janet Flanner:

> She was a nomad de luxe. During her famous season at the New York Century Theatre, she bought up every Easter lily in Manhattan to decorate the theatre the night she opened in Berlioz's *L'Enfance du Christ*, which was her Easter programme. The lilies, whose perfume suffocated the spectators, cost two thousand dollars. Isadora had, at the moment, three thousand dollars to her name. And at midnight, long after all good lily-selling florists were in bed, she gave a champagne supper. It cost the other thousand ... After the lilies faded Isadora and her school sat amid their luggage on the pier where the ship was about to sail for France. They had neither tickets nor money. But they had a classic faith in fate and a determination to go back to Europe, where art was understood. Just before the boat sailed, there appeared a schoolteacher. Isadora had never seen her before. The teacher gave Isadora the savings of years and Isadora sailed away. Herself grand, she could inspire grandeur in others, a tragic and tiring gift. There were always schoolteachers and lilies in Isadora's life.

There are many such apocryphal tales about Isadora, but her name has echoed down the years above all as a symbol of freedom and rebellion, a woman who broke the chains which bound the female body and spirit in her time. Her lover Gordon Craig wrote to a friend:

> If you could see *one* dance you would understand how wonderful it is ... I have seldom been so moved by anything. It's a great, a rare rare gift brought to perfection by eighteen years of persistent labour – and we may all agree to worship such things.

The 'eighteen years of persistent labour' began when Isadora was a child in San Francisco. She was born in 1878, 'when Venus was in the ascendant', as she wrote in her autobiography. The daughter of Scots-Irish immigrants, her father's business ventures failed dramatically and her mother divorced him soon after Isadora's birth. The divorce left Mrs Duncan and her four children in desperate financial straits. They were constantly moving house to escape their creditors and Isadora became adept at securing credit from the local grocery store.

At night, when Mrs Duncan returned home from work, she played the piano and read to her children from the works of mildly radical contemporary thinkers. The family entertained itself with amateur dramatics and readings from Shakespeare – Isadora said later that this was her true education, rather than what she had learnt at school. In her early teenage years she set out, offering her services as a dance teacher at the homes of the wealthy. Even then she had a confident sense of herself and a clear vision of how she might shape her life through dance.

Isadora grew up during the *fin de siècle*, a time of fierce debate about culture and society. Every generation looks back on past glories, and at the end of a millennium a sense of living in a time of cultural decay is especially acute. Western society had undergone radical changes with the growth of industrialization, and the past was seen as a golden age. Isadora was a voracious reader and her home was one where ideas were freely discussed. Among them were those of Robert Ingersoll, an Irish agnostic who travelled around America preaching a gospel of love, kindness and sensuality. He was something of a pagan, a man who adored women, and Isadora's mother was an enthusiast of his ideas about life and art, which she in turn passed on to her children.

At the end of the nineteenth century artificiality permeated every aspect of culture, especially the performing arts. Theatre was a pantomime of over-dramatic gestures and the striking of poses, and it was generally agreed that dance had fallen into a state of decay. 'The first-born and eldest sister of the arts has fallen upon evil times in this old age of the world,' wrote one critic who called for a revival of classical Greek dance as a model for the future.

As an embryonic dancer Isadora listened, watched and absorbed by osmosis the debates and artistic movements of the time. But she was probably influenced most of all by the French ex-actor and philosopher François Delsarte, who devoted his life to studying and analysing physical expression. He was popularized in America by the actor Steele MacKaye, who devised a system for teaching Delsarte's ideas as he understood them (for they had never been written down).

138

Delsarte's teaching was concerned with the rejection of artificial expression in life as much as in art. He wanted to dispense with the language of cliché and formality and replace it with a more natural form of physical expression. Action, he said, should emerge as the expression of an inner state, rather than be something imposed from the outside. His theory was that, instead of short bursts of activity punctuated by the striking of poses, dance movement should travel through the body in a fluid, wavelike manner. Underlying his system was the concept that at the heart of physical harmony lay repose and poise, which should come from a state of inner calm.

This was something of which Isadora became convinced very early on in life: that inner repose carried over into everyday life; that by the way we move we express everything about ourselves. From the many descriptions we have of her it's clear that she was a living example of this ideal. A friend of her youth recalls how Isadora set out to develop this distinctive calm by spending hours moving with painful deliberateness until her movement became natural. Gordon Craig wrote that she was the calmest woman he ever saw; that she never, ever hurried.

From a young age Isadora taught dance as a contribution to the family coffers. But teaching harmonious movement to children was one thing; treading the boards was another:

> You enter. The audience, mostly male, eagerly eyes the stage. The air is heavy – the audience seems heavy. Smoke tickles the nostrils. All are prepared for a 'good time'. They know about exactly what's coming – the blaze of colour, the stupendous efforts to amaze, pretty chorus girls and clever principals – legs, toes, arms, hips, breasts, eyes, hair, the whole *mélange* of stage femininity.

Theatre dance in America meant acrobatic turns, skirt dancing, burlesque and ballet. A ballet consisted of short 'numbers' interrupted by pauses to acknowledge applause, and a great deal of revealing leg work. At that time ballet's biggest fans were men about town who visited theatres to ogle the girls and find themselves a companion for the night. They certainly weren't interested in ballet for artistic reasons and, no doubt, neither were the ballerinas. Quite apart from these considerations, dance was still not a career that a girl entered into for creative reasons. It was considered frivolous, incapable of being anything other than a mildly diverting entertainment.

There were three openings available to Isadora if she wanted to perform: she could join a theatre review; she could become a member of a ballet company; or she could be a 'turn' at society parties. She tried her hand at the first option – working with the Augustin Daly Company in New York – but it didn't suit what she had to offer. The second option she didn't even consider, for she loathed ballet and everything it represented. The third – dancing at society parties – was the most promising for the moment. Hobnobbing with the wealthy was a possible way of making contact with the artists whom she hoped would lead her to her ultimate goal. So she tried it for a while, first in San Francisco, then Chicago, as she gradually drifted east to New York.

When Isadora entertained the wealthy in their mansions it was as an attractive diversion, an 'extra' thoughtfully provided for the guests by their host, along with the food and wine. In such a setting she was little more than a servant, though a rather eccentric one, with a penchant for offering the guests little lectures on the art of the dance as she reclined on a sofa in her Greek draperies. Throughout her life Isadora talked about her theories on art and life to anyone who would listen to them. As she herself said, she would have talked about them to the plumber if he'd come through the door.

In order to distance herself from the cheapness of her profession she dropped the title of 'dancer' and began referring to herself as 'artist'. As the new century drew near, though, she realized she was making slow progress in her native land and turned her gaze towards Europe. She appealed to her society acquaintances for donations, and little by little they began trickling in. On 18 April 1899 she gave a farewell performance. It was reviewed by a New York paper:

> her sole costume for yesterday's dance was a species of surgical bandage or gauze and satin of the hue of a raspberry ice ... When the final dance was finished there was a sigh of relief that it was over and that Miss Duncan's bandages hadn't fallen off as they threatened to during the entire show. Then the entire audience of 67 solemnly filed up on the stage to kiss Miss Duncan, her mamma and sister, and wish them success in introducing 'The Happier Age of Gold' to London drawing-rooms in May. Miss Duncan has fully determined on this reckless course, which is sad, considering that we are at peace with England at present.

With this sneer ringing in her ears Isadora and her family set sail. They travelled steerage in a cattle boat, going in the opposite direction to all those hopeful immigrants flooding into New York, looking for prosperity and a new life. It would be many years before she returned, and when she did, it was as one of the most celebrated women of her day.

***

In *My Life* Isadora writes about the early, penniless days in London, where her family was reduced to sleeping on a park bench for the first few nights. Finally, she took matters into her own hands and marched them into one of the best hotels. She explained to the night porter that their luggage had been held up in Liverpool, and imperiously ordered breakfast to be sent up to their rooms.

> All that day we slept in luxurious beds. Now and then I telephoned down to the porter to complain bitterly that our luggage had not arrived.
> 'It is quite impossible for us to go out without a change of clothes,' I said, and that night we dined in our rooms.
> At dawn of the next day, judging that the ruse had reached its limit, we walked out exactly as we had walked in, but this time without waking the night porter!

If it's true that we make our own luck in life, then Isadora is a great example of how fortune favours the brave. By a series of fortuitous meetings she managed to make contact with London's upper crust and found herself once again dancing at society parties. More often than not she made no money from these engagements. Her hosts fobbed her off by saying that since she would be dancing before so many lords and counts and princes, this opportunity was payment enough. Nor did they think of offering her anything to eat, though one afternoon her hostess gave her a bowl of strawberries: 'I was so ill from not having had any solid food for some days that those strawberries and the rich cream made me very miserable indeed.'

Isadora wryly recorded the lukewarm English response to her dancing – 'How pretty', 'Awfully jolly', 'Thank you so much'. It was only when she found herself moving in intellectual and creative circles that she received the response she craved and, fired by this encouragement, she began developing her dance in earnest.

She moved to Paris in 1900 with her mother and her brother Raymond and took a studio above a printer's for the incredibly low rent of fifty francs a month. At night the floor shook with the thunder and clatter of the printing presses as they crashed into life. An invitation that Isadora sent out to one of her recitals in December 1901 reveals something of the personal charm which was to beguile all who met her:

> Miss Duncan will dance to the sound of harp and flute in her studio next Thursday Evening, and if you feel that seeing this small person dance against the waves of an overpowering destiny is of ten francs benefit to you – why, come along!

It was in Paris that the name of Isadora began to be talked about in appreciative terms. In Paris too she discarded her gold sandals and metamorphosed into 'the barefoot dancer'. The story of how this happened is told by Mary Desti, who met Isadora that year and was to be with her through good times and bad until the end of her life. Desti describes how, one evening, Isadora was preparing to give a recital in her studio:

> While the conference was on, Isadora was getting ready, putting on a costume behind a curtain which cut off the corner of the room which was used as a stage. Isadora wore very high laced gold sandals to dance. Even at this time she liked a little alcohol before the ordeal of dancing, and as the glass of Hunter's rye slipped out of her hand, pouring into one of these sandals and smelling to heaven, we began to giggle and laugh until, try as we would, we could not get the sandal on. The conference finished and the music started.
>
> I grabbed the sandals, threw them in a corner, and pushed Isadora on the stage barefoot. This was the first time that Isadora Duncan ever danced barefoot in her life, and it created such a sensation, everyone raving about the beauty of her feet, that she adopted it forever.

At the 1900 Paris Exposition Isadora met fellow American dancer Loie Fuller. Fuller created a sensation by manipulating hundreds of yards of gossamer fabric, which transformed her into a storm of different shapes: a snake, a butterfly, a conflagration. After meeting Marie Curie, Fuller had experimented with the effects of radium painted onto her costumes; but her great innovation was in using streams of coloured light, which fell on the whirling folds of her costumes to create the most glorious effects.

Fuller had her own theatre at the Paris Expo. She was a capable impresario, generous enough to present other dancers whom she recognized as having something valuable to offer. So it was that she invited Isadora to join her company on their European tour. It was a great opportunity, which Isadora readily accepted, though she broke away from Fuller's company soon afterwards to perform as a soloist. In her autobiography Fuller relates an incident from this tour. She had arranged to present Isadora to a select company in Vienna. Ten minutes before the concert was due to begin, Fuller went backstage to see how Isadora's preparations were coming along:

> I found her with her feet in warm water, in the act of dressing her hair in a very leisurely manner. Startled, I begged her to hurry, explaining that she ran the risk through her negligence of offending an audience that would definitely give her her start. My words were without effect. Very slowly she continued her preparations.

Eventually Isadora was ready and made her entrance, with her usual calm. But something distracted Fuller: 'She appeared to me nude, or very nearly so, to so slight an extent did the gauze which she wore cover her form.' After Isadora's dance there was a silence, and one of the illustrious guests leaned towards Fuller and whispered, 'Why does she dance with so little clothing on?' At this, Fuller decided she must find an explanation: she said loudly that Isadora's luggage had not arrived, and rather than disappoint her expectant audience, she had agreed to perform in her rehearsal costume!

Isadora's revealing costumes, her so-called 'nudity', caused a great stir to begin with. 'I took off my clothes to dance because I felt the rhythm and freedom of my body better that way,' she wrote in her memoirs. Her transparent Greek chitons clung to her skin, and these little wisps of costume may have created the illusion of nudity. But they were more substantial than they appeared. They were anchored securely to her body, fastened with elastic over the shoulders and round the waist, and attached to a silk jersey body-stocking. An elastic harness kept the costume from riding around and held the folds in place.

Many years later, one of Isadora's dancers, Julia Levien, recalled that the company always travelled with bundles of little gold safety pins:

> When we went to have our photos taken by Arnold Genthe (Isadora's favourite photographer) we did not use anything underneath! He thought the undergarments spoiled the line of the body. This of course added to the legend that we wore nothing under the tunics!

Isadora rejected the coloured tights that other dancers wore as a symbolic veil of respectability. Spectators may have thought they were seeing a dancer's legs, but most dancers wore 'fleshings', unlike Isadora, who danced bare-legged. She may also have taken the unusual step of removing her leg and underarm hair. Removing underarm hair wasn't common among American women until after the 1910s, and removing leg hair later still. But female performers adopted the custom earlier than other women. As with other traditions of the day, they set the fashion for other women.

From many anecdotes about her it seems that Isadora had no false modesty and, more than that, a complete carelessness about revealing her body. Her friend Kathleen Bruce recalls a picnic given for the sculptor Auguste Rodin:

> After lunch at the picnic, a fine old Norwegian painter, Fritz von Thaulow, tuned up his fiddle, and somebody said the lovely dancer must dance. Isadora had a long, white, high-waisted Liberty frock on, and shoes. She said she could not dance because her frock was too long. Somebody said, 'Take it off!' and the cry rose, 'Take it off!' So she did, and her shoes too, and as the fiddlers began to play, Isadora, in a little white petticoat and bare feet, began to move, to sway, to rush, to be as a falling leaf in a high gale, and finally to drop at Rodin's feet in an unforgettable pose of childish abandonment.

From 1902 to 1904 Isadora toured Europe to rapturous enthusiasm from press and public alike. In Munich students unharnessed her horses and pulled her carriage through the streets, and one night they swept her off to a cafe where they lifted her from table to table to watch her dance.

That she was offering something completely different to anything they'd ever seen before was a source of great excitement to the young and to her

144 fellow artists. But it didn't prevent some carping from the critics. Isadora never learnt to ignore spiteful reviews, a skill essential to the self-preservation of any performing artist. She always preferred to answer back. Indeed, there was nothing she liked better than the whiff of gunsmoke. When the Berlin *Morgen Post* critic wrote, complaining that she had no technique and her dance could not be considered an art form, she took up her pen:

> Dear Sir,
>
> I was very much embarrassed on reading your esteemed paper to find that you had asked of so many admirable masters of the dance to expend such deep thought and consideration on so insignificant a subject as my humble self. I feel that so much excellent literature was somewhat wasted on so unworthy a subject. And I suggest that instead of asking them, 'Can Miss Duncan Dance?' you should have called their attention to a far more celebrated dancer – one who has been dancing in Berlin for some years before Miss Duncan appeared. A natural dancer who also in her style (which Miss Duncan tries to follow) is in direct opposition to the school of ballet today.
>
> The dancer I allude to is the dancing Maenad in the Berlin museum ...
>
> For this dancer of whom I speak has never tried to walk on the end of her toes. Neither has she spent much time in the practice of leaping into the air to find out how many times she could clap together her heels before she came down again. She neither wears corsets nor tights, and her bare feet rest freely in her sandals.
>
> I believe a prize has been offered for the sculptor who can replace the broken arms in their original position. I suggest it might be even more useful for the art of today to offer a prize for whoever could reproduce in life the heavenly pose of her body and the secret beauty of her movements. I suggest that your excellent paper might offer such a prize and the excellent masters and mistresses of ballet compete for it.
>
> Perhaps after a trial of some years they will have learnt something about human anatomy, something about the beauty, the purity, the intelligence of the movements of the human body. Breathlessly awaiting their learned reply, I remain, most sincerely –
>
> Isadora Duncan

In *My Life* Isadora recalls the handful of ballet lessons she took as a young girl: 'When the teacher told me to stand on my toes I asked him why, and when he replied "Because it is beautiful" I said that it was ugly and against nature and after the third lesson I left his class, never to return.'

It's an amusing story, though probably not entirely accurate, for Isadora liked to alter the facts the better to make a point. One thing is certain though: she loathed everything to do with ballet. Its aesthetic was the antithesis of beauty to her. She loathed the tightly corseted ballet costume, which restricted the body. She loathed the meaningless stops and starts and holding of poses – they couldn't have been more different from her own natural flowing movement, just as the stiff spine of ballet was the opposite of her fluid, supple backbone. She loathed the self-conscious walk to the footlights to acknowledge applause every few minutes, breaking up the flow of a dance. She loathed the taut knees, immobile hips and shoulders, and the pointe shoes which tried to create 'the delusion that the law of gravitation does not exist'. Most of all, she loathed the distortions that ballet technique inflicted on the body and the damage it did: 'Under the tricots are dancing deformed muscles,' she wrote. 'Underneath the muscles are deformed bones.'

Only the briefest film extract exists of Isadora dancing, and this speeded-up fragment from the early days of cinema makes it impossible to gain a real idea of what she did. We see her from a distance in a sunlit garden. She whirls, turns, disappears behind a tree, reappears, whirls, lifts her arms and bows. It's all over in a few maddeningly short seconds. Of course, there are many accounts of her dancing, but these can be deceptive. Some are couched in almost mystical terms and describe only the effect of what she did. Others record how she used the simple movements of everyday life – walking, running, skipping and turning. As a dance performance this in itself would have been extraordinary at the time. One description focuses on the sensual flow of her dancing:

> She moves often in long and lovely sensuous lines across the whole breadth or down the whole depth of the stage. Or she circles it in curves of no less jointless beauty. As she moves, her body is steadily and delicately undulating. One motion flows or ripples or sweeps into another.

What is obvious is that, added to what must then have been an unusual simplicity and grace of movement, she had tremendous stage presence. In the years of her maturity as an artist her movements became even more simple, if that were possible, and those who saw her say that her effect came from her great dramatic gifts. But exactly how she moved, and how this combined with her very great stage presence, must remain something of a mystery.

It's hard for us to imagine how revolutionary Isadora was then, and not just in her dancing. Everything she has come to stand for was centred on the idea of freedom of the body for women: free movement unconstricted by crippling fashions; and the freedom to bear children outside marriage. And if some of these ideas took shape as early as her childhood (when she burned her parents' marriage certificate and vowed never to marry), others were forged on the anvil of experience. Many times she found herself acting in defiance of difficult circumstances. And none were as difficult as those which faced Isadora the day she met the man who was to be the great love of her life.

***

On a winter's day at the end of 1904 Isadora met Edward Gordon Craig in her Berlin apartment. Of all her loves, it was Craig who was to cause her the greatest pain.

A friend was playing the piano, and Craig watched Isadora as he listened to the music. He wrote in his diary that they became friends and lovers from the moment they stood there together at the piano. Craig was to write about Isadora often in letters, notebooks and articles. Many years after her death he wrote most movingly of what the two of them had meant to each other:

> Our meeting first of all was, as I have already written, a marvellous coming together. Not because I saw in her someone who fulfilled my ideas of the perfect dancer, the interpreter of unspoken things, the Figure of Figures for the stage. That may or may not have contributed some slight extra-ness to what I felt in 1904 in Berlin. That coming together was so little to do with art – theatre – dreams. That coming together was a marvellous thing. No small words or thoughts can tell of that. Suppose one had been in a world with one's other half – once – and that world so wonderfully perfect; and

then, suppose that world had dissolved and time had passed over one, and one had woken up in another world – but one's other half not there … Years go by … Life, making sport of us, makes it difficult: it becomes more difficult – but one lives. Life wins. Then suddenly, the marvellous happens – that other half is standing beside one; she too has found her way, after all these centuries and over all those hills and rivers and seas – and here she is – and here am I.

They were together for much of that year, and for a time Craig travelled with her and acted as her tour manager (an uncommon act in a man who normally gave no time or energy to supporting other people's work). But she was constantly touring, and eventually he was forced to return to his own work. She wrote from Frankfurt, longing for his company and cajoling him to join her:

> [*February 1905*]:
> Darling Love, Sweetheart, Come Here – I've been 50 ages alone now, and I Want you right away. I wonder if you'll come – only 8 little hours away – 8 little hours … If you took the train tonight you'd be here by 6 tomorrow morning. O Come along –
> I'll pose for you like an angel –
> I'll stand on my head, I'll do anything – only Come and put a stop to this dreadful Aching …

Craig preserved (and carefully annotated) Isadora's hundreds of letters, which are a poignant testament to her spontaneity and generosity. We do not have his letters to her – only the rough drafts, for, unlike Isadora, who wrote openly, holding nothing back, Craig was in the habit of carefully composing rough drafts of his love letters. From Brussels she wrote:

> [*March 1905*]
> … You need not write 'Never not love me' – I love all that is beautiful and I will always adore you because you are beautiful (Is that Calm and Cool enough?). Besides you have given me Everlasting Joy – I would say more but Joy is the highest – Joy includes Suffering – I suppose Suffering is a part of Joy – Well you have given me joy enough to last a lifetime if need be – (Is that Big and Clear enough?).

Yes you have given me unspeakable joy and made me Happy beyond my dreams of what happiness could be. You have taken me to the heights – the highest – and now whatever comes – I will always be grateful and happy –

(See how Calm I am)

Wonderful isn't it?

The meeting of Isadora and Craig was a meeting of twin souls. Craig revolutionized stage design, just as Isadora revolutionized dance. He sought to sweep away the clutter of naturalistic theatre and turn the stage into an empty space to be filled with light. He and Isadora shared this revolutionary concept. But the two of them differed in that Isadora achieved many of her ideals, as well as fame and success in her lifetime, and Craig did not. Time and again, through pure egotism, Craig alienated those who worked with him and put paid to his chances, ensuring that success remained ultimately elusive.

Almost from the start, the passionate attraction between Isadora and Craig warred with their need for freedom to get on with their individual work. In *My Life*, Isadora writes about the compulsion to devote herself to her work and the simultaneous urge to give it up and devote herself to Craig: 'Why don't you stop this?' he used to say. 'Why do you want to go on the stage and wave your arms about? Why don't you stay at home and sharpen my lead pencils?'

Yet there is no doubt that Craig admired Isadora's work. Years after her death he gave a radio talk, recalling the extraordinary impact she had on all those who saw her dance:

> She came to move as no one had ever seen anyone move before … Only this can we say – that she was telling to the air the very things we longed to hear and until she came we had never dreamed we should hear, and now we heard them, and this sent us all into an unusual state of joy, and [I] sat still and speechless.

Like Isadora, Craig was fearless and outspoken and it's clear that his dynamic energy and physical beauty gave him a potent sexual attractiveness. But Craig did not come into Isadora's life unencumbered. He had an ex-wife and a devoted mistress, Elena Meo, who had already borne him two children and was expecting another, as well as several other illegitimate children. He sometimes expressed wonder at where all these children had sprung from, implying that it was really nothing to do with him, that it was the women's silly fault for allowing it to happen. Throughout his life he provided for none of his children. He was kept afloat financially by his mother, the actress Ellen Terry, and by the other women in his life, including Isadora at the time of their liaison.

When Craig and Isadora became lovers, he told her that he was due to marry Elena Meo in four months' time; Isadora laughed and said she didn't believe in marriage. One wonders if he gave her an accurate picture of his other commitments, for in his dealings with women he was never straightforward. An apologetic letter that Isadora wrote to him hints that she had belatedly learnt the extent of his complicated love life and had reacted negatively to the discovery. 'I feel awfully ashamed … dust and ashes … I'm afraid you will never be able to think of me in the same way again …'

Meanwhile she was having problems with the children's school that she had set up in Germany. When the school committee heard of Isadora's liaison they wrote telling her that they could no longer support an establishment whose founder had such lax ideas of morality. Her response was to hire a hall and give a lecture expounding her thoughts on the subject:

> Of course people will respond, 'But what about the children?' Well, I could give the names of many prominent people who were born out of wedlock. It has not prevented them from obtaining fame and fortune. But, leaving that, I said to myself, How can a woman go into this marriage contract with a man who she thinks is so mean that, in case of a quarrel, he wouldn't even support his own children? If she thinks he is such a man, why should she marry him? I suppose truth and mutual faith are the first principles of love.

It's a poignant passage, considering how Craig neglected every one of his eight children. Isadora's objection to marriage had been forged by her own parents' disastrous experience, as well as her passion for justice. In *My Life* she writes:

> I believe, as a wage-earning woman, that if I make the great sacrifice of strength and health, and even risk my life to have a child, I should certainly not do so if, on some future occasion, the man can say that

the child belongs to him by law, and he will take it from me, and I shall see it only three times a year!

A very witty American writer once replied to his mistress, when she said, 'What would the child think of us if we were not married?' by saying, 'If your child and my child were that sort of child, we would not care what it thought of us.'

From the very start of her love affair with Craig, Isadora longed for a child. Not once, she wrote, had they made love when she'd not whispered, 'Give me a child.' Two years after they met she gave birth to her daughter Deirdre. Isadora did not align herself with what was then known as the 'woman movement' or 'suffragism', but she demonstrated many times in support of women's independence. She fervently believed that women should be free to love and bear children outside of marriage, often finding herself in hot water after speaking out on the subject.

In the social climate of the time, however, longing for a child and actually having one were two different things. It was considered scandalous for an unmarried woman to bear children. And if it happened to women who led unconventional lives – and performers were high on that list – they didn't advertise the fact. It's significant that, during the short life of her longed-for daughter, Isadora never introduced Deirdre as her own child but as 'our youngest pupil, a daughter of Edward Gordon Craig'.

When Isadora's pregnancy started to become apparent, she removed herself from the limelight and decamped with a nurse to a lonely beach in Holland, to wait out the event. She was careful to show Craig only her bright courage, and wrote to him with a cheerfulness that she certainly did not feel:

> *9 July 1906*
> Dearest – When I opened my eyes this morning the old one brought me your letter – a letter from you is like a touch from your hand filled with vitality and gives me new life – also you are dear and sweet to write so often & to send me so many beautiful thoughts and things ... I am what you make me – very happy –
> Your
> Topsy

In reality it was a lonely, desperate time, as her friend Kathleen Bruce records. Bruce received a letter from Isadora, begging her to leave her Paris studio and go to Isadora's aid:

It was a queer cry, childish and pathetic. Would not, could not, I come to her? Her need was very great, very very great. I went at once. I found her pitiful, helpless, and for the first time endearing. 'Poor darling, what is the matter?' 'Can't you see?' cried the dancer, spreading high her lovely arms. Slowly, and with many a lie, the story came out. A well-known personage with a wife, a mistress, children, dissolute habits, and no money, had ensnared her body and mind, and her baby was due in a month or two. .. She had danced as long as she dared. She was lonely and miserable.

Bruce swallowed her qualms – after all, as an Englishwoman of strict upbringing she was shocked by Isadora's condition – and moved into the house on the beach. When a press reporter tried to track down Isadora in her hideout, Bruce helped head him off by disguising herself in a voluminous cloak and running and dancing on the beach. One night Bruce woke up, unaccountably worried. She rose and went to check Isadora's room. The bed was empty, the lights were off and the front door lay open. She ran down the sandy path to the sea where she was horrified to see, far out in deep water, Isadora's hands and outstretched arms:

> The sea was calm. I rushed in. The figure ahead did not move. As I neared it, calling, she turned round with a gentle, rather dazed look, and stretched out her arms to me with a faint, childish smile, saying, 'The tide was so low, I couldn't do it, and I'm so cold.'

One day, Bruce recalls, Craig arrived unexpectedly. Isadora was overjoyed at seeing him and their life was turned upside down in order to create a festive atmosphere for him. According to Bruce's account, the visit wasn't without some wild outbursts of temper, which made her fear for Isadora. But:

> Endowed always with an abundance of generosity towards those around her, [Isadora] seemed now ready to forgive, to condone, to accept, to give herself up to ministering to this unbridled child of mature age whose presence so altered our mode of life.

Craig departed as suddenly as he had appeared and the two women settled down to the long wait. The baby was born after a gruelling labour. Isadora was ill for months afterwards. She struggled to get back to touring as soon as she could but, try as she might, it was impossible for her to go on working. Described at the time as 'neurasthenia', she may well have been suffering from post-natal depression. She must in any case have been exhausted after the difficult birth of Deirdre, as well as the heroic efforts she had made to keep up her spirits while hiding her pregnancy from the world.

Ever since her first taste of success, Isadora had been the breadwinner for everyone around her – her family, her school, even Craig himself. If she couldn't work, who else was going to provide for all those dependants? She also (rashly, considering how money slipped through her fingers) offered to sponsor Craig's theatre projects. It was a promise she had no hope of keeping, so great were her financial commitments by then. Isadora was never good at managing money, only at spending it. Though she was making huge sums of money at the height of her fame, her financial commitments were also huge, considering the number of people she was in the habit of providing for. Agents and promoters found it easy to swindle her, even to the extent that she sometimes came away from a sell-out concert with hardly enough money to travel on to the next one.

Isadora's long illness after the birth of Deirdre was dismissed by her doctor as 'neuralgia – just nerves – nothing'. In the parlance of the day it was termed hysteria, but Isadora may well have been unconsciously relieved that she had to call a halt to her gruelling touring schedule. Relieved too that, for a time, she was released from the hard work of massaging Craig's ego and trying to hold his interest when she knew there was another woman in the background.

Blinded by his *amour propre* and his huge needs, indulged by every woman who had ever entered his life, Craig justified his break with Isadora by citing her broken promise to provide him with money for his work in Florence. To him it was 'a trifle', but Isadora simply couldn't find the money, and it wounded his pride as an artist:

> From that day I have never forgiven this [he wrote]. I don't mind what anyone does or says to me – but if they in any way show disrespect for my work once I am at work (when warm at it) then click goes the apparatus & it's all over between me and whoever has played me the trick.

Isadora wrote to Craig that she was desperate for money herself at the time:

It is all very rum rum rum – extremely rum – I had better go to America & find a millionaire or so – for this dancing business seems to make board & lodging only … Can't your dear Mama find us a millionaire?

In the end, she realized it was hopeless to struggle on:

Dearest Dreamer [she wrote sadly], this is a pretty silly world & I'm afraid you needed someone a bit stronger than your poor Topsy to help you. All my heart's love to you – it can't do you much good though can it?

Isadora had put her considerable resources – her fame, her support, her humour and generosity – at Craig's service and she had fought hard for him. But in the end Craig's self-obsession triumphed and he dropped out of her life. After they parted, however, they continued to write and meet up on occasion over the years. For a while, Isadora even cherished the hope that their love might be rekindled. It was not to be. And though she went on to have other affairs, she was never to meet another man who inspired, even remotely, the all-consuming passion she had felt for Craig.

***

One of Isadora's achievements was to make audiences look at the female body in a new way. Reviews of her performances often noted that her dancing wasn't sexual. This isn't to say that she wasn't sexually alluring, but that she didn't try and stimulate erotic desire through her movements. To dance sexually is to be conscious of the onlooker, to direct dance movement at the audience, and this she never did. She aimed neither at satisfying men's expectations nor stimulating desire for her body. As Craig's friend, the composer Martin Shaw, wrote, 'There was no sex appeal in Isadora's dancing. That in itself was new and strange.'

When she danced, Isadora was in her own world, immersed in the mood and the music and the moment. She expressed a vitality which included sensuality and spirituality as equally valuable, interlocking aspects of the life force. That she set her dances to classical music (the first dancer to do so) lent weight to what she did. But it sometimes outraged composers, who didn't like to be identified with such a disreputable art form as dance. While she was sometimes attacked for her revealing costume, however, she was most often described as 'chaste':

> The fact that her feet and legs are unclothed is forgotten. It is part of the picture. Miss Duncan does not therefore rely upon physical charms to add to her success, as do some of the so-called dancers who are at present doing various sorts of stunts on both sides of the water. Her success comes through her grace and ease of movement, not on account of her ability to kick or wiggle or do acrobatic tricks.

Isadora's Greek-style chitons weren't designed to isolate parts of the body and offer them up for their erotic appeal, unlike the tutus and corseted bodices of ballet. There was no emphasis on bosom or hips, no special kicks, no parading down to the footlights to flutter her eyelashes at the audience. When Isadora danced it was with her whole body. When she lifted her arms in that open, all-embracing gesture which we recognize in so many photos, when she curved her supple spine or threw back her head in abandon, she wasn't offering sexual promise; she was demonstrating the allure of a wild, free spirit in all its seductive, subversive power.

The fashionable female body at the turn of the century had a tiny wasp-waist, a shelf of bosom, and a bustle to emphasize what was known as 'the meat in the seat'. This swaying, serpentine figure echoed the sweep and curve of the then-fashionable art-nouveau style. But, as we've seen, being an S-shaped woman involved considerable discomfort. This hothouse flower who was the visible manifestation of wealth believed it was her duty to attract men at whatever cost to herself, and if she suffered to be beautiful, it was a price she was willing to pay.

The sight of women strolling along with their skirts trailing in the mud, collecting germs and dirt, inspired dress reformers like the American Amelia Bloomer to advocate trousers for women, and by the beginning of the twentieth century a lively dress reform movement was underway. It was some years, though, before it began to take effect, and then it was due to the roles women had taken on during a catastrophic world war.

Even children's clothes needed reforming, as Isadora's pupil Irma Duncan recalls in her autobiography. She remembers the day she went to audition for

Isadora's school. Isadora asked Irma's mother to undress her young daughter, who was forced to stand in an agony of embarrassment while her mother fumbled over the many hooks and buttons on her clothes: 'After she had removed the black stockings, the high-buttoned shoes, and the last petticoat, I stood exposed in a cotton camisole and a pair of lace-edged underpants, from which dangled long black garters.' Irma felt terribly ashamed and couldn't help contrasting her own clothes with Isadora's simple ankle-length white tunic and bare feet.

As an early pupil of Isadora's, Irma was one of the first to take part in her dress reform programme. She remembers people's shock as the young girls walked down Berlin's streets in early spring in their tunics, feet bare in their sandals. Women called after them, 'Oh, you poor, poor, little children! Why, you must be freezing to death with so little on! ... It's cruelty, that's what it is! We ought to get the police after you. Cruel! Cruel! Cruel!' Nor did it end there:

> No one had reckoned with the other children of the neighbourhood, mostly boys, who subjected us poor victims to what amounted to a minor persecution. Like the Christian martyrs of old, we were actually stoned. Frequently (and this was most humiliating) the children pelted us – in this era of horse-drawn carriages – with something else entirely ... It hardly seems credible that, in the first decade of this atomic century, the pupils of Isadora Duncan should have been stoned because of their unconventional dress. But a novel idea was on the march and nothing could stop its progress.

Isadora dispensed with corsets and high-heeled, pointed-toed shoes and in her everyday life she wore an adaptation of her Greek-style stage costume. The culture of ancient Greece had entered people's consciousness following the excavations in Troy, and it was held up as the height of civilization. No matter that the ancient Greeks endorsed slavery and rejected the education of women. Set against Victorian prudery, the Olympic ideal – the beauty and strength of the human body – spoke of a time of innocence and nature. Newly unearthed Greek statues in their simple, flowing drapery offered a glimpse of a world of elegance, grace and nobility.

Back in the early nineteenth century, it had been the custom at society parties for women to pose in wispy Greek chitons made of muslin and cheesecloth. Nelson's mistress, Lady Hamilton, was one beauty who entertained her guests with classical Greek poses while her husband stood behind her with lighted candles. Statue-posing in the Greek style was popular as far back as the 1830s in American theatre. Later on came 'living statues' who moved as well as posed, an idea harking back to Delsarte.

In her early career Isadora was described as reviving the dance of ancient Greece, a label that suited her at the time. Years later she denied that this was what she had tried to do. She claimed that her dance expressed the wide-open prairies of the American West and the expansive, exploring human spirit. Certainly, as the descendant of immigrants who had crossed the continent in a covered wagon, all her life Isadora displayed the ingenuity of an American pioneer.

As she developed her dance it took on a spirit of freedom and rebellion that had little to do with ancient Greece. Her costume, she said, was fashioned after the dancing figures in Botticelli's *Primavera*, a copy of which hung in the Duncan house when she was growing up. That she wore an adaptation of this costume to mingle with elegant society was thought wildly eccentric. When Cosima Wagner asked her whether all Americans dressed like her, she replied with her usual sense of fun, 'Oh no, some wear feathers.'

The biographer of her Russian years, Ilya Ilyich Schneider, remembers Isadora finding some beautiful transparent silk shawls in a Georgian market. She decided to make herself and Irma new dresses for a banquet she was due to attend that evening. Taking up one of the shawls she had bought in the market, she folded it in two, cut a slit for the head and two more down the sides and slipped it over Irma's head. She pulled the two parallel ends through the side slits, tied them in a wide knot and allowed the shawl to fall over Irma's shoulders and down her back in the shape of a cloak. That night the dresses made a great impression, and it's typical of Isadora that she proceeded to lecture the women guests, who thought they were seeing the latest Paris fashion:

> Those dresses you admire so much have been bought in your market and I made them today with the help of only a pair of scissors. You do not value the beauty of what is right in front of you, and you are all trying to keep up with the Parisian fashions which would look ridiculous in this country.

For years Isadora was happy to wear the simple gowns which were an extension of her stage persona. But this changed when she met Paris Singer. In *My Life* she writes that, after Craig left her, she wished long and hard for a millionaire. It was a mantra she carried on repeating until, one afternoon, as she was sitting in her dressing-room at the theatre, her millionaire appeared.

Paris Singer was forty-one when he met Isadora and she was thirty-two. Heir to the Singer sewing-machine fortune, he described himself as *un homme de goût*, and as a man of taste he did indeed collect rare and priceless objects. The rarest item in his collection was undoubtedly Isadora. Throughout their stormy liaison Singer was generous with Isadora. He recognized her worth, financed her schools, offered to build her a theatre, and during some of her worst times of poverty after their parting, came back into her life and settled her bills.

Singer, like Craig, had a complicated set of commitments elsewhere – in this case, a wife and four children. But this was a minor problem for Isadora compared to those she had had with Craig, and in any case, her millionaire was in the process of getting a divorce. Singer introduced Isadora to a life of luxury and it must have been with a sigh of relief that, for the first time ever, she settled down to letting someone else take care of the bills. She who for many years had worn a plain woollen tunic in winter and a plain linen tunic in summer, succumbed to the lure of couturier gowns.

Her favourite designer was Paul Poiret who, in turn, became highly influenced by Isadora – in particular, the classical Greek look that she brought to public attention. Poiret followed her lead in advocating the unpadded, uncorseted female figure. His gowns created a new silhouette for women which emphasized the shoulders as the point of support, rather than a minuscule waist created by the grip of steel and leather stays. The inspiration for his beautiful designs came from many sources, including Orientalism, which was then in vogue. Other designers favoured discreet colours: delicate blues, lavenders, dove greys. Poiret's colours couldn't have been more different. His gowns were vivid with scarlets and peacock blues; he used gorgeous velvets and silks, embroidered and subtly sprinkled with gold and silver. His creations were works of art and their simple lines allowed women to move freely. Within a few years Poiret had become the most influential fashion designer of the period leading up to the First World War.

Isadora loved Poiret's beautiful gowns, just as she loved the fine food and cruises on yachts that Singer's money could buy. Not only that. She was touched by his eagerness to support her work, in particular her school. A year after they met she gave birth to their son Patrick.

But Singer's way of life was not Isadora's scene at all. He proposed marriage: when they were married, he said, she would be able to stop touring. What should she do with her time, she inquired, if she were no longer working? Singer replied that they could spend their time in his London house, in his country mansion, on his yacht ... And then what? Isadora asked. So Singer proposed that they try the life for three months. 'If you don't like it,' he said, 'I shall be much astonished.' They drove down to his Devon house, Oldway Mansion, which had been built in the style of a French chateau. Isadora recalls the visit in her autobiography:

> The English people ... rise and have an early breakfast of eggs and bacon, and ham and kidneys, and porridge. Then they don mackintoshes and go forth into the humid country till lunch, when they eat many courses, ending with Devonshire cream.
>
> From lunch to five o'clock they are supposed to be busy with their correspondence, though I believe they really go to sleep. At five they descend to their tea, consisting of many kinds of cakes and bread and butter and tea and jam. After that they make a pretence of playing bridge, until it is time to proceed to the really important business of the day – dressing for dinner, at which they appear in full evening dress, the ladies very *décolleté*, and the gentlemen in starched shirts to demolish a twenty-course dinner. When this is over they engage in some light political conversation, or touch upon philosophy until the time comes to retire.
>
> You can imagine whether this life pleased me or not. In the course of a couple of weeks I was positively desperate.

There were many aspects of the high life that Isadora embraced. But however much she enjoyed luxury, her sense of social justice was never far away. In the midst of pleasure her conscience looked on, murmuring that luxury for one should be luxury for all; that wealth entailed right behaviour. Years later, she talked to her biographer Sewell Stokes about the more disturbing aspects of her life with Singer:

> With all his money he was not happy. He was a jealous man, with a terrible temper. If his food didn't satisfy him in every detail, he just

flung it in his chef's face. Really, he did that. I used to sit at the table, nervous of the scene I knew he was about to make. When the chef came in from the kitchen, my Millionaire, after pointing out what he considered was wrong with the pheasant, or whatever the dish was, simply picked it up and flung it across the man's face ... How I hated that man at times; and yet, do you know, at times I could feel desperately sorry for him.

The problem with collecting a rare bloom is what to do with it when you've collected it. To gather up an artist who has lived and breathed for her work and then put her in a glass case and admire her is an undertaking doomed to failure. Isadora wasn't happy in idleness. Her mind was too active. For as long as she could remember she had danced; her body didn't suit a life of reclining by the pool or dancing in a Greek temple for an audience of one (something which Singer tried to organize, with disastrous results). At first she may have welcomed the relief Singer offered her, as well as his generosity. But he wasn't an obvious choice of partner for a free spirit like hers. Many times they quarrelled and parted and came together again, yet in the end their affair was doomed to failure.

***

Isadora's brother Raymond once had an affair with the screen vamp Theda Bara. Believing the actress was having a harmful effect on him, Isadora took matters into her own hands by buying him a train ticket and sending him off to Moscow. Feeling guilty, she arranged to go and see the actress and explain what she had done. She begged her friend Mary Desti to go with her for moral support:

> I have never seen Isadora at any time more uncomfortable than she was at this meeting [wrote Desti]. Being very tender-hearted, the last thing she wanted in the world was to hurt anyone. She did not tell [Theda Bara] at once what had happened, but asked her to drive with us and go to lunch. On the way to the studio, however, she finally broke the news that he had gone ... The future cinema star arose, and in a voice trembling with hate, said, 'I curse you. The

gods of my fathers curse you and your children for ever.' And at that very instant we were on the spot where years afterwards the motor-car with Isadora's children entered the Seine.

Desti wrote that, throughout her life, Isadora was troubled by hallucinations and portents of evil. In Russia the stage designer Leon Bakst once read her hand and, discovering two crosses on her palm, told her, 'You will have great glory, but you will lose the two creatures whom you love most on earth.'

The day of the tragedy in Paris in 1913 was a day of heavy rain. Isadora had taken her children to dine with Singer and sent them back to the apartment with their nurse. Crossing a bridge over the Seine, their car stalled and the driver dismounted. Without thinking to apply the handbrake, he set about cranking the car. As the engine spluttered to life the car gave a lurch and began rolling towards the river. The driver watched, helpless, as it plunged into the Seine and sank to the bottom.

Word of the children's death spread rapidly. Overnight, students from the Beaux Arts gathered all the white flowers they could find in Paris and covered the trees and bushes of Isadora's garden with them. In *My Life* she writes that she had always hated the ugly rites of the church: 'the mummery of what one calls Christian burial ... and I think the modern idea of a funeral is ghastly and ugly to a degree of barbarism'. She wanted to replace the tall black hats and macabre horror of the traditional funeral with a ceremony of beauty and light. She refused to put on the black weeds of mourning and at the funeral played uplifting classical music:

> How I wanted, when parting from the remains of my children, and their sweet nurse, some gesture, some last radiance. Surely the day will come when the Intelligence of the World will finally revolt at these ugly rites of the church and create and participate in some final ceremony of beauty for their dead. Already the crematorium is a great advance on the ghastly habit of putting bodies in the ground. There must be many who feel as I do, but of course my endeavour to express this was criticized and resented by many orthodox religionists, who considered that because I wanted to say farewell to my loved ones in harmony, colour, light and beauty, and because I brought their bodies to the crematorium instead of putting them in the earth to be devoured by worms, I was a heartless and terrible woman.

Many years later Craig wrote to a friend, bitterly accusing Isadora of neglecting the children:

> Never need she have lost her loved children had she realized that to have children entails having obligations. Someone must care for them – and that someone is always MOTHER. This truth she never seems to have faced up to – She let them be looked after by a governess or whoever was at hand.

Craig even believed their death was deliberately engineered, that the driver was hired to murder the children and could easily have saved them if he had tried. But he offers no justification for such a conspiracy theory and in another, equally deranged, letter he writes that Isadora 'failed to see it was her own fault – her not really wanting [a child] more than anything else – Ran or walked around the world bewailing the loss she could have prevented ...' It seems to have escaped Craig's notice that Isadora was 'running around the world' trying to earn money to support him and his creative schemes, as well as his daughter.

Isadora never recovered from the loss of her children. Shortly before her death she wrote:

> I believe that, although one may seem to go on living, there are some sorrows that kill ... I have heard people speak of the ennobling influence of sorrow. I can only say that those last days of my life before the blow fell were actually the last few days of my spiritual life. Ever since then I have had only one desire – to fly – to fly from the horror of it ... and my life has been to me but as a phantom ship upon a phantom ocean.

***

No artist works in isolation, and all her life Isadora picked up inspiration, like a magpie, from contemporary currents of thought. At the beginning of her career she looked for a teacher. Finding no one who could guide her on the path she sensed she had to follow, she learnt instead to seize on an idea and develop it alone, through a long process of thought and experimentation. Then, having made her own discoveries in movement, she linked them to what could be loosely termed political and social ideals and tried to pass them on through her teaching.

She was never interested in dance as mere entertainment, or 'merchandise' as she called it. For her it was a question of 'the development of the female sex to beauty and health, of the return to the original strength and to natural movements of woman's body.' The dance of the future, she wrote, should reflect 'the free spirit who will inhabit the body of new woman'. In the early decades of the twentieth century, when dieting was popular, Isadora wrote about Craig's mother, Ellen Terry:

> [She] was then in the full maturity of her magnificent womanhood ... deep bosomed, with swelling hips, and a majestic presence, very different from the present-day ideal! If audiences of today could have seen Ellen Terry in her prime, she would have been besieged with advice on how to become thin by dieting etc., and I venture to say that the greatness of her expression would have suffered had she spent her time, as our actresses do now, trying to appear young and thin.

When Isadora was growing up, social dancing was beginning to be taught as an exercise to promote heath, moral behaviour and refinement. According to one dance manual, 'With children the effort to move gracefully produces a desire also to be gracious in manners, and this is one of the best influences of a dancing school.' Isadora believed this with a passion. She was convinced that we express everything about ourselves by the way we move – that our behaviour mirrors our inner reality – and throughout her career she endeavoured to teach this idea to young children. She did it through setting up schools first in Germany, then France and finally Russia.

When people assumed Isadora was running training schools for dancers, she retorted that her school was for teaching people how to live. For this they must begin early in life; so it was small children she was interested in. But not the children of the rich. She sought to rescue those who, like her, had had a difficult start in life. These, she reasoned, were the ones who had most need of her.

Some years ago I met a woman who had trained with Isadora in Russia. Though she was only thirteen when Isadora died, Lily Dikovski (whom I interviewed when she was in her eighties), has vivid memories of her childhood at the Moscow school:

All she knew was that people could better themselves by moving and expressing themselves. Simplicity is very difficult, you know. We had to be very simple, very plain, in how we moved. She said, your movement should never be uncomfortable. And you know, I never feel uncomfortable in my life. I don't care where I am, whoever I meet. I've never had a feeling that I didn't know how to be, in company with other people. And it's from Isadora, definitely. She gave me that.

Isadora's serenity stood out. Her movements were exquisite. When she walked she floated, she never really walked! It was absolutely beautiful to me, as a child, to see her. And she was always creating, always. When she talked, you could see she was floating somewhere else, thinking about what she was going to do. Her mind was only on one thing: always on dance and how to pass on beauty. That was her aim.

Isadora adored children all her life. After the deaths of Deirdre and Patrick, her school in France was her one surviving child. It had an additional importance though: it was her intention that, through performing and teaching, her dancers could pass on her work to future generations and in this way it would live on. Her touring work was essential in helping fund the schools. What else, she once said, would she want money for? But she had to rely on others to run the schools, a task that fell first to her sister Elizabeth, and then to her principal pupil Irma. It was Irma who ran the Moscow school, as Dikovski recalls:

> I was terrified of Irma. She was so strict! But that's the only way to teach. Isadora knew she couldn't teach, she wasn't strict enough. She had no patience for it. But she put in the seed. For the first two years she was with us constantly, but after that we saw little of her. The first years we learnt how to group. Then how to dance. Then we started travelling, doing matinees around Russia. Just the children. We danced with Isadora at the end of her programme, to The Internationale. She was so warm! After we performed she used to kiss us – I had marks all the way up my arms from the lipstick!

One of the first things that had attracted Isadora to Singer was his offer to underwrite the expenses of her school. He moved it to the south of France, thinking to provide Isadora with a more sunny, relaxed atmosphere in which to create her work. Some time later Singer handed her the keys to a mansion just outside Paris that he had bought for the school. But the grand undertaking which Isadora had in mind needed a constant injection of funds, for she was adamant that she would only take poor children, not those who could afford to pay. The children contributed to their upkeep by performing – sometimes as part of Isadora's own concerts, and sometimes as a company – but even with Isadora's own earnings added to the coffers, it was still a heroic attempt to keep the enterprise going.

In 1920 Isadora appealed to the French government for support. They listened sympathetically, but gave her nothing. Then in 1921 she received an invitation from the Bolshevik government to open a school in communist Russia. She had toured Russia before the revolution and the suffering she saw there had had a profound effect on her. Following the overthrow of the tsarist regime and the freeing of the serfs, she choreographed the Marche Slav:

> With her hands bound behind her back, groping, stumbling, head bowed, knees bent, she struggles forward, clad only in a short red garment that barely covers her thighs. With furtive glances of extreme despair she peers above and ahead. When the strains of God Save The Tsar are first heard in the orchestra she falls to her knees and you see the peasant shuddering under the blows of the knout ...Finally comes the moment of release, and here Isadora makes one of her great effects. She does not spread her arms apart with a wide gesture. She brings them forward slowly and we observe with horror that they have practically forgotten how to move at all. They are crushed, these hands, crushed and bleeding after their long serfdom; they are not hands at all but claws, broken, twisted, piteous claws! The expression of frightened, almost uncomprehending joy with which Isadora concludes the march is another stroke of her vivid imaginative genius.

The invitation from the new communist government to set up a school in Moscow filled Isadora with joy. Here at last, she thought, were people who understood her. Her own politics were simple: she believed in justice and freedom for all. Now here was a government attempting to build a society which matched her ideals. It was a great undertaking and she was eager to contribute to it. When asked if she was a Bolshevik she replied, 'Rot! Rot! Rot!' But, she added, all artists worthy of the name were revolutionaries.

After the revolution Russia was in a state of utter devastation. It was a country under siege, both from aristocratic groups within, and from those working outside the country, with the support of Western governments, to overthrow the communist regime. It was something of a heroic attempt to even think of starting a school then, but Isadora wasn't a woman to be easily deterred.

In Russia Isadora broke a long-time vow and married the poet Sergei Esenin. Since she spoke only a few words of Russian, and Esenin just as little English, their relationship turned into an *opéra bouffe* of drinking, carousing and fighting. When Isadora decided to tour outside Russia in order to earn money for her school, she naturally included Esenin in her plans. But she knew it would be difficult for them if they weren't married. In the process of becoming Esenin's wife, she forfeited her American citizenship, which was later to cause her problems. For, as a Russian, she was a citizen of a country under siege, making her, in effect, stateless.

The fact that Isadora had been to communist Russia and come back and danced in a red dress was enough to cause suspicion in her native land (her hennaed hair was described as a Bolshevik shade of red). When she accidentally bared a breast during a performance in Boston, one reporter wrote that she looked pink, talked red and acted scarlet. Even her marriage to Esenin failed to work in her favour, for he was fifteen years her junior. Here was another cause for gossip.

Esenin's behaviour on tour did nothing to help Isadora. He broke up hotel rooms and got into drunken brawls like any modern rock star. Meanwhile, he kept a small suitcase with him, and if anyone went near it, he yelled in fury. Years later, after his death, Isadora opened the case and discovered that it was packed with fancy clothes and bundles of money – money she had given him whenever he asked for it on that fateful American tour.

Dikovski remembers Esenin as an unwelcome presence at the Moscow school:

> First of all, he used to drink a lot. At night he used to wander into our bedrooms, drunk. One of the girls woke up one night and there he was, sitting on the end of the bed, drunk. Isadora never lost her temper, never, with the children, but she did with that idiot. He was

very good-looking, beautiful blue eyes, a mop of blonde hair, but absolutely uncouth, unbearable. She used to call him Devil and Angel, I remember, in Russian. But he wasn't in her league at all. He was a barbarian.

Years after they parted, Esenin booked into the Hotel Angleterre in Leningrad, where he and Isadora had stayed on their first trip together as lovers, and hanged himself. When Isadora was told that she had inherited his money (they did not divorce) she refused to take it, even though she was desperate for funds for her school. Instead she insisted that it go to the woman with whom Esenin was living at the time of his death.

**

After the loss of her children Isadora was like a rudderless ship. For some years she drifted from place to place, still dancing, still touring and trying to keep her school open. Towards the end of her life, broken but unbowed, she had nothing more to lose and became – if it were possible – even more defiant than in her youth. All her life she had challenged the status quo, and her achievements had come about in the face of opposition and even ridicule. She discovered early on that she had to fight for her ideals, and perhaps the Irish in her enjoyed those battles.

In the second half of her career her dances became darker, more powerful, as she explored the great, tragic themes of existence. In 1927 Sewell Stokes, who was helping her with her memoirs, described a performance she gave in her studio along the seafront at Nice (where she was then living). It was a cold night, and she advised the few friends who came to watch her to keep their coats on:

> Then she bent down to wind up the gramophone. None of us dared to do this for fear of breaking it. After that she threw a sheet over her shoulders, draping it about herself quickly, and went and stood before the dark curtains at the opposite side of the room ... Nothing mattered, when Isadora danced, except her dance. She herself did not matter. One forgot, watching her move very slowly, that she was there at all. She drove out of the mind, with one slight movement of

her foot, or of her hand, the impression one had had a short time before of a large red-headed woman drinking lager beer. Her largeness, with everything else about her, disappeared. In its place was a spiritual vitality that defied the body it animated. Her dance, one felt, had been in that room since the beginning of time. It would be there until the end of time.

***

In later years something of an unspoken rift developed between Isadora and Irma Duncan, who by then was the school's chief teacher and the mainstay of the children's tours. Dikovski told me that Irma felt the school belonged to her because she did so much of the work:

> Irma wanted the group to herself, I think. She didn't want Isadora to have too much say. Irma wanted us to go with her to America. 'We will open schools,' she said. We'd been brought up to only teach ordinary children, poor children. I said, 'Are we going to teach rich children?' And instead of saying, that won't be necessary, Irma pulled out a dollar and waved it at us. You know, we were making a fantastic sum of money then. This was in 1929, 1930. We started off earning sixty dollars a week each. This was when for one dollar you could live nearly a whole week. The second contract, we were getting a hundred dollars. For children! So Irma took out this dollar and she said, 'This is the most important thing.' To us it was never important.

Threatened by encroaching shadows, Isadora even began to doubt the convictions upon which she had based her entire life and work. When a journalist who saw her dance one night told her she was the only genius he had ever met, Isadora replied:

> I used to believe that anybody who showed signs of genius should be encouraged ... But of course I was wrong; perfectly absurd. Now I am wiser. I know the world. I know the world so well that I'd say to anyone who asked me what was the best thing to do with a child

who showed signs of genius, 'Shoot it!' Really, I would. I'd stand children of genius up against the wall and shoot them all. It would be the kindest thing to do. Then they would never know what an unhappy place this world can be for those whose thoughts are not the thoughts of the majority.

In 1925 Isadora was living at the luxurious Hotel Negresco in Nice. 'When in doubt, always go to the best hotel,' she said. But once installed at the Negresco she couldn't leave because she couldn't pay the bill. She kept a rented studio at the far end of the Promenade Anglais, facing the sea. It was described by one who saw it as:

> a kind of large shed or garage, stuccoed a faded pink salmon; the windows were boarded up, and on the peeling blue paint on the small door were a lot of graffiti ... The building looked abandoned and unoccupied, as a lot of rubbish was piled around it.

From being the toast of two continents Isadora had become the subject of gossip columns, and it was reported in the papers more than once that she had tried to commit suicide by walking into the sea. She was stony broke and her debts were considerable. Having developed a taste for the good things in life, Isadora refused to go back to living frugally.

She had put on weight and the choreographer Balanchine, who saw her dance at that time, reported that she was 'fat and drunk, rolling around the stage like a pig'. But others were moved to tears by the beauty of what she did. Dikovski recalls Isadora's great dramatic power: 'I never saw her when she was young, so I don't know how she danced then. By the time I saw her she was more of an actress than a dancer. Really, she was a very great actress.' Sewell Stokes described the last performance her ever saw her give, in that same studio in Nice:

> 'I'll do one more dance for you,' she said, standing up suddenly. 'For this dance I shan't need any music.'
> Her last dance, the last dance I ever saw her perform, would scarcely be judged a dance by ordinary standards. Isadora stood at one end of the studio, a motionless white figure clutching her draperies. Very slowly – so slowly, in fact, that one scarcely saw her move – she made her way across the room, from time to time

glancing fearfully behind her at the imagined shadow of death. Gradually the shadow, which one could almost believe one saw – so great was the power of her acting – advanced upon her, until at the end she remained standing perfectly upright, frozen in its grip.

A few months later, she arranged to go for a drive in an open-topped sports car, to distract herself from her troubles. It was 14 September 1927. As the car set off, the long train of the shawl that she had flung round her neck caught in the axle of the wheel and strangled her. She died instantly.

After her death the car was sold at auction. It was knocked down for what was then the incredible sum of 200,000 francs. Meanwhile, her beautiful crimson shawl was ripped to shreds by onlookers of the fatal accident in their quest for souvenirs.

Isadora's great achievement as an artist was to introduce the notion that dance was capable of exploring the great themes of existence. Shortly after her death, Jean Cocteau wrote of her:

> She did not narrow her eyes, like a painter, and she did not stand back. She wanted to live massively, beyond beauty and ugliness, to seize hold of life and live it face to face, eye to eye . . . Here was a dancer who did not much care if her dress slipped and revealed shapeless shapes, if her flesh trembled or if sweat ran down her. All these things lagged behind her inspiration.

She once improvised an encore in which she said she would 'dance the philosophy of my life'. She appeared to be standing in front of a great door. Time and again she hurled herself against this unyielding, invisible door, and time and again she was thrown to the ground. Summoning all her strength, she lifted herself up and hurled herself one last time against that door so that it finally fell open.

Isadora forced open the prison door of puritanism, letting in light and liberation and a new way of thinking about women's experience and their lives as artists. In her time she had more female admirers of her work than any other performer, and it is fitting that, today, dance libraries report more requests for books about her than about any other dancer.

Black Bottoms

I want someone to go wild with me!
Eva Tanguay

It has been said that, at a time when New York's musical establishment was wondering when the inventive American spirit would produce its own 'classical' music, it was being produced right under people's noses. But they failed to recognize it for it wasn't, as expected, a product of highbrow culture. It was born instead in New Orleans' black community in the form of jazz.

Once the yoke of slavery was lifted in 1866 a powerful creativity was unleashed and black Americans set about stamping their identity on Western culture with a vengeance. It was they who taught white dancers to move their hips and torsos freely for the first time – and to music full of such explosive energy, such infectious gaiety, that it became America's popular music and remained so well into the 1940s.

There are various ideas about the derivation of the word jazz, which was initially spelt 'jass': one theory has it that it referred to women's jasmine perfume; another, that it was the black pronunciation of 'ass'; or that it was simply black slang for sex. Another intriguing notion holds that, French being the common tongue of early Southern whites, the term comes from the French for gossip – *jaser*. Whatever the case, jazz christened an age when people went wild for pleasure, dancing, drinking and partying into the night.

Jazz began as the music of outsiders defining their identity in a new land. And despite the deep melancholy, born of bitter experience, which lies at its heart, jazz was marked from the start by a gutsy, shrug-of-the-shoulders humour. As improvisatory music it was ideal for dancing, and in the symbiotic relationship between the two, jazz helped nurture a host of social dances rooted in the African way of moving to music. Yet during the darkest hours in African history, and by the cruellest of ironies, the continent's celebratory, life-affirming dancing was turned into a grotesque means of survival.

On board the slaving ships which plied their trade between Africa, the West Indies and the Americas, male slaves were permanently shackled. Female slaves were allowed to go about unchained, but this was by no means to their advantage, for it made them easy prey to the sailors' sexual advances. Every once in a while, all slaves were taken up on deck and forced to dance for the amusement of the crew. This grim entertainment was also intended to keep them healthy so that, on arriving at their destination, they looked better and fetched a higher price when they went to auction. Female slaves danced among the men, who were obliged to shuffle about and rattle their chains in a travesty of dancing. Anyone reluctant to oblige was encouraged with the lash.

Blacks were one of the least numerous of the many ethnic groups in the United States. Only five per cent of African slaves (around half a million people) were taken directly to the United States. All the others went to the Caribbean and Brazil, though many later migrated from there to the cities of the north. During the nineteenth century those already in the Northern states worked as domestics, while Southern African-Americans toiled in the sugar and cotton fields. Just as they'd been forced to dance on board ship for their survival, and even on the auction block itself, they were also called upon to entertain up at the big house in the evenings. Despite the indignity of their situation, being forced to dance helped them maintain a vital link with their past. Some plantation owners even allowed their slaves to visit neighbouring plantations, where they held their own parties – though, once again, this was largely for reasons of health and morale.

The pages of *Gumbo Ya-Ya*, a chronicle of life in Louisiana, are full of testaments from ex-slaves reminiscing about these gatherings. George Blisset was one of them:

> Our marster couldn't stand noise. Us slaves used get together in one of the houses in the quarter and take a big iron pot with three laigs – the kind you use for killin' hawgs – and dance and sing around that, and there wouldn't be no noise could be heard, 'cause all the noise go right into the pot. Us held balls by candlelight, though they was strictly against orders.

These secretly organized slave parties grew to such an extent that whites finally began complaining about them in their newspapers. On 22 May 1860 the following letter appeared in *The Vigilante*:

> For the last two or three months the balls for white persons have given place to balls and parties for Negroes. When a new house is built, following an old custom, it is christened by our slaves having a grand ball at night in the building. Twice to my knowledge, this 'privileged' class has given a ball so close to our Donaldson Ballroom that I nearly walked right into their place ... Besides the balls, our slaves have musicals at night, mixed with games and round dances, etc. Mr Editor, how can this state of things go on ...?

The slaves also used their music and singing to tell each other when an escape or mutiny was being planned. There were sporadic rebellions, during which they turned on the plantation owners, and many slaves managed, in this way, to flee north. As a result their freedom of movement between the plantations was severely curbed. When it was realized that drums were being used to send out long-distance signals to spark off a revolt, percussion instruments were banned as well.

Laws were passed relating to sexual mixing between blacks and whites. But the Southern Code Noir of 1724, which prohibited intermarriage or concubinage, was never enforced. Some mulatto children born as a result of these mixed unions were sold as slaves by their white fathers. Others fared better. Having a single drop of white blood could mean freedom from slavery; and some white men freed not only the children they sired from slaves, but the women too. Considering the number of children born of mixed-race unions, however, as well as the numerous black women raped by plantation owners, it would be rash to speculate what proportion of them went free.

The Code Noir prohibited freed mulatto women from marrying either slaves or whites. They could only marry other mulattos. By becoming a white man's mistress, however, a mulatto woman could get herself an education, own property and enjoy privileges unknown to other black women in America at that time.

By 1790 there were a considerable number of unmarried 'women of colour' living in the city of New Orleans. Every year the most beautiful and best educated among them were presented at quadroon balls, which they organized themselves. The purpose of these events was to meet well-connected white men. A quadroon was officially a quarter Negro, but many were so fair skinned – some had blonde hair and blue eyes – they could have been mistaken for whites. On a visit to New Orleans, the Duke of Saxe-Weimar Eisenach wrote of them:

> The quadroons are almost entirely white: from their skin no one would detect their origin ... Formerly they were known by their black hair and eyes, but at present there are completely fair quadroon males and females. Still, however, the strongest prejudice reigns against them on account of their black blood, and the white ladies maintain, or affect to maintain, the most violent aversion towards them.

The quadroon ball was one of the sights of New Orleans. It was the same kind of cattle mart held by the European aristocracy to marry off their daughters, only with the difference that marriage itself wasn't on the cards. For many quadroon women a liaison with a white man – together with all the privileges it brought – was preferable to the single marriage option open to them. Only quadroon women and upper-class white men were allowed to attend these balls, and it's said that most men who visited New Orleans went to at least one of them, such was their fame. Some men even persuaded themselves that it was their 'duty' to go, in order to understand the New Orleans way of life.

Those who attended a quadroon ball invariably remarked on the stunning beauty and graceful dancing (not to mention the wealth) of mixed-race women. An English actor compared the event favourably to its equivalent in London or Paris and noted how the mothers sat 'watchful as owls, and wrinkled as Hecate', keeping a vigilant eye on their daughters. It was with these women that arrangements had to be made.

Every liaison began with the handing over of money, followed by a celebration party. A suitable property was found and furnished in the quadroon section of the old quarter, with the man's father footing the bills. It was quite the tradition to take on a quadroon mistress, though these relationships weren't without their problems and many came to an end when the young man married. A financial settlement was usually made for the ex-mistress, who would usually go on to marry or set up her own rooming-house business. Sometimes these women were rejected by their own people after their liasons with white men, but children born of such affairs were generally well looked after and educated.

In her study of black dance in America, Lynne Fauley Emery notes occasions when a quadroon ball clashed with a masked ball being held for white society. Men knew they had to show their faces at the white event first, even if they were planning to sneak off to the quadroon ball later on. And it wasn't without a certain fear of being found out that they did so, for their disappearance left women far outnumbering men and condemned them to sitting around as wallflowers, or 'tapestry', for the rest of the night.

One reason for the popularity of quadroon balls was that they were more relaxed events than those organized by white society, as the Duke of Saxe-Weimar Eisenach noted:

> I must avow I found it much more decent than the masked ball ... Cotillions and waltzes were danced, and several of the ladies performed elegantly. I did not remain long there that I might not utterly destroy my standing in New Orleans, but returned to the masked ball and took great care not to disclose to the white ladies where I had been. I could not however refrain from making comparisons, which in no wise redounded to the advantage of the white assembly. As soon as I entered I found a state of formality.
>
> If it be known that a stranger, who has pretensions to mix with good society, frequents such [quadroom] balls as these, he may rely upon a cold reception from the white ladies.

Quadroons of both sexes embraced aspects of white culture through which they could advance their fortunes and some came to despise their African heritage. Along with mulattos and Creoles (those with a more even mix of black and white blood) quadroons were brought up to play European music and perform European social dances.

So it was that the waltz and polka, jig and clog dance came to influence African-American dancing. Not only that. Mixed-race men, valuing their European heritage, contributed new melodies and instruments to the hybrid which was to become jazz. At the root of this new music were the powerful rhythms of Africa. But jazz didn't look back nostalgically to either Africa or Europe. It was a product of the New World's unique cultural mixing and it was uniquely American in its jaunty, irreverent spirit.

***

In the early years of the twentieth century the US was a country bursting with confidence. Eager to shuffle off the stifling conventions of the past, young people turned for inspiration to African-American culture. Women especially discovered in its dance a freedom of movement unlike anything they'd known so far. They were engaged in struggles which involved an unprecedented break with tradition. They were fighting for a place in public life and for the right to engage in meaningful work alongside men.

The First World War decimated the male population and radically altered everyone's lives. Whatever rung they occupied on the social ladder, women who had held the fort and stepped into men's jobs during those four years of slaughter learnt practical, confidence-building skills. War turned them into independent earners and freed them to spend their money as they chose. The daughters of immigrants staffed factories, stood behind the counters of department stores and were drafted in to help with the war effort. They began socializing without male escorts, they took up sport, they travelled and drove themselves around in their own cars and they got into the habit of dancing with strangers more freely than ever before. In 1920, two years after British women, American women won the right to vote. By then, the rate of social change had shifted up a gear.

The giant of American economic might arose in the late nineteenth century and by 1914 the United States was overtaking Britain as the world's leading manufacturer. A new kind of society, based on consumerism, was being fashioned under the cynical direction of men like Sigmund Freud's nephew Edward Bernays. Bernays took on board Freud's belief that human beings are riddled with instinctive drives which have to be kept in check, in order to prevent society descending into anarchy.

New York's banks had founded chains of department stores as outlets for the mass-produced goods which were appearing in ever-greater numbers. People had to be persuaded that they not only wanted all these easily available goods, but that they actually couldn't do without them. Bernays realized that, by playing on people's irrational motives, he could create a constant greed for the ever-changing variety of merchandise pouring off the assembly lines.

One of his most inspired projects involved persuading women to smoke, a habit then considered unladylike. When the American Tobacco

Corporation realized it wasn't reaching half its potential market, Bernays was brought in. He turned to a psychologist to discover what exactly cigarettes meant to women: back came the reply that they symbolized the penis. Bernays realized that if he could persuade women to connect the act of smoking with challenging male power they would soon acquire the habit. So he planned a publicity stunt to coincide with New York's Easter Parade. He arranged for a group of wealthy debutantes to hide cigarettes in their garters and, at a given signal, to light up. Meanwhile he told the press that a group of 'suffragettes' was going to stage a protest by lighting up what they called 'torches of freedom'. The stunt worked like a dream. The idea that smoking could make women feel more powerful and independent had plenty of takers, and from then on sales of cigarettes to women began to rise.

Soon women were aping other male habits in similar bids to hijack their power. They drank to excess, took to wearing monocles and began cross-dressing. As this last custom was beginning to be viewed as a symptom of sexual deviance, it made lesbianism something of a fashion as well. Even before the war women had flirted with the androgynous look. Now Coco Chanel stepped forward, and frills and the kind of clothes designed for reclining on sofas were consigned to the dustbin. The most influential designer of her day, Chanel created tailoring for women and also made imitation jewellery popular. Wearing a man's suit gave the illusion of redressing the balance, now that there were fewer men around, following the ravages of war. It also served as a statement that women were just as capable as men to enter the arena of public life.

For the first time in history ready-made clothes gave poorer women access to fashion. Any shop assistant could wear a swinging skirt and a cloche hat tilted at a jaunty angle. Only from the quality of fabric and the cut of her clothes could you tell how well-off she was. Eye make-up – previously the badge of immorality – became just another aspect of the morning routine; and at night women used make-up in especially dramatic ways, outlining their eyes in thick kohl and giving themselves bright red cupid bow lips.

The way women were now able to dress gave them confidence. They began signalling their desire not just to be physically active but to be at the heart of events, rather than supporting from the sidelines. Moral crusaders warned women that their short skirts and make-up and the slim hip flasks they kept in their garters made them indistinguishable from whores. But their words went unheeded. Women carried on binding their breasts and cropping their hair, either adding a pert little fringe or sweeping it back in an Eton cut. It was said that American ballroom dancer Irene Castle inaugurated the fashion for bobbing the hair.

Irene and her husband Vernon gave ballroom dancing respectability. They emphasized skill, elegance and refinement on the dance floor and it was largely through their efforts that social dancing became accepted as a 'civilizing' and 'aesthetically pleasing' social activity. The Castles were so wholesome they reassured middle-class parents that dancing was a harmless pastime – in moderation. As Irene Castle wrote in her memoirs, 'We were clean-cut, we were married, and when we danced there was nothing suggestive about it.' The Castles emphasized the health aspects of dancing and compiled a table of do's and don't's on the ballroom floor: 'Do not shuffle, do not bob up and down or trot.' Above all, they maintained, you should be able to see 'daylight' between the bodies of dancing couples.

If Irene Castle epitomized the New Woman, cutting her hair came about by accident. Admitted to hospital for an appendectomy, she wrote that what she dreaded was not the operation, but having the nurse come in and comb her hair twice a day. So she picked up a pair of scissors and lopped it off. At first she felt shy about revealing her shorn locks in public, but she realized she had to take the plunge some time. One night, preparing for an event at New York's Knickerbocker Hotel, she rummaged through her jewellery box and came up with a seed-pearl necklace which she sewed together to fit over her forehead:

> I walked into the Knickerbocker that night with my head held high, looking neither to the right nor left ... Evidently women were just waiting for someone to do it first and give them enough nerve to face their outraged husbands. The first week there were a hundred and fifty Castle bobs; the next week twenty-five hundred. Stores began to feature the 'Castle Band to hold your hair in place'. Men's barbershops began to hang out signs reading 'Castle Clips here' and cartoonists pictured men dressing like women so they could stand a chance of getting a haircut in a barbershop filled with women. It was a departure from long-established custom and so radical that one Connecticut newspaper spread the news in bannered type across its front page: IRENE CASTLE CUTS HAIR.
>
> Cecil Beaton wrote about me in *The Book of Beauty*: 'If any one person is responsible for the appearance of the modern young lady

of fashion whom we admire so much today, it is certainly Mrs Vernon Castle, who was the first to cut her hair into the curly locks of the bob, who loosened hobble skirts with her voluminous chiffons and long flowing sleeves, and who, with her boyish figure, tight waist, sloping torso and arrow-like legs, discovered a new grace and fluid elegance so fresh and attractive that in comparison classic beauties were considered stolid and lifeless.'

Irene and Vernon Castle standardized the steps of dances they picked up from the black community, which, they said, 'reach New York in a very primitive condition, and have to be considerably toned down before they can be used in the drawing-room'. Segregated dance halls, known as juke joints (from *dzugu*, meaning 'wicked'), had existed for years all over the South. Often they were little more than shacks. Abandoned churches were also turned into black dance halls and in one of these in Columbia, South Carolina, a dance dubbed the 'big apple' was first seen. It began with a shuffling entrance, everyone moving in a conga line, swinging their hips and waving their arms in the air.

In the African tradition people dance as individuals within the group. When men and women danced together as a couple it was to satirize European conventions. The cakewalk, popular in the late nineteenth century on Southern plantations, was this kind of dance. It began as a walk, carrying a bucket of water on the head, with a prize awarded to the one who spilled the least liquid. Couples dressed up in all their finery and paraded around, parodying the close couple dancing of the plantation owners that they'd learnt from black house servants. They began with precise little steps and complicated figures; then suddenly they'd slip in a folderol, a courtly bow or, more startling, a leap in the air. As couples vied to outdo each other in ever more preposterous combinations, a good-humoured competitive spirit entered into the proceedings. It was then only a short step to establishing the custom of presenting a cake to the best parody of high-tone white dancing. The cakewalk was the first popular black dance to capture the imagination of white America. It became the finale of minstrel shows in which whites blacked up to perform, by rubbing a mixture of burnt cork and water on their faces.

If laughter is the best medicine, it was certainly the case that African-Americans used humour to make light of the untold ways in which they'd been stripped of their dignity. Satire and parody aside, white America was increasingly attracted to the vibrant energy of dances like the cakewalk and the new black music which mixed African rhythms with European folk melodies. But so many warnings were sounded about this being the culture of 'primitive' races that at first they held back. In 1913 the *New York Herald* wrote:

> Can it be said that America is falling prey to the collective soul of the Negro through the influence of what is popularly known as ragtime music? If there is any tendency towards such a natural disaster it should be definitely pointed out and extreme measures taken to inhibit the influence and avert the increasing danger, if it has not already gone too far. American ragtime music is symbolic of the primitive morality and perceptible moral limitations of the Negro type.

Of course, once the door had been cranked open there was no slamming it shut again. In the years before and after the First World War ragtime was America's most popular music and it gave birth to a barnyard of dances. The turkey trot, the foxtrot, the grizzly bear, the buzzard lope and the bunny hug all shared a driving rhythm and a sense of humour. Their popularity cut across boundaries of race and class, their vigour and freedom proving irresistible to young Americans. Dances like these couldn't have been more different from the waltz, which had reigned over the dance floors of white society for the previous hundred years.

***

In the early decades of the twentieth century dancing was the favourite social activity among all classes of society. Places were needed where people could go and practise and (for those with money to spare) learn to dance properly. George Rector, who owned one of the most popular restaurants in New York, laid down a floor capable of accommodating 1,500 dancers at any one time. It attracted such huge crowds that, he noted wryly on one occasion, 'The entire fifteen hundred all tried to dance on this postage stamp at the same time.' Such was the demand for dance venues that floors were even set aside in hotel foyers. Once they were there, people wanted to be entertained by watching a more skilled and inventive version of the dances they themselves could do. So began the phenomenon of exhibition dancing, and gifted amateurs like Irene and Vernon Castle found themselves with a new means of livelihood. What's more, it brought fame and fortune within their grasp.

As ballroom dancing moved out of a private setting and into the milieu of public life it fostered the growth of nightclubs, or cabarets. The cabaret, where an entertainer mingled with the audience in between performing his or her act on a tiny platform stage, was a Parisian invention. French cabarets were intimate, somewhat scruffy, and the performers' material political in tone. This didn't suit Americans, who set about inventing a grander, more glorious kind of cabaret.

Exhibition dancing became one of the most popular kinds of theatre entertainment, and flourished at tea dances, where amateurs went to learn the latest steps. On both sides of the Atlantic tea dancing became a feature of cafés and department stores as an after-shopping activity, and provided an outlet for those desperate to dance in the middle of the day. Women knew they could go to a tea dance quite safely without compromising their reputation. As one London tea-dance fan commented:

> What could be pleasanter, on a dull wintry afternoon, at five o'clock or so, when calls or shopping are over, than to drop into one of the cheery little *thé dansant* clubs, which have sprung up in the West End during the last month or two, and take one's place at a tiny table – one of the many which surround the dancing floor – set forth with the prettiest of gold and white china; to enjoy a most elaborate and delicious tea, served within a moment of one's arrival, while listening to an excellent string band playing delicious, haunting tango airs, with an occasional waltz, or lively ragtime melody, introduced from time to time.

In New York, tea-dance customers paid a dollar admission, out of which they were entitled to fifty cents' worth of tea or alcohol. Social commentators like Ethel Watts Mumford were concerned that the large numbers attending in gangs of girls would fall prey to the gigolos haunting these events. She inquired, 'Where is your daughter this afternoon? Just what is an afternoon tea? Do you picture it, Oh New York Mother, as a peaceful gathering over a silver teapot and a gleaming cup?'

Writers on contemporary etiquette realized reluctantly that, since so many dance venues were springing up – not only tea dances, but social clubs and dance halls as well:

> no one under the age of Methuselah is immune from the present craze for dancing ... With old and young spinning about the room like so many dancing dervishes, the visitor must thread her way warily between the couples, lest she be run down as by a motor-car.

Back in the 1890s industrialists had begun meeting to do business in hotels and restaurants. Prominent families like the Vanderbilts and the Astors knew that, if they didn't want to forfeit their hard-won social position, they had to mix with America's *nouveaux riches*. So it was that hotels and restaurants began offering their customers plush surroundings and gourmet food. A natural development of this was to include entertainment, and from this period dates the growth of a grander style of cabaret which offered a combination of dinner, dancing and live entertainment.

It was after the war that people started dining out in earnest. And what could be more delightful on a hot summer night than to get up and dance on one of those tiled rooftop floors, with the lights of New York twinkling below? All the pieces were in place for the jazz age to explode. And when it did, it was, as songwriter Hoagy Carmichael put it, 'with a bang of bad booze, flappers with bare legs, jangled morals and wild weekends'.

***

The 1920s was an age of satire and excess, an age when everything became a joke and New York, with its buzzing energy and inventiveness, became known as the centre of the wisecrack. Novelist F. Scott Fitzgerald chronicled the era and christened it the jazz age:

> We were the most powerful nation. Who could tell us any longer what was fashionable and what was fun? It was a whole race going hedonistic, deciding on pleasure. The jazz age now raced along under its own power, served by great filling stations full of money.

The biggest innovation of the twenties' social dance scene was that people danced alone, rather than in couples. In the individualistic, anything-goes climate of the times, dancing like an animal became the thing. In the turkey trot a man strutted towards his partner, flapping his arms like an aroused barnyard fowl, while she did the same, only backwards. In the grizzly bear and bunny hug dancers embraced, as in the waltz, but less gracefully. (Many of these dances became the rage with white couples months, even years, after they'd been popular among African-Americans.) Intimate couple dancing became a thing of the past as people started expressing themselves as individuals, and never more exuberantly than in the greatest dance craze of the twenties.

For a few brief years, if you couldn't dance the charleston you were a social outcast. In some white households a black maid seeking work went to the top of the list if she said she could teach her employers this dance. In the charleston you flung your arms wide and swung your legs backwards and sideways. You made little leaps to the side, squatted down and slapped your body; you could even change partners (known as 'cutting in') in midstream. Doing the 'fan', you leaned forward, plonked your hands on your knees, then opened and closed your legs while switching hands from one knee to the other, to make it look as if you were crossing your legs. (One telling photo from the period shows a baby monkey demonstrating this move alongside a dance instructor and his partner.)

New York's Roseland Ballroom held a charleston marathon that lasted twenty-four hours, while in cafés which ran charleston contests you couldn't get in unless you arrived early. One thing this dance had going for it was that it didn't involve travelling across the floor. Performed on the spot, it required minimum space. Flappers were filmed dancing in the street, on building sites, on the narrow parapet walls of skyscrapers. Their loose dresses concealed the shape of their bodies and were ideal for the wild dancing coming out of juke joints and black honky-tonks, where women worked as hostesses. By now the meaning of the word flapper, which once meant whore, had softened.

The new dances weren't about grace and elegance and smoothness and flow. Their exaggerated pelvic movements made them a prime target for the anti-dance lobby, who feared they would 'niggerize' (and, by implication, over-sexualize) American culture. Even their names – fanny bump, funky butt, grind, itch, mooche – were inflammatory. The slow drag, in which partners clung to each other, grinding interminably to and fro, was seen as especially dangerous.

At the same time as all this was going on, jazz music was being attacked by the press and musicians' unions as 'socially demeaning', the music of clowns and escaped madmen. It was described as an assault on the piano, which, 'poor thing, is pulverized with arpeggi and chromatics until you can think of nothing else than a clumsy waiter with a tin tray full of china and cutlery taking a "header" down a flight of concrete steps'.

Words connected with black music had a strong sexual undertone. Boogie-woogie originally meant syphilis, while a host of food terms, including jelly-roll and shortening bread, were slang for sex. Rock 'n' roll had the same meaning, while jazz belles (originally jezebels) were whores. The terriers of moral panic are never far away and they continued to yap at the ankles of jazz-lovers and dancers alike. Books with titles like *From Dance Hell to White Slavery* appeared and in 1914 the Pope denounced the turkey trot and the tango. Some women did consider these dances too close for comfort. One ingenious inventor produced the 'bumper belt', a wide cloth belt with a number of padded sticks emerging from the front, which successfully kept a woman's male partner several inches away from her belly while dancing the bunny hug.

In *Adversaries of Dance* Ann Wagner examines the ongoing anti-dance phenomenon, which included condemnation of even moderate dancing as 'damnation in baby clothes'! Her book ranges widely over the fire-and-brimstone writings of the lobbyists, one of them a Southern Baptist preacher by the name of J. W. Porter:

> The wave of licentiousness, now sweeping over the country, and threatening the very foundations of our civilization, is due in large measure to the ballroom ... Liquor and the dance hall are responsible for 50 per cent of the murders of America.

Dancing was condemned as a 'moral cancer eating at the vitals of the nation'. It was stated that young women under the influence of alcohol and the lust engendered by dancing surrendered to gigolos who took them off to nearby hotel rooms or back alleys to consummate what the dance-hall atmosphere had begun. Even if women didn't succumb, the men were well primed, after an evening of sweaty hip-wiggling, for a visit to the local whorehouse. Loathsome diseases, abnormal sexual urges and white slavery were the result. Meanwhile, all that familiarity between women and men who weren't their partners couldn't help but breed jealousy and infidelity.

Masked balls were suspected of causing incest, which was only discovered when a couple removed their masks after having sex.

Self-appointed guardians of morality are always on hand to slap people down when they start losing their inhibitions and enjoying themselves, and they bred like rabbits in those years. One of the most powerful was Billy Sunday, the same mean-spirited rabble-rouser who had denounced Isadora Duncan as a woman who 'looked pink, spoke red and acted scarlet'. Sunday's gift for passionate oratory won over thousands of converts to his cause. Jacket thrown aside, sleeves rolled up, he leant over his pulpit and boomed into the crowd's upturned faces beneath him:

> Don't you go with that young man; don't you go to that dance ... I say, young girl, don't go to that dance; it has proved to be the moral graveyard that has caused more ruination than anything that was ever spewed out of the mouth of hell.

Most disturbing of all the new dance venues springing up were taxi dance halls, which played host to an all-male clientele. These places catered largely to poor customers, with occasional visits from the well-heeled, out slumming. In these 'closed' venues the line between social dancing and performance became blurred, as an article in *Collier's* magazine entitled 'The Devil's Dance Dens' attested: 'Dancing was once a diversion. Now it is a trade.' Girls who worked in taxi dance halls were hired to dance by individual customers and paid in proportion to the time they spent with them. As their name implied, they had to accept any fare who hailed them. A case worker who studied their lives in 1925 reported that they were often from broken homes. Many of them either kept their profession secret or broke all ties with their families. It seems that a career as a taxi-dancer was brief. It began in a girl's adolescence and came to an end by the time she reached her twenties, when she either married or moved into the world of prostitution. In 1928 an evangelist from California put pen to paper on the subject:

> With each passing year 5,000 girls slip out of sight never to be seen again by parents or loved ones in the city of Los Angeles. In a century over 7,000,000 girls are lost in a life of shame and sorrow. It is estimated that 600,000 girls, soiled doves, travel up and down, in and out, wandering to and fro as a great army. They have been

ensnared into a life of sin. Six hundred thousand soiled doves. A careful survey of all these girls was made and they were asked to tell frankly the cause that led them into this life. This survey revealed that 68 per cent or 375,000 attributed their downfall to the modern-day dance.

Later on, when swing was all the rage, it too was lambasted as being 'nothing but orchestrated sex … a phallic symbol set to sound'.

It wasn't only white Americans who sounded the dance alarm. Black middle-class Americans were upset by the tag of vulgarity being levelled at their culture. The Rev. Adam Clayton-Powell Senior of the Abyssinian Baptist Church claimed that his people were dancing themselves to death and that the detrimental effects of dancing could be seen in the way they talked and moved around the house.

Moderate social critics pointed out that there were all sorts of dangers in modern life just as pernicious as dancing, if not more so. One was sitting huddled in dark cinemas or going to theatres to watch 'suggestive sex-problem dramas'. A doctor contributed to the debate with the comment, 'Ten thousand people injure themselves by the abuse of eating, for one who does so by that of dancing.' Irene Castle commented that, if dancing was a sin, half the population of the large cities was in danger. New places were opening daily to cater to the businessmen who dropped everything early in the afternoon and trotted off to the nearest dance parlour for a lap or two around the floor. This practice began to cut into working hours and a prominent magazine editor fired fifteen girls for doing the turkey trot during their lunch hour.

One of my favourite newspaper stories concerns the New Jersey girl who was hauled into court for singing 'Everybody's Doing It Now' and turkey-trotting down the street in a residential neighbourhood. When the case came to trial a small riot ensued as the defence attorney insisted on singing the song and the spectators joined in when he reached the chorus. When the jury requested an encore the lawyer sang it again and did a fast turkey trot in front of the judge's bench, to great applause. The judge found the girl not guilty.

Rudolph Fisher too sounded a lighter note:

Now Negroes go to their own cabarets to see how white people act and what do they see? Why, we see them actually playing Negro games. I watch them in that epidemic Negroism, the charleston. I look on and envy them. They camel and fishtail and turkey. They black bottom and scrunch, they skate and buzzard and mess around. And they do them all better than I. This interest in the Negro is an active and participating interest. It is almost as if a traveller from the north stood watching an African tribe dance then suddenly found himself swept wildly into it, caught in its tribal rhythm. Maybe these Nordics at last have tuned into our wavelength. Maybe they are at last learning to speak our language.

**

In the twenties and thirties Harlem was the place to go and be part of things in New York. Since the dawn of the twentieth century more than a million African-Americans had migrated north from the southern plantations, driven out by years of poor crops and lynchings. With plenty of work in the defence industry after the outbreak of the First World War, people from all over the country saw their opportunity. Many black Americans fetched up in New York City, the greatest number arriving during the 1920s. At first they settled in the tenderloin or red-light district around Times Square. At that time Harlem's elegant brownstones were home to a community of Irish, Dutch and German immigrants, but as these groups grew more prosperous they began moving out. When property fell empty in Harlem black families moved up there, along with Latin Americans, and this in itself hastened the exodus of European Americans, who felt menaced by their new neighbours.

It was in Harlem that the heartbeat of black America, its music and dance and art and lifestyle, could be found. In 1914 its black community numbered 50,000; by 1930 it had reached 200,000. From dance halls and cabarets and speakeasies came the pulsating throb of jazz, the moan of the blues and the irresistible rhythms of dance music. At clubs like the Bucket of Blood you could pay a quarter of a dollar and go 'howling and stomping sometimes well into dawn in a miasma of smoke, booze, collard greens and hot music'. For music and dance lovers Harlem was paradise, a place to lose your inhibitions, dance away your troubles and be in on the most innovative entertainment scene of the time.

Harlem was also where well-heeled white folk went slumming. Harlem, savage Harlem, was a thrilling, dangerous place. It was the black heart of darkness, the end of the jungle line. With its flamboyant night life, its low dives and drug dens, it became known as the home of what Americans call 'vice' (not 'the English vice', as homosexuality used to be known, but prostitution).

In Harlem's more ritzy night spots white punters enjoyed watching chorus lines of black female dancers in glittering costumes snaking across the stage in the dance known as the big apple: a conga-line of swaying hips, waving arms and swinging bottoms. One of the top places to see a floor show was the Cotton Club, as Claude McCay recalls:

> They danced, Rose and the boy. Oh, they danced! There was no motion she made that he did not imitate. They reared and pranced together, smacking palm against palm, working knee between knee, grinning with real joy. They shimmied, breast to breast, bent themselves far back and shimmied again.

At the Cotton Club the cream of black entertainers played and danced for a strictly white clientele for, like other nightspots, the club was segregated. (The Castles' black orchestra, whose music made a great contribution to the pair's success, was barred from using the main entrance at the smart hotels and restaurants where the couple performed and had to go in by the back door instead). Looking back on that time, the black American writer Langston Hughes wrote that Harlem's black population didn't care for the influx of white visitors after dark:

> flooding the little cabarets and bars where formerly only coloured people laughed and sang, and where now the strangers were given the best ringside tables to sit and stare at the Negro customers – like amusing animals in a zoo.
>
> The Negroes said, 'We can't go downtown and sit and stare at you in your clubs. You won't even let us in your clubs.' But they didn't say it out loud – for Negroes are practically never rude to white people. So thousands of whites came to Harlem night after night, thinking the Negroes loved to have them there, and firmly believing that all Harlemites left their houses at sundown to sing and dance in cabarets ... The ordinary Negroes hadn't heard of the Negro Renaissance. And if they had, it hadn't raised their wages any.

It was in the roaring twenties that the mafia rose to power, largely as a result of Prohibition, and it was to Harlem that racketeers went for their enjoyment. A billion-dollar tax-free business had fallen into their laps and they weren't about to let it slip away. Given that alcohol had been one of the most popular social drugs for thousands of years it was naive – to say the least – to imagine that a law would radically change this. But in 1919 such a law was passed. It closed down the saloons, sent restaurant profits plummeting (especially at the ritzy end of the market) and sent people into nightclubs and speakeasies, where they drank their spirits out of teacups.

Never before had there been such a binge. 'The Pekin Restaurant was a madhouse,' recalls bandleader Vincent Lopez. 'People came with baskets and bought liquor by the quart to hoard. That night they used it for shampoo, in their soup, in their finger bowls …' But Delmonico's Restaurant wasn't so lucky. It was closed down after a raid in which an undercover agent at a tea dance was given a teapot full of something stronger than he expected!

By 1921 bootlegging was in full swing. Beyond the three-mile limit of the Atlantic seaboard (known as Rum Row), a fleet of boats did a roaring trade. The real high rollers put to sea in luxury liners where they paid for their cocktails with 100-dollar bills. Canny wine-growers switched to producing grape concentrate which, they loudly warned, would turn into wine if left to ferment. Lest customers miss the message, the label included detailed instructions on just how this catastrophe might be encouraged.

During Prohibition wine consumption trebled in the US and California's vineyards grew sevenfold. It's even said that Prohibition turned millions of people who had never touched alcohol before into seasoned drinkers, purely out of a desire to flout the law. Meanwhile drugs like opium and ether were becoming a feature of social life and provoking their own bad press. Freud's favourite drug, cocaine, was included in the original recipe for coca cola. (It was also an ingredient of chewing gum, which throws an interesting light on those eternally gum-chewing villains and news hounds in old black and white films.)

Methodist minister Clovis G. Chappell wasn't one to pass up the chance to link dancing with what was becoming yet another social problem. 'Whether you are a dancer or not a dancer,' he wrote, 'you must agree with me that nothing short of the dope habit holds its habitués in so tight a grip.' Later on, in the swing era, psychologist Dr A. A. Brill appeared on TV with a similar warning. He claimed that swing 'acts as a narcotic and makes [people] forget reality. They forget their depression, the loss of their jobs. It is like taking a drug.'

In Harlem's nightspots high society enjoyed the *frisson* of rubbing shoulders with drug dealers, racketeers and whores. There were even dances which dramatized the criminal subculture – notably the apache, which came from Paris. In this dance a whore and her pimp fight a duel to the death, with the whore inevitably coming off worst. (Looking back on her days in Paris, Irene Castle wrote about the case of a professional performer who died after injuries she sustained performing this dance.)

There was nothing new in the idea of slumming. Visiting working-class haunts for sexual initiation and titillation had been a diversion of well-heeled men for centuries. What was new was that women were getting in on the act. And it wasn't only a matter of well-off women going to Harlem nightspots as observers. Working-class women were going slumming in the burlesque halls of white districts. Burlesque was a European export from the 1860s, a pot pourri of suggestive songs, dances and comedy sketches. In New York it could be found in saloons and variety theatres and by the beginning of the twentieth century it had started moving into the world of legitimate theatre. In burlesque the house lights were left up bright, so that theatre managers could spot the police if they came barging in on raids.

Most people who went to burlesque theatres didn't go for the jokes or the singing; they went to see the dancers in their skimpy costumes. The chorus line was chosen for having the kind of plump body which had become old-fashioned in those androgynous times – the fleshy contours and voluptuous padding associated with sexual appetite and whores. (Medical research of the time came up with the interesting conclusion that whores were 'peculiarly plump'.) The most daring dance of burlesque was the hoochie coochie. Inspired by Little Egypt and other Middle Eastern dancers who performed at the 1893 Chicago Trade Fair, the 'cootch' became a byword for the ultimate in shameless dancing. One of the most notorious cootch dancers was Millie de Leon, whose 1915 act was vividly described by a reporter for the *Philadelphia North American*:

> From knee to neck she was convulsive. Every muscle became eloquent of primitive emotion. Standing suddenly erect, with a deft movement she revealed her nude right leg from knee almost to waist ... Streaked and sweaty, her face took on the aspect of epilepsy. She bit her lips, rolled her eyes, pulled fiercely at great handfuls of her

black curly hair. Indescribable noises and loud suggestions mingled in the hot breath of the audience. Men in the audience rose with shouts. A woman – one of six present – hissed. Laughter became uproarious. And then Millie de Leon gave a little cry that was more a yelp, and ceased.

It sounds funny now, but at the time, it shocked audiences to the core.

Arabic dance was nothing new as a spectacle, thanks to the nineteenth-century fashion for Orientalism. There had been many public demonstration of it (often by dancers calling themselves 'Millie', mistaking this abbreviation of 'mademoiselle' and seeking to give themselves a little French cachet). Of course, the only women who were expected to sway and shimmy their hips were showgirls, who were assumed to be parading their bodies for hire. And though women in London, Paris and Chicago may have secretly practised the *danse du ventre* in private, to undulate their bodies in public was still rather daring. So it was quite something when ordinary women began swinging their hips in public dance halls – as they did in earnest, in response to the infectious rhythms and dancing of black Americans.

***

Sexual liberation was an important item on women's agenda for change. In the early years of the twentieth century women began experimenting with sex and demanding the right to choose their own partners. For centuries 'virtuous' women had denied their sexuality. They'd learnt to toe the line, cover up and keep themselves pure for marriage. Sexual purity was the basis of their dignity and power. But there's not much fun denying yourself the pleasures of the flesh when everyone else is enjoying them in ever more flagrant ways, and the 1920s were all about enjoying yourself. A spirit of *après moi le déluge* was in the air and women didn't want to be left out of the fun:

> The average girl today [wrote Billy Sunday] is turning her home into a gambling shop and a social beer-and-champagne-drinking joint, and her society is made up of poker players, champagne-, wine- and beer-drinkers, grass-widowers and jilted jades and slander-mongers … She is becoming a matinee-gadder and fudge-eater.

By 1925 smoking, drinking and 'free love' were common. Looking back on the period years later, American playwright Lillian Hellman doubted whether women derived as great an enjoyment as people imagined from indulging in their new freedoms. Commenting dryly on the sexual liberation of the 1920s, she wrote that women had all either slept with a man or claimed to have done so. The flappers, she says, were so shocked by their new freedoms that they set out to shock others with them too. (Perhaps it was like the 1960s, when more women slept around openly than in the past, only to confess, years later, that it happened more because it was expected than because it gave them great pleasure at the time.)

Among New York's working-class women a subculture was developing, centred on dance halls and cheap vaudeville theatres. On the dance floor, young girls swivelled their hips in a dance style called 'spieling'. These 'tough girls', as they were known, didn't wait to be introduced; they walked up to unknown men, traded wisecracks with them and asked them to dance. Social reformers like Elisabeth Marbury (who also happened to be Irene Castle's agent) pointed the finger at these girls for lowering the moral tone of Broadway. It was, she claimed, female enthusiasm for blatantly sexy entertainment which was the problem. As Marybeth Hamilton comments in *When I'm Bad, I'm Better*:

> Marbury and her colleagues were certainly not imagining this new abundance of female patrons, but their relentless emphasis on it, in such heated terms, points to a broader crisis those patrons seemed to represent ... Nineteenth-century theatre chroniclers had credited the middle-class female audience with the creation of a legitimate stage, their very presence encouraging a bawdy institution to reshape itself into a decent and refined one. For women to shift their patronage to sex and sensationalism was a severe symptom of cultural upheaval, a sign that the world moralists valued was on the verge of extinction.

The fact that the traditional upholders of virtue were seen as hungering after risqué entertainment was viewed with special alarm. And it was a woman herself who caused the biggest headlines in offering it up to the public: Mae West turned her slow, swinging-hipped swagger into a walk, a dance, an entrance and an exit with which she would forever be identified. In 1914 she went to a cafe in Chicago where she saw an unfamiliar dance:

We went to the Elite Number One and the coloured couples on the dance floor were doing the 'shimmy-shawobble'. Big black men with razor-slashed faces, fancy high yellows and beginner browns – in the smoke of gin-scented tobacco to the music of Gin House Blues. They got up from the tables, got out to the dance floor, and stood in one spot, with hardly any movement of the feet, and just shook their shoulders, torsos and pelvises. We thought it was funny and were trebly amused by it. But there was a naked, aching sensual agony about it, too.

The next day on-stage at the matinee, the other actors were standing in the wings watching my act. I always did a dance for an encore. Then, inspired by the night before, during the dance music I suddenly stood still and started to shake in a kidding way, for the benefit of the actors in the wings backstage, recalling to them what we had seen the night before at the Elite Number One. The theatre began to hum.

West used the shaking shoulders and hips, which are a staple of African dance, to outrage the press. She knew this would draw bigger audiences, and throughout her career she deliberately used shock tactics like this to increase interest in her shows. She even made use of the strap-breaking trick to expose her bosom as she sauntered off-stage; indeed, she did everything she possibly could to cause a stir.

Only once, when she tried to present black Harlem in her novel *Babe Gordon* and its stage version *The Constant Sinner*, did she miscalculate. In her novel the unthinkable happens: a white woman, Babe, takes black racketeer Money Johnson as her lover. West describes her hero as an animal, a sexual primitive, whose desires are evenly matched by those of Babe. Contrary to received wisdom, West was inferring, women have as strong a sexual appetite as men. She describes Harlem as 'a museum of occult sex, a sensual oasis in the sterile desert of white civilization, where conventional people can indulge in unconventional excesses'.

But Harlem wasn't a museum, for museums aren't remotely threatening places. And it certainly wasn't a museum of 'occult' sex, which brings to mind the excesses of the Marquis de Sade. Harlem was, however, everything polite society has feared and been fascinated by down the ages. It was a place of sensual letting-go, with the added *frisson* of blackness.

In the battle between high and low culture, working-class entertainment is viewed as a kind of swamp, from which are extracted promising elements to be turned into the gold of art. In the 1920s jazz and black dancing became the new raw materials of high art. Sophisticated Parisians had already been treated to the faux-Orientalism of the Ballets Russes. Now they were ready for the next big thing to titillate their jaded palettes.

In the 1920s the French went jazz crazy and they also went crazy for Josephine Baker. Middle Eastern women had long been tagged exotic and sexually rampant. Now it was the turn of black women, only with an additional twist. For the French chose to glorify Baker as an embodiment of the noble savage.

Josephine Baker was nineteen when she set sail for France in the autumn of 1925. She had found success in New York in the show *Shuffle Along*. As the last member of the chorus line, she had drawn attention to herself by crossing her eyes and generally clowning around and it earned her a spot as a featured dancer. So it happened that she was booked for the first black revue to be mounted in Paris. The Revue Nègre was designed to cater to the current French passion for jazz and all things African. But it wasn't booked into the Folies Bergère or the Casino de Paris, or one of the other music halls. Instead its setting was a little art-nouveau theatre tucked away in a side street, the Théâtre des Champs Elysées.

The theatre's facade and interior were dominated by statues modelled after Isadora Duncan in her classical Greek poses. These figures of graceful female dancers in flowing gowns served as a poignant reminder of Duncan, who had fallen out of fashion and was to die tragically two years later in the south of France. Her radiant ideals for a new dance were already a thing of the past. So too was the art-nouveau style in which the theatre was decorated. The war had ushered in a more angular style of modern art: the fragmentation of Cubism, and the wild music and dance which reflected modern life in all its brassy, hard-driving pace and energy.

The Revue Nègre couldn't have offered a dance more different from Isadora's; and it was the right dance for the time. People were looking to be reborn after the horrors of war, and for that they were going back to their fantasies about the primitive, which now homed in on African culture. Jacques Charles from the Moulin Rouge was brought in to pep up the costumes and dances of the Revue Nègre. The Moulin Rouge, once the scene of riotous, high-kicking *cancaneuses*, had become a temple of nude female flesh. And one of the first suggestions that Charles made to Josephine Baker was that she dance bare-breasted, clad only in a girdle of feathers.

During the twentieth century the French did their best to convince everyone that a tasteful exhibition could be made of bare-breasted women on the music-hall stage; that. indeed, you had to be socially gauche to be embarrassed by female nudity. By 1918 the all-but-naked chorus line was an established attraction of Parisian cabaret.

But Baker was shocked at the suggestion that she dance nude. She was not, she said, a stripper. Meanwhile, Paul Colin had the task of creating a poster for the Revue. He decided that Josephine's unusual body would make an eye-catching image and asked her to pose for him – in the nude, of course. Once again she refused, and kept her underwear on. Colin spent two entire days sketching her. By the second sitting she had got used to the idea and did take her clothes off. (Indeed, over the next few years she was to become perfectly at ease dancing bare-breasted, Parisian style.) The final poster that Colin came up with, a crude cartoon image of African-Americans, shows a hip-thrusting Baker flanked by the faces of two grinning piccaninnies. But it suited the Revue Nègre, for the show was based on the stereotype of primitive, befeathered jungle dwellers. In Baker's *danse sauvage* she wore feathers as a skirt, in her hair and round her neck and ankles. She also, rather incongruously, wore flat black pumps on her feet.

Journalist Janet Flanner remembers Baker entering nude, save for a pink flamingo feather between her legs. She was carried on-stage on the back of her partner, upside down and with her legs splayed. After being lowered to the ground she set off in what was described as a 'stomach dance', shimmying, shaking and undulating and moving her bottom with the speed of a hummingbird, all the while travelling across the stage. Films show how incredibly quickly she moved. No eye could keep pace with her movements, which may have looked effortless, but were based on a good deal of technique. She played the different parts of her body like the instruments of a jazz band, each part answering the other with unexpected trills and notes thrown in seemingly at random. According to Flanner, Baker's partner:

> swung her in a slow cartwheel to the stage floor, where she stood like his magnificent discarded burden, in an instant of complete silence. She was an unforgettable ebony statue. A scream of salutation

spread through the theatre. Whatever happened next was unimportant.

But some members of the audience were disgusted and one woman called out, 'We didn't come to see this ugliness!' What had they come to see? Nothing more nor less than the fulfilment of their deepest fantasies about the erotic, exotic black body. These fantasies were born back in the sixteenth century, with the fashion for having young black servants who were treated like pets and pampered for their rarity value. Before the dawn of tourism few Africans lived in Europe, but from the earliest days of empire sexual fantasies about black women were rampant.

In 1810 an African woman named Saartje Baartman was brought to Britain and dubbed the Hottentot Venus. She became famous for the size of her bottom, and a typical cartoon of the day shows an explorer examining it with his telescope. She was displayed for the delectation of paying gentlemen visitors, in much the same way that lunatics at that time were displayed in asylums. Five years later she died, aged twenty-five, in Paris. This was a period obsessed with racial difference, as well as a period of intense scientific scrutiny. After her death, Baartman's body was cut open in a series of autopsies whose ostensible motive was to solve the mysteries of racial difference and female sexuality. A presentation was made to the Académie Française of 'the genital organs of the woman prepared in a way so as to allow one to see the nature of the labia'. This sad curio was exhibited at the Musée de l'Homme in Paris until as recently as the 1970s.

For all the whistles of disapproval at Baker's wildly shimmying bottom, it wasn't as if French fantasies about black women were new, nor were the French unused to the display of female sensuality. They'd already had the cancan, the *danse du ventre* and the tango. What more shocking moves could a woman make on-stage? But Baker was performing all but nude. And she was black. She was, in the eyes of her audience, a living primitive. In truth, though the French may have craved the primitive, to be so energetically confronted by Baker's wild, free energy was more than they expected. Flanner writes that, within half an hour of the curtain coming down, news about the Baker phenomenon had spread all the way up the Champs-Elysées:

> Witnesses of her triumph sat over their drinks, excitedly repeating their report of what they had just seen – themselves unsatiated in the retelling, the listeners hungry for further fantastic truths. So

tremendous was the public acclaim that for the first week's run the cast and the routine of the performance were completely disorganized. Drunken on the appreciation they had received, and on champagne, to which they were not accustomed, the Negro choruses split up into single acts consisting of whichever males or females could still keep their feet, or had not lost their voices from the fatigues of pleasure ... Most of us in Paris who had seen the opening night went back for the next two or three nights as well; they were never twice alike.

The critics tried to pin Baker down by analysing the meaning of her wild gyrations. But what they came up with was a critique of their own society:

> Our romanticism is desperate for renewal and escape. But unknown lands are rare. Alas, we can no longer roam over maps of the world with unexplored corners ... We lean on our own unconscious and our dreams. As for reality, we like it exotic. These blacks feed our double taste for exoticism and mystery. We are charmed and upset by them, and most satisfied when they mix something upsetting in with their enchantments.

In his revue, André Levinson wrote astutely that the dances in the Revue Nègre weren't exactly African, they were a jazz fusion, the product of the black American experience. With some perspicacity he predicted that black culture was destined to become part of American culture, though he doubted whether this would be the case in Europe:

> There seemed to emanate from her violently shuddering body, her bold dislocations, her springing movements, a gushing stream of rhythm. It was she who led the spellbound drummer and the fascinated saxophonist in the harsh rhythm of the 'blues'. It was as though the jazz, catching on the wing the vibrations of this body, was interpreting word by word its fantastic monologue. The music is born from the dance, and what a dance! The gyrations of this cynical, yet merry mountebank, the good-natured grin on her large mouth, suddenly give way to visions from which good humour is entirely absent. In the short *pas de deux* of the savages ... there was a wild splendour and magnificent animality. Certain of Miss Baker's

poses, back arched, haunches protruding, arms entwined and uplifted in a phallic symbol, had the compelling potency of the finest examples of Negro sculpture.

He ended with the comment that Baker was no longer simply 'a grotesque dancing girl' but 'the black Venus that haunted Baudelaire'.

Many who saw Baker dance wrote that what she presented on-stage in no way inspired lust. When publisher and diplomat Harry Kessler met her in Berlin he wrote, 'Watching her inspires as little sexual excitement as does the sight of a beautiful beast of prey.'

Kessler wasn't the only member of high society who invited Baker home for supper and expected her to dance for it. The common assumption, still made to this day by the well-heeled, is that performers should feel honoured to be invited socially by them and will naturally want to get up and entertain. In Baker's case, rumour had it that she was happy to perform without pay, indeed that she often carried on dancing naked long into the night. It was also rumoured that she ate spaghetti with her hands. ('The white imagination sure is something, when it comes to blacks,' she commented wryly.)

In 1926 the 'Baker look' was all the rage. Baker's gleaming cap of slicked-back hair gave rise to a fashion, sending Parisians out to the shops to buy 'Bakerfix' for plastering on their own shorn locks. A year earlier Parisian women had shielded their delicate complexions from the sun. Now they rubbed walnut oil on their skin to darken it. It was the first time ever that a brown body had been fashionable in Western society.

The attention that the Hottentot Venus had received for her bottom was echoed in the case of Josephine Baker. The French naturalist Baron Cuvier observed that, 'The protuberances of her buttocks were not muscular but of an elastic trembling consistency – whenever the woman moved, she vibrated!' It was written that she had composed an entire dance out of moving her bottom. As one of her lovers, the French crime-writer Georges Simenon, commented, it had to be the most famous posterior in the world: 'It must be the only bottom which has become the centre of a cult. And it is everywhere, on sheet music, magazine covers plastered all over the city walls.' Simenon described it as the only bottom that laughed; others said it had something audacious about it. For her part, Baker commented, 'The rear end exists. I see no reason to be ashamed of it. It's true there are rear ends so stupid, so pretentious, so insignificant that they're good only for sitting on.'

In later years, weighed down by towering headdresses of diamanté and feathers, Baker sang and danced at France's two great monuments to tackiness, the Casino de Paris and the Folies Bergère. At the Folies she wore a skirt of bananas which jiggled merrily around her hips as she danced. This time, though, she wasn't surrounded by other black entertainers, but wiggled her bottom for the pleasure of two pith-helmeted white explorers resting beneath a tree. And no tired old colonial fantasy could be more explicit than that.

Baker was the perfect subject for this kind of fantasy, for she was good-humoured and funny. She played the poor girl in rags and entertained the audience by mugging for them – crossing her eyes and puffing out her cheeks, doing the splits and the crossed-knees of the charleston. Nor was she conventionally beautiful, with her heavy thighs, over-painted mouth and toothy grin. In this sense, she didn't inspire the awe that a conventional beauty would have done; everything about her was unthreatening.

Baker may have been fooled into thinking her fame had opened the door to the upper echelons of French society, but it was never the case. None of her wealthy lovers went as far as to propose marriage (though she apparently received 40,000 proposals from her fans). According to one of the men who enjoyed the honours of her bed, it wasn't so much her colour which disqualified her as the fact that she was a dancer, and a half-naked one at that. Baker was keen to marry this particular man, and in *Jazz Cleopatra* her biographer Phyllis Rose tells the humiliating story of how the dancer bought three dozen white roses and paid a call on his disapproving mother. When Baker presented her with the flowers and asked for her son's hand in marriage, Maman burst out laughing: 'Mademoiselle, it is true that there have been some scapegraces in our family, but not for two generations, and nothing like this. No, no, what you want is quite impossible.'

Critics were fond of comparing her to an animal – a panther, a giraffe, a kangaroo. Ironically, her great success turned her into Paris's pet monkey. But who were the real animals, the real savages, in this scenario? As actress Louise Brooks commented of the audience's response, the first time she saw Baker appear on-stage, 'They rage there as in a menagerie when the meat appears at the cage.'

**

Beneath the fascination for Baker and jazz, the boil of racial prejudice which was to burst with the Second World War was rising slowly to the surface. All that walnut oil that women were rubbing on their faces was making people nervous. In Germany jazz was labelled the art of degenerates and savages.

An article in *Le Figaro* dubbed the Revue Nègre 'a lamentable transatlantic exhibitionism which makes us revert to the ape in less time than it took us to descend from it'. It went on to say that, far from the performers being noble savages, they were poor people, degenerates, the dregs of civilization. The article echoed the American condemnation of jazz-age dances: that they were a means by which the human race was in danger of reverting to its animal origins. Unless it was brought under control, black influence threatened to overwhelm white civilization. Oswald Kirke's piece, 'Are We Going Black?', was symptomatic of the fears engendered by the prominence of black culture in Europe and America:

> What can you make of it when you read as I did only this week that artists, anthropologists and medical men are getting concerned about the way the Londoner is growing darker in complexion and in colouring of eyes and hair?

This article appeared in 1929, the year the Wall Street stock market crashed. The rapid, artificially engineered growth of consumerism had helped create a boom in the stock market that came to an abrupt end on 24 October. The crash brought ruin, suicide and despair, and along with it the death of the roaring twenties. As F. Scott Fitzgerald wrote, the most expensive orgy in history was over.

On the day of the crash the song *Happy Days Are Here Again* was introduced to wealthy diners in New York. It was written by Jack Yellen, who recalls that fateful night:

> In the big dining-room of the hotel a handful of gloom-stricken diners were feasting on gall and wormwood. [The band leader] looked at the title on the orchestration and passed out the parts. 'Sing it for the corpses,' he said to the soloist. After a couple of choruses the corpses joined in sardonically, hysterically, like doomed prisoners on their way to the firing squad. Before the night was over, the hotel lobby resounded with what had become the theme tune of ruined stock-market speculators as they leaped from hotel windows.

Other members of socially prominent families put a bullet through their brains. One of them, Henry Grew Crosby, danced away his youth in Paris and died in a suicide pact at the age of thirty-two. Of those heady years he recorded in his diary:

> We play (taking turns at winding the gramophone) the *Broadway Melody* from before breakfast till after supper (over a hundred times in all) ... And when the records wore out, there were new ones to take their place, new orchestras hot and sweet, jazz omnipresent and always carrying the same message of violent escape towards Mandalay, Michigan, Carolina in the morning, one's childhood love, a new day. Everywhere was the atmosphere of a long debauch that had to end; the orchestra played too fast, the stakes were too high at gambling tables, the players were so empty, so tired, secretly hoping to vanish altogether into sleep and ... maybe wake on a very distant morning and hear nothing whatsoever, no shouting no crooning, to find all things are changed.

The exuberance of the 1920s sprang from relief after the tensions of war, as well as from a desire to have done with the tightly buttoned-up Victorian age. But at the heart of youth's rebellion lay a kind of desperation. When the crash came it marked the culmination of a lifestyle which had grown up and been supported by a diet of increasing stimulation and sensation.

In 1933 Prohibition was repealed and a flood of speakeasies reopened as nightclubs. Now that people could drink cheaply at home they had no need to venture out at night in search of alcohol. Nightclub managers soon realized they had to offer more glamorous entertainment if they were to revive their flagging business.

Meanwhile, for the poorest Americans there wasn't even money for essentials, let alone to throw away on frivolous pursuits. Record companies shut down as radio came to the fore, enabling millions to hear music free of charge. However little money people had, though, they still went out dancing. They had to have something to make them feel good, something which made life worth living, and when they entered the dance hall they left their troubles at the door.

Swing was incubating, a music of such irresistible gaiety it couldn't help but lift people's morale. It was music you just couldn't sit still to; when you heard it you got up and danced and felt good to be alive again. As the stock market crashed for a second time and the Depression settled in, the swing craze kept on growing, despite the deepening financial gloom. It was almost as if its vitality fed on the desperation of the times. Swing was electrifying music. Its driving energy dragged people up out of their seats for the sugar foot stomp, the shag and the jitterbug. Frank Manning, a regular at the Savoy Ballroom in New York City, recalls the joy of those days: 'The only way you know who you are sometimes has to do with what you can do when you go home from work, change your clothes, get with your partner and dance all night long.'

Up in Harlem rent parties became widespread. These were pot-luck suppers with entertainment and food brought in by the neighbours. A small admission fee was charged and entertainment provided by piano players, and sometimes a drummer (who muffled the noise of his drums by covering them with a blanket). Rent parties had existed before the Depression. They originally came about as a way of helping Harlem's poor, who had been hard hit by skyrocketing rents. Housing experts estimate that, in Harlem in the 1920s, as many as 5,000 to 7,000 people lived in a single block. Before black Americans started moving up there, apartments could be had for a song and were even a bit of a white elephant for landlords. But after the European immigrants moved out prices soared. Black families became used to living like sardines. Large rooms were converted into tiny cubby-holes in which 'shift-sleeping' wasn't unknown, as day and night workers switched places in beds which never had the chance to grow cold.

The Saturday-night rent party benefited everyone and had the added bonus of allowing African-Americans to have a good time without being gawped at by white strangers, who liked to stand behind them and imitate their dance moves.

> Almost every Saturday night that I was in Harlem [wrote Langston Hughes], I went to a house rent party ... I met ladies' maids and truck drivers, laundry workers and shoeshine boys, seamstresses and porters. I can still hear their laughter in my ears, hear the soft slow music, and feel the floor shaking as the dancers danced.

Overnight these parties became all the rage, as more and more families began flinging their doors open. Some went on well into Sunday morning, with guests helping themselves to fried chicken, pig's trotters and pork chops before getting out on the floor to dance. When Prohibition was still in force,

homemade corn liquor could be had from bars set up in the hall. As Frank
Byrd recalls:

> The thing that makes the house rent party (even now) so colourful
> and fascinating is the unequalled picture created by the dancers
> themselves. When the band gets hot the dancers get hotter. They
> would stir, throw or bounce themselves about with complete
> abandon; their wild, grotesque movements silhouetted in the semi-
> darkness like flashes from some ancient tribal ceremony. They
> apparently worked themselves up into a frenzy but never lost time
> with the music despite their frantic acrobatics. Theirs is a co-
> ordination absolutely unexcelled. It is simple, primitive, inspired. As
> far as dancing is concerned there are no conventions. You do what
> you like, express what you feel, take the lid off if you happen to be
> in the mood. In short, anything goes.

Along the way there were impromptu contests between the dancers to invent
new steps. In the early hours of the morning the hilarity reached a peak, as
everyone got down to some serious enjoyment:

> They spin, tug, and fling their buxom, amiable partners in all
> directions. When the music finally stops, they are soaked and
> steaming with perspiration. 'The girls' … set their hats at a jaunty
> angle and kick up their heels with glee. Their tantalizing grins and
> the uniformly wicked gleam in their eyes dare the full-blooded
> young bucks to do their darndest. They may have been utter
> strangers during the early part of the evening but before the night is
> over, they are all happily sweating and laughing together in the best
> of spirits.

From time to time the odd white punter wandered into one of these parties
and would 'gasp and titter (with cultured restraint, of course) at the
primitive, untutored Negroes who apparently had so much fun wriggling
their bodies about to the accompaniment of such mad, riotously abandoned
music'.

Whatever other function they may have had, rent parties were part of the
black American response to being shut out of their own clubs, where they
provided the entertainment but weren't allowed in as members of the

audience. There was only one place which allowed total racial integration, and it was the first building in the US to do so.

The Savoy Ballroom – the stomping ground of the most devoted dancers, black and white alike – was the best-loved ballroom in Harlem. An entire block long, it could handle up to 4,000 dancers at a time, and its floor was so well stomped, it had to be replaced every three years. Walking down the street to the Savoy, Norma Miller recalls, you could hear the music even before you reached the door, and already you were in the mood. In the days before air conditioning was common, people flung open their windows on hot summer nights. Fifty years later, when those for whom the Savoy was their nightly haunt talk about it, their eyes light up and they laugh out loud at the memory.

Norma Miller lived right opposite the Savoy and recalls being rocked to sleep by the music pouring out of the ballroom into the warm night air. She used to watch the shadows of the dancers, silhouetted against the windows of the ballroom. By practising what she saw, at home and outside on the pavement, she taught herself to dance and was soon invited in. She was unaware that the Savoy was unique in allowing black and white to mix. Everyone who wanted to dance was welcomed. In Cats' Corner a friendly rivalry arose between couples seeking to outdo each other with the most complicated steps. Partners practised for hours at home before displaying their new moves on the dance floor.

The big dance of the time was the lindy hop. If the charleston had a certain jerkiness, the lindy was smooth. In the 'swing out' of the lindy you let go of your partner and improvised for a short space, and the improvisations became ever more acrobatic and outrageous. According to Langston Hughes, black couples threw in outlandish moves purely to impress the white dancers, moves 'that probably never would have entered their heads to attempt merely for their own effortless amusement'. Friendly competition arose between black and white couples as the tempo accelerated, making it more demanding to dance to:

> We had an edge. This will be something you will not do better than me, I don't care who you are [recalls Miller]. We wanted our tempos fast and white dancers didn't like that. There was always a battle because we didn't want them taking our dance. They had everything else, so we couldn't allow them to take the lindy hop!

There's nothing like a war for sending people scurrying into the dance halls. The wild cavortings of the First World War years had been known as 'dances of death'. People danced as if driven, throwing caution to the winds in a desperate attempt to banish the mental horror and live, however briefly, in the warm lights and whirl of the dance floor. Now, as economic depression segued into war, the same thing happened all over again. Swing tunes became anthems of wartime on both sides of the Atlantic. Many of the best-known big band leaders were Jewish or black, and swing came to epitomize the idea of racial freedom and justice in a war which was all about prejudice and injustice.

Ironically, in the US itself, entertainment was still segregated. The ritzy clubs where well-heeled white audiences went to watch the best black music and dance remained closed to African-American audiences. The only unsegregated dance hall was the Savoy Ballroom. So it was a sad day for everyone when, on 21 April 1943, the Savoy was shut down. The dance floor, it was suggested, was operating as a place where sexual and racial barriers were being broken down. City and military authorities claimed that men in the armed forces had caught venereal disease from black women they'd not just danced with but gone home with. But while shutting down the Savoy may have been a great blow to New York's black population, it did nothing to halt the pulsating tide of their energy and inventiveness, which continued to break over the shores of Western culture.

For if the twentieth century was the American century, in terms of music and dance it was the century of African-Americans. Black dancing brought into the open a body language which had been suppressed and dubbed primitive. It offered white society a way of connecting with a source of energy and spontaneity after centuries of languishing beneath the weight of inhibition and self-consciousness. As for music, jazz and swing dominated the first half of the century, and today's rock music would be unrecognizable were black influence to be stripped away.

During the past hundred years this vibrant, soulful music and dance have been the biggest single influence on entertainment throughout the Western world. Given the relatively recent, and tragic, circumstances of African arrival in Europe and America, such cultural conquest is no small triumph.

Battle of the Sexes

The tango is man and woman in search of each other.
It is the search for an embrace, a way to be together.
Juan Carlos Copes

Confitería Ideal is one of Buenos Aires' last remaining grand cafés, where strangers while away the afternoon circling the floor in a tea-dance tradition going back to the 1920s. Today the cafe retains only traces of its former splendour. The big glass display cases which were once filled with mouth-watering pastries stand empty, save for one which contains a violin and a collection of faded women's hats in pastel colours with little net veils attached to them. The walls are tobacco-stained. The huge framed mirror in the toilet has lost its silvering and you have to peer closely if you want to see your face in it. The dusty chandeliers give out a soft yellow glow infinitely more flattering than the strip lights, which have been fixed crookedly to the ceiling to provide additional illumination.

Confitería Ideal is run by a handful of octogenarians who look as if they've spent their entire lives pottering about behind the dark wood counter. Every afternoon around three o'clock, customers who have been enjoying a coffee downstairs migrate en masse to the first floor, abandoning the tables covered in frayed pink cloths and leaving the teashop empty. Upstairs a score of noisy fans clatter and rattle and whir, stirring the warm air as couples tango round the pitted marble floor. Most of the small tables around the perimeter are occupied by a clientele of middle-aged women, tourists and the kind of men who used to be known as lounge lizards or gigolos. Most customers sit alone. For the gigolos the prize is a lone Western woman visiting Buenos Aires to improve her tango skills, who may well engage a guide for a tour of the country to round off her holiday.

I found myself sitting next to an ex-ballerina. Like me she'd come to Buenos Aires on a tango course, and said she'd hoped to find herself dancing with smouldering Romeos. 'I still haven't found the right person to dance with,' she confessed. Still, she wasn't short of partners. It's only beginners who are left to sit and watch, for no one wants to tango with someone who doesn't know the ropes and has to be carried round the floor like a sack of potatoes. One thing is certain, from the most casual observation of tango: you can't talk and dance at the same time. And if tango couples look serious, it's because they're concentrating hard on picking up each other's subtle signals as they go gliding past.

Languid, slinky and playful, this social or 'salon' tango as it's known is a far cry from the dazzling display of 'show' tango, whose interlaced legs and physical collision make it a dance of mutual danger as well as mutual dependence. Today in Buenos Aires there is plenty of show tango on display in the theatres around Avenida Corrientes. At one I watched a stern, skinny dancer in a dress slit to the crotch. She jabbed her leg up between her partner's legs from every angle: facing him, with her back to him, sideways on, circling him with such lightning speed I was convinced she was going to do him an injury. He was the still centre at the eye of the storm raging around him as she sought out fresh angles of onslaught.

This is the kind of tango that journalists write about. They like to reduce the dance to the cliché of being steamy and sexy: women in black fishnets and stilettos and shiny skirts slit to the thigh; macho men with slicked-back hair and a bit of a paunch. But the tango has always been more than its stereotype. It's a dance full of mischief, with a melancholy which reflects the struggle of generations of immigrants who shaped it. And among those who share a passion for the tango you find many intriguing definitions of what it has to offer. It has been described as 'an opera in three minutes', 'a sorrowful thought that can be danced' and 'two people just doodling to music.' One *tanguero* (male tango dancer) insists, 'It's sensual, not sexual. You dance tango with the girlfriend of your best friend.'

The tango is all this and more, and in Buenos Aires today it's enjoying a popular revival. On Avenida Corrientes there's a kiosk which sells nothing but tango literature. *Milongas* (tango dance halls) thrive in every part of the city. They open their doors around eleven at night and the dancing is still going strong at four in the morning. Ten years ago these places were dying on their feet: now they're the hangout of young and old alike. Some *milongas* offer free classes before the general dancing begins, and you can find a place to tango every night of the week by thumbing through the pages of the free glossy magazine *Tanguero*, which can be picked up from shoeshine boys in the city centre. Like other countries which use images of dancers to attract tourists, Argentina employs a picture of a tangoing couple to symbolize its passionate sensuality. A popular pose shows the man upright and the woman sliding down with her back leg outstretched, her face on a level with his crotch.

On Sundays couples tango around the flea market on Plaza Dorrega. Cafés in the recently derelict port of La Boca have been spruced up and given a gay lick of pink and turquoise and orange paint; murals on the sides of buildings depict scenes from tango life and loudspeakers waft lilting tango airs into the cobblestoned streets. A few minutes' walk away, the huge meat-packing factory disgorges a continuous stream of beef-laden lorries which rumble noisily past Calle Necocea. A quiet, shabby street with the odd garish *cantina*, Necocea is part of the meat trade in more ways than one. Situated in the heart of an immigrant quarter once known for its low-life dives and brothels, it was in streets like this that the tango was born.

***

Buenos Aires was once a port of entry for the slave trade and by the second half of the nineteenth century a quarter of its population were descendants of black slaves. La Boca was becoming an increasingly busy unloading point, not for a reluctant cargo this time, but for thousands of willing immigrants flocking to the city in search of a new life. In 1880 the city was enjoying an unprecedented wave of prosperity, thanks to the beef trade, and Buenos Aires became Argentina's capital. Steamships and railroads made the rapid transport of food possible for the first time in history, and as the century drew to a close the country was fast becoming one of the richest in the world. So it was that Buenos Aires found itself vying with New York as the first port of call for thousands of immigrants fleeing poverty and oppression in their homelands.

The city's new wide boulevards and elegant mansions were built by Europeans in European style and materials. They were like any you might find in Paris, Madrid or Rome. But, like other great capitals, this splendid new metropolis was soon surrounded by shanty towns. It was in these *barrios*, with their corrugated-iron dwellings and tenements where families lived crowded into single rooms, that the immigrants settled. They travelled from all over Europe, from Germany and Russia and Poland, from Spain and France. Spanish was the common tongue of Argentina. But the majority of immigrants came from Italy and, like any underclass, they used a secret language to protect themselves: in *lunfardo* the syllables of a word are swapped round and spoken in reverse order. Incomprehensible to the middle and upper classes, it was the slang of the poor, the language of shady deals, and in time it became the language of tango poems and lyrics.

Strangers in a strange land, the first loss faced by some immigrants on arrival was the loss of their name. With the pressure of so many people to process, if a man didn't speak Spanish and couldn't make his name quickly understood, he was given a new one. So someone who said he was from Rome ended up with the name DiRoma. The enforced adoption of a new name must have added to the immigrant's insecurity. But loss can be a liberating elixir and this new identity may well have served to reinforce the feeling of having made a fresh start in life. One tango film was to describe the immigrants, with their sentimental, passionate Latin temperament, as visionaries who dreamed of conquering the big city. Yet many who crossed the Atlantic to escape war and poverty discovered that this wasn't as easy as it looked, and some ended up returning home again. For most of them, though, turning round and going back wasn't an option, for they had sunk every last penny on their steamship fare.

Like many people before and since who crossed continents and found themselves washed up on an unfamiliar shore, these immigrants used music and dance to keep their culture alive and tell their story. Ports have always been fertile cultural spawning grounds. And at the same time as jazz was being born in the port of New Orleans, so, in Buenos Aires, tango music was stirring – a hybrid which, as it turned out, was to have much in common with jazz. Both were born on the American continent; both were essentially improvisatory, the music of outsiders defining their identity in a new land; and both were ideal for dancing. In time, jazz became a great river of sound with many tributaries. Tango music, by contrast, remained a quiet current flowing through the immigrant experience. It has never lost the inherent melancholy of either its melodies or its lyrics, which are a poetry of loss, rage, nostalgia and regret:

> The tango is an argument that you dance [runs one of these songs].
> And that argument isn't just about who will go home with whom. It
> broadens to take in destiny. Perhaps there will be love, but perhaps
> you'll just wake up in the morning with an empty whisky bottle.

Among the thousands of immigrants pouring into Buenos Aires men vastly outnumbered women. By 1914 the discrepancy would become huge, with more than 10,000 extra men to every woman. The few women who did accompany their husbands in the great adventure of immigration were shielded from the outside world, protected from temptation – especially of the sexual kind – and forbidden to venture far from their homes on the outskirts of the city. Most women, though, were left behind in Europe, hoping their men would be able to send for them or at least send money home once they had established themselves in the New World.

The scarcity of women resulted in brothels growing up around the port of La Boca, many of them staffed by Europeans. Some had left home with the intention of working as prostitutes in Buenos Aires. A 1992 study reveals that they were recruited for the trade by French, Italian and Jewish organizations, many in cahoots with the city's police department. By the first decade of the twentieth century, Buenos Aires had acquired a reputation for being the centre of the white slave trade, and though this sounds like a typical press exaggeration, it is a fact that both legal and unlicensed brothels prospered in every area of the city and many of the women who staffed them were foreign-born. Some single European women entered the profession by accident. They had emigrated with the promise of an honourable marriage at the end of their voyage across the Atlantic; but though a marriage may well have taken place, it was often to pimps whose goal was to put their 'wives' on the market as whores. And once the women became dependent on these men it was hard for them to escape their situation.

Like other social dances, the tango grew up wherever people went to let their hair down: in streets and squares and under the trees. It wasn't purely a product of brothel life, though brothels had an interesting part to play in how it took shape. For there, men danced together as a way of passing the time while they were waiting. With demand for prostitutes far exceeding supply, brothel owners began providing music in order to stop their customers growing restless and leaving. They hired trios – a guitarist, fiddler and flautist – to play waltzes and polkas. And, given the scarcity of female partners, no doubt the time came when two men stood up and began dancing together. After a while the custom spread and these men found themselves creating a duet which, in time, grew more elaborate and inventive. The tango became a duel in which each man sought to outdo his partner's skills, make fun of him even, in order to attract a woman's attention. Later the dance came to describe other kinds of relationships, including the struggle between a whore and her pimp.

From such encounters there evolved a dance forever marked by the poignant nature of its origins. The first dancers were men without women. They needed physical contact and they discovered it in the tango. In the early dance women were physically absent. But they were always there in spirit, a vital presence whose very absence was a burning obsession among the men who danced together in the bars and brothels of La Boca.

***

In the early days only disreputable women danced the tango and some of the 'whores' seen tangoing on street corners were actually men in drag. The tango was raw and rough, and among immigrants themselves there was a split between the *tolerantes* and the *prohibicionistas*, who wanted to outlaw it for the sake of establishing a respectable image in their country of adoption. Outside its own milieu it was abhorred and remained controversial for years.

It's said that one of the greatest influences on the emerging tango was the Spanish-Cuban *habanera*, a languid, sentimental dance with a sleepy hold and 'something of a gentle hammock swing' about it. This combined with elements of the waltz and polka to produce the popular *milonga*, which had a jaunty rhythmic pattern derived from a black dance called *candomblé*. The *milonga* (a word meaning 'mix-up' or 'unruly gathering') is the direct forerunner of the tango. It has been described as two people tangling themselves up into a braid, the man dragging the woman against his hip.

The local venues for black social dancing may well have given the dance that eventually came out of the *milonga* its name, for these venues were known as 'tangos'. Black social dancing had little in common with that of Europe. And though couples embraced in the *milonga*, it lacked the formality of a European ballroom hold. It's been suggested that African-Argentines performed European dances such as the polka to gain acceptance in white society. Similarly, streetwise young toughs known as *compraditos* took to calling in at African 'tangos' and imitating what they found there. One observer of the time, Ventura Lynch, comments, 'The *milonga* is danced only by the *compadritos* ... as a mockery of the dances of the blacks.' We can imagine, too, that African-Argentines, who danced with lithe, fluid torsos, may have parodied the restrained and formal manoeuvrings of European couple dancing (just as they did in the North American cakewalk).

The tango was marked by a kind of self-conscious bravado in the face of loneliness. Supremely male, it played out the toughness and desire for control at the heart of macho culture. Being a good dancer was how a man advertised himself. Showing grace and strength on the dance floor was important if he wanted a woman to dance with him, given her wide choice of partners. Later on, when tango schools were established, men were obliged to master the women's steps first, so that they could anticipate their partners' moves before learning their own leading steps. (This was even more crucial in the thirties and forties, when men outnumbered women by 500 to 1. Any man who wanted to get hold of a partner, and keep her, had to know how to make a woman feel good on the dance floor; yet another incentive to be a skilled dancer.)

The tango took shape as a ritual of seduction. It described the man's desire to capture and possess a woman, and it mirrored the immigrant's desperate desire to be in control of his destiny. The sons of immigrants had seen their fathers grovel for acceptance and some of them weren't prepared to do the same. They took the path of outlaws and advertised their defiance by dressing in streetwise style: tough guys with a slouch hat pulled low over the forehead, cowboy boots, a scarf round the neck and a knife tucked in the belt. And in a culture where arguments and old scores were settled by fights, this element too fastened onto the new dance. In competition for a woman's attention, a knife might be brandished and the dance turn into a battle.

We can only imagine what the early tango looked like, but all indications are that it was jaunty and brazen and that the music had none of the languorous, suggestive pauses which later gave it its seductive allure. Couples travelled across the floor with the man flaunting his mastery over his partner:

> In this agitated dance, women were led by their partner's whim and the impulse of the figures that he provoked. It was easy for them to lose track of the rhythm, and they had to cultivate the faculty of divination in order to follow such fidgeting about. [In addition], the strong shaking to which they were subjected should be taken into account; they were led backwards, pushed back and forth, sometimes led to sit on the thigh of their partner, sometimes led to bend and lean back.

One photo from the period shows a man with one hand clasping his partner round the waist, holding a cigarette out of the way, behind his back. When a man eventually did manage to get hold of one of the few available women, he certainly wasn't going to hold her at arm's length. But there's a quality of casual ownership in the way he holds her which is very unlike the predatory tension and tight embrace of later years:

> The *compañera* threw her left arm over his right shoulder and rested her hand on his shoulder-blade, holding a handkerchief to combat the sweat that smeared her white powder, or else a cigarette that she smoked distractedly. The legs were apparently locked. The heads very close to each other, almost touching when not temple to temple.

The man led. He dictated the rules of the game, and early eyewitness accounts of the dance make the woman sound as if she had as much power as a rag doll to choose her movements. She looked instead as if she was being carried round the floor against her will.

As more women entered the dance scene the tango came to reflect the age-old power struggle between men and women in a more dynamic way. One of the city's tango bars was presided over by Luciana Acosta, whose sensuous walk and dark good looks earned her the name La Moreira (the Moorish one). The daughter of Andalusian gypsies, she wore a red polka-dot blouse done up with a ribbon, a green pleated skirt, big gold earrings and high boots, in one of which she carried a knife. Together with her south Italian pimp, she lived a life which seems to have included a good deal of violent jealousy and fighting, in which La Moreira apparently gave as good as she got.

Acosta was a typical *milonguita*, as tango women who were paid to dance with customers were called. Like *milonguero* (male tango dancer), this was a term of insult. The *milonguitas* of the early days, who worked as dancer-prostitutes, weren't all as tough as La Moreira. They danced in *academias* (combined whorehouses and dance halls) until they were ready to drop. It was a tough life, and they kept going on alcohol and cigarettes. A few of them managed to pull themselves up by their bootstraps to run these *academias*, and in such a position of strength they received a kind of grudging respect from the men. But they were not welcomed for making innovations in the tango and were secretly scorned for being intruders in a man's world. Essentially, they were seen as having lost their natural shyness and delicacy; by definition, their femininity. Lacking a husband – who might or might not have protected them, both in the short and long term – what they enjoyed instead was independence and freedom.

Brothels and tango dance halls came in all shapes and sizes. In some you could hear the chink of billiard cues from behind a wooden screen and the slap of cards on the table. These places operated as social clubs, catering to different classes of men, and most of them offered entertainment of some kind. One of the places where the tango was known was Hansen's Caffee, situated downtown. Hansen's played host to two different types of customer. At weekends the aristocracy flocked there, but after midnight the sons of the wealthy mingled with poorer citizens who went to dance and listen to tango music – men like Adolfo Bioy, who recorded in his memoir, *Antes del 1900* (Before 1900):

> Hansen's Restaurant was the entertainment centre of light-headed women. They danced the tango before this music became fashionable and accepted in the high circles of the city. We used to attend once in a while when we wanted to have fun, no matter the risks of getting into trouble with the dangerous men that one could find there.

For men like Bioy it was quite the thing to go slumming in La Boca. The tango was their flirtation with danger, and they took care to go down to the port in groups for their own safety. This didn't always prevent them being rolled. The women they danced with in the brothels worked, like La Moreira, in cahoots with their pimps and were adept at getting the men drunk and filching their wallets. By the early years of the twentieth century the tango's underworld reputation had spread to Europe:

> In Buenos Aires tango is a dance belonging distinctly to ill-famed clubs and taverns of the worst repute. It is never danced in tasteful salons, or among distinguished people. The purpose of the tango is to describe the obscene. It summarizes the choreography of the brothels, and its fundamental task is the pornographic spectacle. When the ladies of the twentieth century dance tango they know, or they ought to know, that they are behaving like prostitutes.

Ironically, it was only after crossing the Atlantic and becoming a craze in Europe that the tango was finally accepted in Argentina.

***

The 'reptile from the brothel', as it was known, was first seen outside the land of its birth in Paris, a city which continued to dictate fashion throughout the Western world. It's said that playboy Ricardo Güiraldes was responsible for introducing the tango to Europe. A poet and sometime writer, Güiraldes liked to frequent the fleshpots of La Boca where he often got into fights with the *compadritos*, and he's reported to have danced a mean tango. He was to draw on his memories of the dance in his novella *Raucho,* whose hero is described dancing at Maxim's with a blonde stranger before going off to a brothel with his friends:

> Her body bent pliantly to his. Timorous at first, he made single steps; then, seeing the skill of his partner, he took courage and danced without thinking, letting himself go to the dedicated rhythm. She followed him, bent to his will, anticipating the special movements, her eyes concentrated in a sad smile, voraciously sensual.

Like other wealthy young Argentinians, Güiraldes went to Paris to acquire a little Old World sophistication. There he created a stir by introducing the tango at a society ball one night. As Countess Melanie de Pourtales was heard to murmur, 'Is one supposed to dance it standing up?'

Outside France there began appearing lurid descriptions of the dance which was creating a scandal in Europe's fashion capital. An English-language newspaper in Buenos Aires reported:

> It is really impossible to give an exact description of what is to be seen in Paris. However, one can say that the tango appears as a double belly dance whose lasciviousness is accentuated by exaggerated contortions. One would think one was seeing a couple of Arabs under the influence of opium.

When the tango found its way to other European countries, the authorities were appalled. In Italy the Pope condemned it as a 'shameless pagan dance that is an attack on family and social life'. In 1913 a Dresden police chief commented, 'The dance offends modest feelings, since the woman spreads her legs so wide that you can see her underwear and stockings.' But the gold star for conservatism must go to Kaiser Wilhelm II, who had not yet accepted the waltz and polka, which had long since been adopted by high society in the rest of Europe. He banned the tango throughout the country, and at court events he permitted only the (elsewhere defunct) minuet and gavotte to be performed.

To tell a familiar tale, once those with a more rebellious spirit took up the dance others were quick to follow. In Paris the tango became so essential to the best parties that anyone who wanted to be à la mode felt obliged to give tango balls even when they hated dancing, as the Duchesse de Clermont-Tonnerre commented wryly:

> I went to the Rue de Varenne to an old lady who traditionally gave quiet little parties at which orangeade was served. But when I arrived, the racket of the music made the portraits of her ancestors vibrate on the walls. Young women were wandering around, cigarette in hand, and gauchos, their hair awry from sweat, grasped their partners, whose calves were visible. 'Where are the usual guests from the gratin?' I asked a friend. 'They must have sought refuge elsewhere,' came the reply.

The dance was still making waves in Paris in December 1913 when an interesting new play by Jean Richepan opened. The plot of *Le Tango* centred on a young newly married couple who were only able to consummate their marriage after liberating their sexuality by practising the tango. This shocking idea was made even more scandalous by the fact that both the main characters were played by actresses. And though cross-dressing on-stage was to become fashionable in the 1920s, it was still sufficiently daring seven years earlier to provoke a *frisson* of excitement.

It was only a matter of time before the tango became accepted. Part of its acceptance came from the fact that, in the ballrooms of Paris, the dance was deliberately turned into something glamorous and tame. Jean Cocteau has left us an amusing account of the new, artificial tango fashioned by Parisian sensibilities:

> Knotted couples, their shoulders immobile, performed the slow Argentine promenade. Fat gentlemen advanced on sliding little steps, squarely in front of their partners. From time to time they halted, turned, lifted a foot and inspected the sole, as if they had trodden in something horrible.

The journalist Sem enthused about the new 'ballroom' tango, with its extended armhold, marching walk and balletic postures:

> It is a miracle to see how the French, with their exquisite sense of moderation, have transformed it, putting it *au pointe* ... a tango a bit caramelized, a bit *parigoté*, with a decent and light grace, an air of scarcely any touching, a bit of a better tone ... where the good taste and tact of its followers is demonstrated, making of this dance of savages an elegant flirt of fine and modest legs.

The stylish Parisian tango had an interesting influence on fashion. Different dances require freedom of movement in different parts of the body, and tango movements involve a turning of the head and torso. The corsets which women were still wearing in the early years of the twentieth century kept the torso rigid. Women also wore hats when they danced, with long feathers which tended to get in their partners' faces. Their floor-length gowns made it impossible for the man to perform one of the basic tango steps in which he slips his leg between hers.

The tango was responsible for two truly revolutionary innovations in women's dress. One was divided skirts. The other was the elasticated corset, which allowed flexible movement in the torso. It also saved women from the damage inflicted on their internal organs by whalebone and steel corsets. There was even a colour named for the dance. Legend has it that a silk manufacturer was finding it hard to dispose of a large stock of shop-soiled satin dyed a rather brash orange. So he put it on sale at a knock-down price, christened it 'satin tango' and, within days, the entire stock had been snapped up, with customers clamouring for more. Thus tango orange was born. Unfortunately the manufacturer lost the recipe for that particular shade, so the name 'tango' came to be applied to an entire range of orange tints.

As with other dance crazes, an entire business grew up around the tango. Giving birth to a new colour is only one example of its influence on fashion. The dance dictated how people dressed, both on and off the dance floor, for women liked to look 'fashionably dancey' even when they didn't dance. Just as European women had once worn the billowing trousers and turbans of Egyptian dancers, so they now took to wearing the elegant new tango styles in their social life.

People are often drawn to a dance (especially one outside their own class or culture) because it offers a chance for passionate expression and liberation from constricting social expectations. In the process of becoming socially acceptable, though, the passion in a dance is often refined out of existence, its liberating improvisational tone jettisoned in favour of rules and set routines. This is what happened to the tango once it had settled into its niche as a civilized ballroom dance. Whereas the original tango had been danced by couples glued together, the ballroom version (like all 'proper' dance, as it was known) insisted that light be seen between the two bodies. Years later, Irene Castle wrote of the furore that the tango initially caused:

> It was against the law to dance too close to your partner at the time, and bouncers in restaurants tapped their patrons on the shoulder when they got closer than nine inches. One inventor went so far as to try to market a pair of metal belts with a nine-inch bar connecting them, to teach people how to dance with the correct space between them. The one big target for the crusaders was the tango. I suppose its opponents objected to the man bending the

woman over backwards and peering into her eyes with a smouldering, passionate look. If Vernon had ever looked into my eyes with smouldering passion during the tango, we would both have burst out laughing. As I look back on the tango, it doesn't seem possible that so many people could have been quite so worked up over something so very foolish, but I can remember quite vividly the furore it caused. A public school in Boston split down the middle over the tango when one educator suggested adding it to the curriculum.

Despite growing acceptance, controversy about the tango continued to rage for many years, as this 1913 letter to the London *Times* testifies:

I am one of the many matrons upon whom devolves the task of guiding a girl through the mazes of the London season. My grandmother has often told me of the shock she experienced on first beholding the polka, but I wonder what she would have said, had she been asked to introduce a well-brought-up girl of eighteen to the scandalous travesties of dancing which are, for the first time in my recollection, bringing more young men to parties than are needed. I would ask hostesses to let one know what houses to avoid by indicating in some way on their invitation card whether the turkey trot, the boston and the tango will be permitted.

The letter was signed 'a Peeress'. The Editor replied, 'We can all guess what her grandmother would have said, because we know exactly how our grandmothers fought tooth and nail against the introduction of the polka and waltz into England.'

By the 1920s the ballroom-style tango had become accepted at nearly every level of European society. When word got back to Buenos Aires, high society, formerly so disapproving, welcomed the dance home with open arms. Yet the tango which was finally accepted in the land of its birth was nothing like its early ancestor. A dance born as a cry of protest, a raw, rough, sexually suggestive ritual, had become tamed like so many dances before it. An expression of immigrant consciousness, a form of rebellion and protest, the tango was ultimately to end up as light entertainment for polite society. Some years ago film-maker Jana Bokova visited Buenos Aires to find out what had happened to the dance in the city of its birth. She found clubs which had never lost the atmosphere of the old days, when the tango still served to express the life of the people who had created it:

> On my second night I was taken to a small cafe in the quarter known as La Boca. No room for an orchestra here: the music came from one guitar and a *bandoneón*, the squeeze-box whose plaintive wail is at the heart of tango music. As they played, a dark-haired, dark-skinned woman took the centre of the floor, between the crowded tables and the bar. She was handsome, gypsy-looking, about sixty years old but dressed like a young woman, a split skirt showing tanned legs, a blouse that left bare her shoulders and arms. She threw her body into the music almost violently, jerking her limbs, curling her fingers, and she began to sing. The voice was loud, husky, defiant: 'Tango, you used to be king. But the rot set in when you went sophisticated. Tango, it makes me sad to see you've deserted the mean dirt streets for a carpeted drawing-room.'

But there is always a quid pro quo, and for many women the gentrification of the tango proved their financial salvation.

***

Like the gypsies, who migrated from India to southern Spain and created flamenco from multicultural roots, Europe's migrants to Buenos Aires forged a fascinating hybrid in tango music. Old World folk songs, Italian opera and black rhythms all had a part to play in shaping early tango music. It was played on paper combs, flutes, violins and the guitar. In time the *bandoneón*, a smaller version of the accordion, with a similar heavy, organ-like resonance, would give tango music its distinctive, jazzy wail. Tango songs were soon heard everywhere. Organ-grinders played the new melodies in the streets, bus drivers whistled them as they went along, and they were heard too on the wind-up gramophones in barbershops. It wasn't long before this music superseded even opera, the Italians' favourite. There was no resisting the subtle, insinuating lure of the tango.

In the early days brothels were the most likely places to offer musicians regular employment, but most of them couldn't earn a living playing tango music. As it became more popular, though, cafe managers in the smarter establishments began hiring tango trios to entertain their customers and the old stigma of its birth slowly faded away.

The tango's golden age dawned in the 1920s in the stylish downtown cabarets which catered to those with money to throw away. Very French in flavour, they were aimed at a middle class who had experienced the Belle Epoque in Paris. All kinds of tango venues sprang up. In some you could listen to the best bands, in others you could watch tango films, eat fine food and dance with the most skilled *milonguitas*.

A certain amount of disapproval was attached to having a daughter working in the still-dubious world of professional tango, despite the popularity of the dance. Female singers who worked in cabarets often dressed as men, while female songwriters, for their part, used male pen-names in order to protect their families. On one level this gender-swapping gave them a dangerous ambiguity and sent a shiver through some members of the audience.

The lives of women who sang and wrote tango songs and played in all-female tango bands remain, to some extent, unknown. They played at afternoon tea dances, weddings and other special occasions, and in the golden age they were as popular and famous as their male colleagues. Yet they proved a temporary phenomenon and seldom feature in histories of the tango. The attitude of their male contemporaries is that those who showed real talent were an exception. One gets the feeling, reading between the lines, that they were elbowed out of the game. Carlos Gardel, tango's most celebrated singer, had nothing to lose by championing other performers, yet he was patronizing of them and grudging in his praise. The most he could find to say of popular *bandoneón*-player Paquita Bernardo was that she was 'the only female who has mastered the macho character of the *bandoneón*'.

Even during its golden age, tango was still essentially a man's thing, and if female musicians received scant praise then so did dancers. Felix Weingarten, writing in the 1920s, was of the opinion that, 'The majority of women who dance tango do so quite badly, while the men are almost all excellent dancers.' Women involved professionally in the tango were on the sidelines of its history, and this remains true of musicians today. Tango literature contains many accounts of famous male musicians and singers, but few about the women for whom tango was an economic godsend.

One benefit of the dance was that it caused a good deal of social mixing. Women from poor families who worked in the new ritzy joints danced with politicians, landowners and industrialists. By becoming a skilled dancer a woman gained the kind of control over her destiny that she could never have aspired to as the wife of a poor immigrant. Dancing gave her economic independence and a way of making contact with the rich and powerful and even – who knows? – making a permanent connection with them. Ana Luciana Devis has written about the cabarets and the men who frequented them:

> The patrons were all men of leisure – they had never worked. They drank bottle after bottle of champagne and consumed vast quantities of caviar. They were nice, generous, but irresponsible people. It was not unknown for one of them to give a dancer a country house as a present. The nights passed slowly – they didn't have to rush off anywhere. Even love affairs where money changed hands were subject to a lengthy, patient ceremony: from the time the gentleman approached the *milonguera*, plying her with drinks, four days would often pass before the adventure actually took place.

If working-class women found it easy to operate in a social setting so far removed from their own lives, this wasn't the case for their menfolk. It isn't surprising that men resented the apparent ease with which women were able to better themselves, on the arm of wealthy men. The women had something for which there is always a demand. And those *milonguitas* who danced their way out of the slums became the frequent subject of bitter tango laments.

The subdued rage in lyrics written by men reflects their failure to rise on the social ladder and to provide for their own women. In the competition for a woman, wealth always won out over mere sexual attraction. Tango songs reflect the frustration of the poor man who has to find someone to blame for his lack of worldly success, and that someone is generally a woman. Lyrics like those of 'Champagne Tango' chronicle the class betrayal of gold-digging viragos:

> *Those broads who did as they were told have gone,*
> *today all they want is frocks, expensive jewellery,*
> *a convertible for driving around the city.*

No one wants a slum,
or to be a struggling seamstress.
Better to be a friend of the guy with big money,
who can rent her an apartment
and take her out to the Pigalle.

There are many tango songs which bemoan the faithlessness of women and warn them that they'll eventually be abandoned. Even though you may think you're moving up, they say, you're bound to fall back when your youth and beauty are gone and your protector tires of you. Remember, his patronage is uncertain. He will betray you just as you have betrayed me, and your old age will be miserable and lonely.

Milongueras were far from ignorant of their precarious position, as the lyrics of 'Campaneando la Vejez' (Thinking about Old Age) demonstrate:

I was never blinded by the lights of the dance hall,
And the tango, the blessed tango, to whom I sang my love song,
Was not my misfortune, as some would say.
Tango was my spur to struggle with honour.

If many tango songs are laments over the woman who got away, there are others which chronicle the immigrants' hankering after a lost way of life, their cynicism and the struggle for survival. They rejoice in the private wounds which are normally kept hidden in intimate letters and diaries. Like the words of flamenco songs, they are a cry of protest against poor living conditions and lack of work. Like the blues, they were improvised according to mood and they often portrayed men as duped, castrated beings, nostalgic for the protective bosom of their mothers.

The Argentinian writer Jorge Luis Borges was a great tango enthusiast. He writes that early tango songs were bold and jaunty, and complains that tango's later lyrics came to indulge in 'loud self-pity, while shamelessly rejoicing in the misfortunes of others'. These songs, which came from a male point of view, were full of maudlin sentimentality and blame, and even when women sang them they didn't change the sex of the protagonist.

As for male dancers, perhaps they didn't want to look as if they were trying too hard. A *tanguero* made only as many steps as were necessary to enable his partner to perform her fancy footwork and there developed the

notion that it was effeminate for a man to put too much effort into his
dancing.

Milonguitas, on the other hand, gave it everything they had. They had
made up their minds to survive and they weren't about to let their spirit be
crushed, nor live ground down by poverty. And if they were going to be
exploited, at least it should be for a reasonable financial return. Being a
pimp's moll or a poor man's wife was, by no stretch of the imagination, their
best prospect. Tango historian Marta Sevigliano writes that, even though
tango women didn't have a great deal of power, those who found their way
as far as the smart cafés in the city centre were far from passive. They were,
she comments, 'passionate objects, not passive ones. Objects that had, if not
a say, at least a move to make in the power game.'

***

It's easy to underestimate the effect that social dancing had on women's lives
during the first half of the twentieth century. For a long time the dance floor
had been the place where strangers met and talked and got to know each
other. For European women, who weren't nearly as bold as Americans, tea
dances were especially popular in the hiatus between the two world wars and
provided a genteel setting for middle-class women to enjoy themselves. At
tea dances it wasn't unusual to find women partnering each other, though
men generally assumed that women couldn't possibly derive much pleasure
from dancing with their own sex. Management often hired professional male
dancers to partner lone women, a situation that Dorothy L Sayers exploits in
her thriller *Have His Carcase*:

> 'I'm afraid I'm not a very good dancer,' she remarked apologetically.
> Mr Antoine clasped her more firmly in his competent professional
> arm, and replied,
> 'You dance very correctly, mademoiselle. It is only the entrain that
> is a little lacking. It is possible that you are awaiting the perfect
> partner. When the heart dances with the feet, then it will be à
> merveille.' He met her eyes with a delicately calculated expression of
> encouragement.

'Is that the kind of thing you have to say to all these old ladies?' asked Harriet, smiling.

Antoine opened his eyes a trifle and then, mocking back at her mockery, said:

'I'm afraid so. That is a part of our job, you know.'

'It must be very tedious.'

Antoine contrived to shrug his exquisite shoulders without in any way affecting the lithe grace of his motion.

'Que voulez-vous? All work has its tedious moments, which are repaid by those that are more agreeable. One may say truthfully to mademoiselle what might in another case be a mere politeness.'

The music stopped. He handed her back to her table with a smile, and she saw him gather up a vast and billowy lady in a tightly fitting gown and move smoothly away with her, the eternal semi-sensuous smile fixed upon his lips as though it was painted there.

The tango has gathered to itself a wide range of clichés: among those which have stuck is that of the unwanted female and the professional gigolo engaged in a mental fantasy of sex on the dance floor. At the other end of the spectrum is the lazy journalistic cliché of tango as 'sex on legs'. There will always be people who regard dancing in general as a substitute for sex. But dance lovers know that dancing is a source of pleasure and an expression of creative energy for its own sake. And, in hard times, it's one of life's least expensive ways of keeping up one's spirits. After Argentina's financial collapse in 2002, tango became more popular than ever in Buenos Aires. Some months after the crash, new milongas began appearing, adding to the thriving dancehall scene. What's more, the new exchange rate made it cheap for foreign enthusiasts to go and brush up their dance skills at the many tango festivals and courses held for non-Argentinians. There was no shortage of work for the dance teachers who have contributed to the recent tango revival there in recent years.

The celebrated performer María Nieves has been teaching and creating theatre work for several decades. Recalling her youth in the 1950s, she says:

To me, el baile [dance] represents life, love, death, hate. It makes my hair stand on end. I used to go dancing on both Saturdays and Sundays. On Thursdays and Fridays we used to go every single time

2222222222222222

a *baile* was held . . . A decent girl went to the clubs just to dance, and
she would dance with tough guys and swarthy types and with
mummy's boys – mummy's boys were hardly ever good dancers. We
were swept away by our love for the tango, we just loved to go
dancing. We didn't go out looking for sex, none of the girls in our
gang did.

There was an etiquette surrounding the tango in those days, and it persists
even now. A man indicates to a woman from across the room that he would
like to dance with her, but he doesn't approach her directly. This would be to
risk rejection. He uses the *cabaceo* – a subtle raising of the eyebrows. If she
wants to dance with him she nods. Otherwise she quickly looks away. Three
tangos are played, all danced with the same partner. Then the couples thank
each other and part, going off in separate directions to their own tables.
While they're taking the opportunity to sit down for a few minutes, collect
their energies and have a drink, 'curtain' music is played, which no one
dances to. Then a man will come over and invite a different woman to dance,
and so it goes on.

In Buenos Aires tango is danced with torsos fused, moving in a single
block as if glued together. The leading is done largely from the torso and
solar plexus, and by the subtlest of signals: a shoulder movement, a slight
turn of the chest, a lift of the arm, a squeeze of the hand. Dancers have to
develop acute sensitivity to their partner's energy, reading their slightest
movement and acting on it. The skill lies in doing nothing. Instead, the
woman has to wait in a state of relaxed, yet alert, concentration for the
man's lead.

At Confitería Ideal I sat and watched my ballerina friend dance with one
stranger after another. One of them was bent on correcting her, even down
to the angle at which she held her head ('You must lower your head, look
down'). She returned to her chair, exhausted, pulling off her shoes and
waggling her toes luxuriously. 'If you don't have a partner who's right for
you, you can't do anything,' she said. 'You can't follow and you can't
improvise, and it's all based on improvisation. It's true what they say, you
know: tango's the search for the perfect partner.'

We watched an Argentinian woman dance. Sometimes it was with
women, sometimes with a man who was working his way round the floor,
partnering different customers. Even when there was no one to partner her

she refused to sit still. She mooched around, frowning in concentration, intent on her steps. Sometimes she held out her arms as if embracing an invisible body. She sat down reluctantly at the next table and picked up a menu to use as a fan. 'Me, I live for the moment,' she said to us, her eyes darting about for the next partner. 'I'm crazy for the tango.'

There was one couple who caught our attention: a young blonde with an impish face and a thin little ferret of a man with a receding chin. But when they began to dance there occurred one of those magical transformations, between two apparently unsuited people, which only happen on the dance floor. Suddenly they became the perfect match for each other. She traced slinky figure-eight patterns around him, slipping her leg between his and flashing her foot behind her. He stuck out a foot to block her path. With slow deliberation she lifted hers, grazing it against his leg, stepped over it and, with a cheeky hip swivel, reversed her direction and freed herself from the impasse he had set up. Now their feet began to fly. They curled their legs round each other and, as the long, final wailing flourish of music sounded, he flung her back in a falling arc, her head barely skimming the floor. Our Argentinian friend who had been sitting, menu aloft, transfixed by this display, began wildly fanning herself. 'Now that', she growled, 'is what I call dancing!'

***

Sally Potter's film *The Tango Lesson* captures perfectly the subtle male-female relationship at the heart of this most sophisticated of couple dances. The raw material for Potter's film was her own passion for the tango and her experience learning it with one of Argentina's best-known dancers, Pablo Verón. It explores the theme of tango as a battle of the sexes which is resolved when the man and woman come to an understanding of each other. Questions of closeness and distance, freedom of expression and collaboration arise and manifest themselves in the attempt to dance with a partner.

At one point, after performing in a show together for the first time, Verón tells Potter angrily, 'Do nothing when you dance. Just follow. Otherwise you block my freedom to move. You destroy my liberty. And then I can't dance.

I can do nothing.' To which she replies that he danced as if she wasn't there. As the couple rehearse together Verón tells Potter, 'Let go. Stop thinking. Do less. You're blocking, using too much force, just centre yourself and let go.' The French for 'Let go' – *Lâchez prise* – literally means 'Let yourself be taken.' Potter, who has been trying hard, mocks him, '*Lâchez prise. Lâchez prise.* I'm trying to *lâchez prise.*' At one point she tells him, 'I've done almost nothing this last year. Except follow. Badly. Because it doesn't suit me to follow. It suits me to lead.'

The leading and following in tango is sometimes described as 'action and reaction'. And in a less macho society than that of Buenos Aires you may well hear men say, 'I'd rather you led' or 'I'm not sure how I feel about this business of leading.' But in any relationship someone has to make the first move, and the beauty of tango is that when a couple give each other space to create, you can't tell who is leading. It becomes a true partnership. As Potter writes, 'The tango is as complex as its own roots and as simple as the primal impulse for two human beings to move as one.'

And though male dancers often insist that they are the leaders, tango subverts the tradition of couple dancing in a fascinating way. The way a woman slips a leg into her partner's stride goes against all the conventions and turns her into a teasing aggressor rather than a simple follower. In show tango a woman's partner sometimes looks as if he's only there to provide her with a solid frame within which she can dazzle, via an array of swift and potentially deadly leg movements.

Dancing tango is like having a conversation, with all the hesitations and interruptions and negotiations of any verbal exchange. And sometimes the conversation turns into an argument, even a battle! In the words of Borges, 'The tango is a direct expression of something that poets have often tried to state in words: the belief that a fight may be a celebration.'

The bizarre idea at the heart of tango is that you set off in a dancing embrace then, contrary to every tradition of partner dancing, you interrupt your walk to perform figures on the spot. These pauses offer dramatic opportunities for intriguing things to happen. The man may bring the dance to one of its pauses, enabling his partner to move into a step which she then decides to embellish. If he's alert he'll pick up on what she's doing and not rush in with the next step, for the woman is the guardian of the flow. He'll wait for her to finish before leading her off again on their travels across the floor.

Tango reflects a more complex male-female relationship than other couple dances, and perhaps this is one reason for its current popularity in Europe and the United States. There are plenty of men who have caught the tango bug; but, as with most dances, there are always more women than men at classes. Men go along when they're looking for a partner and tend to stop going when they've found one. But women carry on for the sheer pleasure of dancing, confirming the old adage that women enjoy themselves most intensely through the body.

Tango enthusiasts find themselves becoming hooked before they even notice it. Suddenly they're going to classes or tango events every night of the week and sneaking in a bit of practice at home during the day. Kate Channel is one. In the British documentary *Travels with My Tutu* she tells ballerina-presenter Deborah Bull:

> At first it was very difficult for me. I came from a culture where women didn't go into bars alone and certainly didn't go and approach men. But I was sitting one night in a venue when I took all my courage and went and asked a man to dance. And, fortunately for me, his face lit up and he said, 'Oh, I'd love to!' And I've never sat out a dance since. It taught me that, in life, you generally get what you ask for. If you want something, go and get it. You can only be told no, in which case you're not any worse off than when you began.

Liz Tomlin keeps a set of boards which fit together into a dance floor. Laid on the lawn, on days when the capricious English weather is warm enough for outdoor socializing, it can hold quite a few of her tango friends. 'Sometimes,' she says, 'you get to the end of a dance and you stand there and you can't move because it's been so extreme, so fulfilling. You think, I can't breathe yet. Being that close, you can't help but transmit your feelings. At the end of my first dance with someone I feel I know their character, I know if I like them, if I trust them. I know if they're honest.'

Mary Brown is a tango amateur who featured in the documentary *Strictly Dancing*. She talks eloquently of a phenomenon understood by anyone with a passion for dancing: that sense of unleashing hidden aspects of herself when she takes to the floor, including a love of dressing-up. Her fortieth birthday fell on the night of a tango ball. One of the men from the class presented her with a surprise birthday cake that he'd made, decorated with a tangoing couple in red and black icing.

After everyone had sung Happy Birthday came a true tango tradition: during one piece of music, each man stepped up in turn to dance with her for a few moments while everyone stood around the floor, watching and smiling. 'In what other activity can you go from the arms of one man to the other in one night without any problems whatsoever? It's wonderful!', she laughed. Then she added, 'If I spend a day without dancing, I begin to wonder if I'm losing it. I think, oh my god, I'm not going to be able to dance next time, I'm going to be rusty! If you're having a good dance with someone you enjoy dancing with, it's magic. It makes it worthwhile being alive.'

Danse Macabre

If people knew how physically cruel ballet really is,
nobody would watch
– only those people who enjoy bullfights.
Margot Fonteyn

Ballet stands like a colossus bestriding the world of dance. It has dominated Western dance for years with its assertion of cultural superiority and its claim that no other dance can be so expressive. And maybe it's fitting that an art which rejoices in the artificial, and celebrates human triumph over nature, has come to represent the Western ideal. For our society has a thousand-year-old distrust – both religious and philosophical – of the natural body.

Much Western literature is based on stories of failed, unhappy love and classical ballet, with its doomed lovers and not-quite-human heroines who carry men off to the land of the living dead, is the perfect expression of our continuing neurotic sexual sensibility. Ballet is the dance little girls grow up wanting to do. The fairy tales of the classical repertoire are irresistible, with their dolls who come to life, their heroines who metamorphose into animals, their girly sprites who fly through the air. It's not surprising that children reach for the glittering tiaras.

They cannot know that ballet is the most concerted attack on the female body of any dance ever invented. More than that: a ballerina's career is as brief as a fashion model's and there are many similarities in the two professions. Like models, ballerinas spend a great deal of their time looking in mirrors, watching their weight and scrutinizing themselves for imperfections. Few develop the bodies of mature women; most retain the flat breasts, tiny boys' bottoms and lean flanks of adolescents. Even as students, there are ballerinas whose female hormones become so depressed that their periods stop and they become infertile. Many are on a constant diet and smoke to depress their appetite, and this combination of poor nutrition and a post-menopausal hormone condition leads to a thinning of the bones. It leaves them as vulnerable to broken bones, especially in the legs and feet, as old ladies. Not only that; so great is the wear and tear on the hip joints resulting from the unnatural demands of ballet that by the time they reach the age of forty, some ex-ballerinas are fitted with plastic hips.

Injuries among ballet dancers are so common that they're talked about in the most matter-of-fact way imaginable. An interview with prima ballerina Sarah Wildor revealed that she'd danced through a season at London's Royal Ballet in such pain that some nights she wasn't even able to put on her own socks before setting out for the Opera House. She was determined to finish the season, but on the day she decided she simply had to give in and stop, she discovered that she'd torn a disc in her spine: 'It's really typical of a dancer's mentality ... you treat absolute agony as if it's just inconvenient.' It wasn't her first serious injury. As a member of the Royal Ballet School she'd suffered stress fractures in her back at the age of sixteen. For four months she wore a plaster cast which extended from beneath her armpits down to her hipbones. She almost decided to give up dancing for good but, she said, 'When you can't dance, everything is taken away from you, your fitness, your joy ... that's why you have to come back for more.'

When the curtain goes up at 7.30, ballerinas have already gone through hours of preparation that day: classes in the morning, rehearsals in the afternoon and a warm-up before the show begins. They may be dancing for nine hours in any one day. They live with the exhaustion of this schedule, yet the moment the lights dim and the performance begins they're expected to look as fresh as if they had spent the day lying on the sofa, resting up for this, their great effort.

Those who manage to live with this gruelling schedule – not to speak of the humiliation which is a way of life in the profession, as well as the injuries which arise through ballet's abnormal demands on the body – still have to contend with unremitting pain in the exercise of their art. The final indignity occurs in their mid-thirties, when they are considered more or less past it and thrown on the scrap heap.

At the end of what some of us might consider a mercifully short career, given its mental, emotional and physical toll, ballerinas are cast adrift to seek a new means of livelihood. For them it's not a merciful release, but a tragedy. From the tender age of eleven they have been locked away in a hermetically sealed world in which nothing matters except the all-consuming demands of ballet. Having learnt to think of themselves as the Rolls Royces of the dance world they wake up one day to discover that they have become obsolete. Some of them cannot accept this and they take to haunting their old workplace. For others it's too painful to go back and they cut themselves off from all contact with their former life. For many a deep depression sets in. To be finished in their chosen career, even before reaching their mature powers of expression, must be a terrible experience.

But the fairy-tale world of ballet isn't about strong, powerful women in their prime. And though women hugely outnumber men in the profession, it's always been men who have called the shots. It's largely through male eyes that women are portrayed in ballet, and even when a woman has been at the helm of a ballet company, it has made little difference. As head of the Royal Ballet, Ninette de Valois did nothing to promote other women to her inner circle. She declared that once ballet was established in Britain it should pass into the care of the mature male element; that its real history was the history of great male choreographers, directors and teachers.

The 'real' history of ballet, though, isn't only the story of steps; it's the story of the 'real' lives of dancers. Their power to move an audience lies not just in technical skill but in the experience they bring to their performing. Ironically, a full life, including relationships and childbearing, is still, even in the twenty-first century, seen as somewhat irrelevant to a dancer's life by the antiquated ballet world, where dancers are expected to put no other loyalty above dedication to their calling.

The fairy-tale game of ballet is seductive, and aspiring baby ballerinas don't know just how dark the dark side of fairy tales can be. They want to be eternal child-women and what they don't know is that there's a price to pay for being a princess.

***

Ballet was designed to be more than simple entertainment. The first ballet dancers were members of the nobility and their dancing reflected the rituals of courtly life. These became woven into the classical ballet language and there they have remained fixed. At the heart of the aristocracy's power lies its ceremonial. The trappings of pomp offer more than mere spectacle; they help engender obedience and humility by reinforcing royalty's idea of its own importance. All that splendid display extends into fashion and the smallest details of behaviour as well. In courtly life form is everything, content and feeling count for little, and a vital aspect of form is the suppression of spontaneity.

The aristocracy's drive to distinguish itself from the *hoi polloi* has left no stone unturned. In the past the upper classes used a different vocabulary and accent, they ate and dressed differently; and towards the middle of the seventeenth century, they decided to walk differently as well. Turned-out walking, which probably originated at the French court, involved swinging each leg out to the side before bringing it round to the front. Walking like this with the feet pointing forward looks comical. Strange as it may seem, turning the feet out as well as the leg looks less clumsy. In time the outward swing of the leg disappeared, leaving only the feet turned-out. This aristocratic fashion for silly walks was incorporated into the dance by choreographer Jean-Georges Noverre, who thought the normal position of the legs awkward and ugly! Ever since then, the duck-like waddle of turnout has remained pivotal to classical ballet, to the detriment of dancers' health.

In terms of the almost superhuman strength it demands, ballet can be compared to athletics. But ballet exerts greater physical strain than athletics, for it requires the body to move in ways for which it simply isn't designed. Much has been written about how ballet dancers overcome the 'limitations' of the human body. To this way of thinking the incredibly complex instrument with which we're all blessed – a wondrous piece of work by any standards – is a machine which has to be bludgeoned (euphemistically described as 'trained') into submission.

Turnout allows dancers to lift their legs higher, move sideways more quickly and change direction more smoothly. To achieve turnout the femur (hipbone) is slowly coaxed to rotate outwards in its socket from its natural position until the entire body opens out. No one can master this technique unless they begin training in early childhood, while the bones are still malleable. One early nineteenth-century-dancer recalls, 'Every morning my teacher imprisoned my feet in a grooved box. There, heel to heel, with knees pointing outwards, my martyred feet became used to remaining in a parallel line by themselves.'

One of the most famous ballerinas of the time, Carlotta Grisi, achieved her turnout by having her lover stand on her hips while she lay belly-down on the floor with her legs spread. She commented dryly that these sessions were the high point of their liaison. Théophile Gautier, a poet and fiction writer by choice, a critic by necessity, was wildly in love with Grisi. The first real dance critic, he made his name from reviewing ballet, though he began by disliking it, especially the turned-out position which he described as 'one of the most abominable positions ever invented by the pedantry of the past'.

Barry Grimaldi has wide experience treating dancers. Writing of the damage caused by turnout, he states that the incidence of osteoarthritis is greater among ballerinas than among other women as they age. This is especially true of the hips and knees, which suffer accelerated wear and tear. A hip replacement at the age of forty-five is not unusual. A hundred years after Isadora Duncan fired off her broadside against the deformed skeletons of ballerinas, the situation has gone from bad to worse; for the technical demands of ballet are far greater now than they were in the past.

Turnout is required of all ballet dancers, and it isn't the only distortion that this dance inflicts on the body. Even more damaging is the need for ballerinas to dance on pointe. This was originally a requirement of fashion and, as we know, fashion isn't about practicality but about offering something new, even comical or outrageous, which will attract attention and give individuals a sense of their own distinction. To this end, there will always be women who are happy to dress in uncomfortable clothes which limit their freedom of movement and even alter the shape of their body.

Over the years fashion has thrown different parts of the female body into relief as a source of erotic attention. Bosom, bottom and legs have all taken their turn, and as we journey from country to country we find that other parts of the body have been equally fetishized. Among the Padong of northern Thailand, little girls as young as eight years old are fitted with brass collars. The macabre gift of another collar is added on every birthday, causing the neck to be elongated. So completely do the neck muscles atrophy over the years that, were these collars to be removed, the women would not be able to hold their heads up.

The association of beauty and pain isn't peculiar to Western culture. The story of how women the world over have colluded with the reshaping of their bodies in ways which damage their health goes back many years. In the past women's acquiescence in their own suffering occurred because they had little economic power. Dependent on men and obliged to please, they conformed to every popular trend, however much pain it caused them.

So it came about that, to exaggerate their supposed spirituality, nineteenth-century ballerinas went up onto their toes, supported by their male partners. A flying apparatus of harness and wires was devised, enabling dancers to lift off into the air and come down so gracefully that their toes barely grazed the stage. It may be that this trick of flight inspired choreographers to try and keep ballerinas in the air (or at least as far removed from the ground as possible) without their harnesses, for dancing on pointe soon entered the ballet repertoire. Pointework helped create the illusion of the airbound heroine. It gave ballerinas the air of being not quite human and not quite women. They were eternal virgins with dangerous, un-virgin-like powers.

A Natural History of the Ballet Girl, published in 1847, described the corps de ballet dancer 'in her leisure time, when she gets any, which is but seldom ... sitting in a peculiarly agonizing pair of stocks, which induce the power of pointing the toes until they form a line with the leg'. As ballerinas patter across the stage, the sound of their stubby, blocked-toe shoes hitting the floor draws our attention. Dancing on pointe, eight stone of body weight bears down through the ankle to a tiny area at the tip of the toes, producing huge pressure on the feet. A contemporary of Anna Pavlova who was once present in her dressing-room when she came off-stage wrote that the Russian ballerina was so reluctant to be faced with the sight of her bleeding toes, she delayed removing her shoes for as long as possible.

Today's pointe shoes consist of elaborately layered canvas, brown paper and glue. They are baked in a hot oven to harden the blocks and preserve their slightly curved shape, which emphasizes the arched instep to which every ballerina aspires. The ideal foot for these shoes has the first three toes all the same length. If the second toe is longer (as it is in any normal, healthy foot) the toes become squashed together and a bump is created.

A surgeon who once attended to the British ballerina Margot Fonteyn commented that the first time he saw her feet he couldn't believe she could stand up, let alone dance on them. 'The first ballerina I ever examined,' he went on to say, 'I asked her if she was in pain and she looked at me strangely. Because they're all in pain. It's just a matter of, what do you mean by pain?'

Recent research has shown that the pain threshhold of ballerinas is three times higher than that of other people. Only ballet – among all the theatre dances of the world – requires that women systematically endure pain and damage to the very part of the body which carries them across the stage and without which they would simply not be able to dance at all.

Dancing on pointe has never been required of men. One of today's male dancers who had to get up on his toes for a modern ballet gasped that it was pure agony. He only managed to carry on, he said, by gulping down painkillers and gritting his teeth.

A pair of toe shoes lasts only a few days and the first thing all ballerinas do with a new pair is try and soften them up. They hit them with hammers, slam them in door jambs, bang them up and down on steps, anything to make them more comfortable. Inside these shoes they cushion their toes with plasters, cotton wool, tissues, J-cloths, bits of old tights. Some use a second skin or a jelly mould. Yet none of these remedies prevents pain entirely when you are dancing non-stop for a couple of hours, and members of the corps de ballet confess to playing mental games to divert themselves from their discomfort. Behind the grinding smiles of all those fluffy white swans lies a steely spirit of endurance.

Toe shoes can cause the toenails to curve inwards like claws, and the feet to become so hardened that the skin splits. Photographer Colin Jones comments, 'I've often seen girls with blood seeping through the satin of their shoes after dancing on pointe for two hours in a three-act ballet.' According to prima ballerina Tamara Rojo:

> My feet are usually covered in blisters, calluses and corns and most of my toenails are either black or falling off because of the pointe shoes. You can't actually wear pointes until you're about ten because your feet aren't strong enough. It's extremely painful for the first year and it's quite scary because you don't really have the strength to keep on balance, so you feel like you've twisted your ankles. You bleed and your feet are not used to it and you don't really know how to deal with it. When I walk off the stage sometimes … my feet are so sore that I can't even be bothered to untie the ribbons – I just cut them off.

Since a high arch is prized by choreographers, some dancers try and impress them at auditions by wearing a silicone instep under their tights, moulded to the top of the foot. In her autobiography *Dancing On My Grave*, the American dancer Gelsey Kirkland recalls a classmate who resorted to cosmetic surgery in order to alter the line of her foot. She had the arches surgically broken and the bones realigned to enhance her pointe, and if we think this is unusual, there are many dancers today who consider having this operation, to give themselves an edge in the highly competitive ballet world.

Kirkland worked with the Russian choreographer Balanchine during the 1970s and '80s. In ballet mythology Balanchine is a man who 'adored' women (he married five, one of whom divorced him because he refused to let her have children). He described ballet as 'Woman', a garden of beautiful flowers, with man as the gardener. We seem to be back in the nineteenth century, contemplating those wilting flower children of the Romantic era. 'Women are naturally inferior in matters requiring action and imagination,' Balanchine wrote in all seriousness as recently as the 1970s. 'Woman obligingly accepts her lowly place.'

Balanchine wasn't the only late-twentieth-century male choreographer with an old-fashioned reverence for the feminine mystique. He wasn't the only one who hesitated to delve beneath the surface where he might encounter a more complex reality. His reverence hides distaste, if not repugnance, and one only has to look at the way he treated his dancers to understand his contempt for women. He discouraged them from dating (they took it for granted that marriage would bring an end to their careers) and kept them in a permanent state of apprehension by warning them that they were expendable and could easily be replaced.

Kirkland recalls how once, when Balanchine couldn't find words to explain what he wanted of her, he wrenched her leg, pulling and tearing the muscles, as he tried to mould her into the required position. 'He was the only teacher at the school of American Ballet whom I would have forgiven for such an offence,' she writes, illustrating the kind of blind devotion which has ultimately led many ballerinas into a professional hell. Kirkland's story is the most chilling example – certainly the most courageous, for she went into print with it – of the contemptuous and violent male arrogance towards women that she encountered in the sado-masochistic world of ballet.

Aspiring ballerinas are taught from childhood that they have to suffer for their art, that they have to endure broken, bleeding toes and constant discomfort of one kind or another. They put up with it because they've been brainwashed into believing that ballet is the most beautiful and sophisticated of all dance forms, and in time pain and pleasure become inextricably linked in their psyche. Even when they're in agony they grit their teeth and soldier on, poor sad little soldiers, for they know how short their performing days are. They know there are always young hopefuls coming up behind them, ready to jump into their place.

The pain does not diminish with time, as Patricia Ruanne attests:

> Your body doesn't want to move in the daytime, and it shrieks louder when you go home at night. But your pain threshold increases. You can go on longer. Your body learns to take a little bit more and a little bit more.

Many testify that it is always a battle to carry on. Natalia Makarova was reported as saying, 'Even with arthritis, which I have in several places, muscles eventually respond. I'm used to pain. We all are. Some days when you don't have pain it's strange.' One 24-year-old ballerina says her body is bent double with stiffness most mornings and she has to lie in a bath for half an hour before she feels human again. Ex-prima ballerina Deborah Bull once commented lightly that dancers keep the Nurofen company going single-handed.

Kirkland, who already had bunions at the age of eleven, was no different in her acceptance of pain as a 'normal' hazard of her profession. To assist her extension she improvised a kind of rack out of her bed on which to stretch herself; assuming a position to force her extension beyond its natural limit, she told a friend to hold her down and not let go, however much she begged for release: 'She sat on me, disregarding my groans, allowing her body weight to restrain me until the pain became so excruciating that I collapsed into tears.'

While a part of her strove valiantly to please her taskmaster, her creative, rebellious side was engaged in a continuous fight with Balanchine, who told her, 'You have to be vairy careful when you use your mind ... or you will get into trouble.' When she asked for his advice on her physical agony he sighed and told her, 'Young people don't have injuries. Go home and read fairy tales. Try a little red wine.' She describes herself limping through rehearsals, her legs often bandaged to the knee beneath her leg warmers.

One time on tour Kirkland was so ill and emaciated that she told

Balanchine she was unable to perform that night. He gave her a 'vitamin' pill and said she would feel better – as indeed she did. The pill made her feel terrific and she danced as if her feet had wings. Afterwards Balanchine congratulated her on her performance and, lowering his voice, said that if she ever felt ill again she should ask him for another of these vitamins. Of course, they were no such thing: they were amphetamines, and from this small beginning Kirkland was to descend into cocaine addiction. Obtaining her supply was never a problem. She claims that there were always small-time dealers in the company and that, on tour, a member of the corps de ballet carried a stash for the stars: 'The dealers were warned by at least one influential member of management not to let things get out of hand. One of the dealers was told to stay away from me. I was out of hand.'

Like others before and since, Kirkland resorted to drugs as a way of coping with life in a super-stressful profession. Her claims that management knew about drug use in the company and tolerated it have been denied. This must make the ballet world unique in the performing arts in its failure to detect the obvious symptoms of drug abuse. At a time when she was completely out of her head, Kirkland was receiving the greatest eulogies of her career. In 1983 the *New York Times* critic Jennifer Dunning wrote of her appearance in Balanchine's *La Sonnambula*:

> Miss Kirkland's Sleepwalker – the mysterious woman who appears from out of her dark tower in the midst of a party, enchants a strange young poet, causes his death and then carries him back into the tower and away with her into the night – had the grandeur of madness and the fine detail of a nightmare, though a beautiful one … Her turns looked blown by some unearthly wind. And the almost convulsive gesture of her arms and head when she came flush with his suddenly dead body, her white sleeves hanging like sculptured wings, had a look of terrifying, cataclysmic truth.

Thin as a rail from anorexia and hopelessly dependent on cocaine, Kirkland turned herself in real life into the martyred classical heroine. She didn't even need to act in order to portray those doomed child-women who expired of broken hearts and betrayal or jumped over the ramparts to their untimely death. Kirkland's memoir is a testament to her rebellion. When her book appeared she was reviled by the ballet fraternity, who closed ranks against her (well they would, wouldn't they?) and denied her allegations about misconduct in the profession.

If you ask ballerinas why they're willing to accept pain and physical deformity as part of their work, and why modern choreographers continue to demand pointework, they'll glaze over, refusing to even consider this question. Since ballerinas are above all obedient, they'll tell you it's beautiful, it's a necessary aspect of ballet technique and there's an end of it. But beauty is in the eye of the beholder, and close-up camera-work shows that even the most technically skilled, not to say famous, ballerina looks like a wobbly stork as she clings to her partner for support and tries to remain upright on the tip of one fragile foot.

One of the best-known *pas de deux*, the Rose Adagio in *The Sleeping Beauty*, shows Princess Aurora's three suitors each, in turn, displaying her as she balances on pointe. She revolves slowly on the spot, holding onto her beau as her body revolves like a mechanical doll on its plinth; then, her back to the audience for a brief moment, she provides the audience with a full-on view of her knickers.

When a cancan dancer lifted her leg and showed the audience her knickers it was considered scandalous, for it was done in a spirit of wild rebellion. But there was no such scandal when a ballerina was held aloft, a choice cut of meat, legs open like a pair of scissors, while her partner marched her round the stage, displaying her crotch to the ogling audience. Every dance has its own body language and includes movements that may be richly comic when we analyse them. But only in ballet are we expected to think that utterly ludicrous moves are sublimely beautiful.

***

At the end of the eighteenth century the French Revolution swept away constricting dress for women and replaced it with loose-fitting robes after the style of ancient Greece. Ballerinas performed in their everyday clothes rather than specially designed dance costumes. So when a more comfortable fashion, as well as soft shoes, became popular they were seized on. Freedom from the cumbersome layers of clothing which had limited women's movement naturally affected how they danced, and a more fluid style began developing. In time the pendulum of fashion swung back towards the artificial once again. Ballerinas stayed put in their gauzy skirts, but they adopted the boned bodices which constricted the upper body and supported a rigid, unmoving torso, and even today these uncomfortable corseted tops are still worn for the classical repertoire.

In an age when it was still considered shocking to see a woman's ankles, the costumes of these gossamer-winged creatures, who pirouetted across the stage like a breath of scented air, were designed to show off their bodies. The tutu was a risqué little number whose length gradually crept up from twelve inches off the floor in the 1830s to mid-thigh length by the end of the century. The propriety of these costumes was a constant subject of debate. For modesty's sake, opaque tights or 'fleshings' were worn beneath the tutu. In Italy the Pope decreed that, in theatres under his authority, dancers' fleshings had to be blue, so as not to incite wanton thoughts.

After the 1830 revolution court patronage of the Paris Opéra gave way to commercial enterprise. With increasing numbers of the bourgeoisie frequenting the opera for their evening's entertainment, their wealth and influence began dictating the kind of work presented there. By the 1860s it had become fashionable to attend the Opéra. The wonderfully gossipy Goncourt brothers described an evening there in their journal:

> It is wonderful what a centre of debauchery the theatre is ... invisible threads criss-cross between dancers' legs, actresses' smiles and spectators' opera glasses, presenting an overall picture of Pleasure, Orgy and Intrigue. It would be impossible to gather together in a smaller space a greater number of sexual stimulants, of invitations to copulation. It is like a stock exchange dealing in women's nights.

Spending an evening at this state-subsidized bastion of French culture was a complicated business. There were intervals for refreshments and milling around, for seeing and being seen, and patrons rarely bothered arriving at the beginning and staying to the end. What was crucial, though, was to be there for the short ballets inserted into the main action.

Men about town attended rehearsals, creating a busy backstage traffic. While exhausted young ballerinas wiped off the sweat and sat, legs outstretched on the dusty wooden floor, suitors presented their credentials to their gimlet-eyed mothers who waited in the wings. It was considered a great coup to gain access to the dimly lit backstage area, with its practice barre and floor sloping down to the giant mirror which reflected the goings-on there. It was in this rehearsal space that wild parties were organized (and, it is said, ballerinas were sometimes served up on silver platters). In the words of the Comte de Maugny, one of the toffs who hung around backstage:

> I have seen maidens departing triumphantly on an admirer's arm after a good quarter of an hour's discussion with maman. I have seen some disappear secretly behind their duenna's back, leaving her prey to epileptic seizure, and others carrying on brazenly beneath their very nose and receiving a volley of blows that would have terrified a stout porter.

It wasn't easy to obtain a backstage pass, and demand was greater than supply. Many of the men who hung around were members of the exclusive Jockey Club, whose president, the Vicomte Paul Daru, was described striding around at the ballet like a sultan in a seraglio. Others familiar with backstage life were fashionable men about town, ballet critics like Théophile Gautier and the artist Degas.

Degas' portraits of ballerinas are so well known to us from the walls of schools and hospitals and town halls that we give them no more than a passing glance. So it's interesting to look at these paintings, knowing it was the Parisian underworld which Degas was chronicling; that the sylphs in their pastel tutus and the hobgoblins who preyed on them were playing out their fairy-tale stage roles for real. Degas' *Backstage at the Paris Opéra* includes more portly, top-hatted gents than dancers. Ballerinas are shown smiling timidly up at white-haired, mustachioed men who stand, legs straddled, looking down on them. They lean on their walking sticks, appraising the girls from on high, while stage-hands go about their business humping scenery.

Degas maintained, tongue in cheek, that taking dancers as his subject was 'a pretext for painting pretty costumes and representing movements'. Like other Impressionist painters he set out to chronicle contemporary urban life, and he homed in on the world of laundresses and ballerinas, especially the little *rats* of the corps de ballet. He was fascinated by the contrasting professions: the drudgery of one, the glamour of the other; fascinated by the effort and sweat involved in both of them. His stout laundresses labour away at their tubs, a lock of hair falling over their faces, doubled over with exhaustion. Sisters under the skin, Degas' washerwomen and dancers are shown straining and rubbing their aching muscles in just the same way. We can see a beauty in all their effort and it's interesting that Degas was reviled in his time for showing us the sweat and exhaustion of ballet, rather than the end result of all that labour.

The nineteenth-century ballet heroine is an enchanting, superhuman creature who appears to the hero in a dream. There she goes, flying through the air, luring mortal men into her magical kingdom. But being ethereal involves leaping about, which requires immense effort as well as good lungs and strong ankles. In those days ballet slippers didn't have blocked toes and ballerinas had to elevate the body and work their leg muscles hard in order to stay up on their toes. Classes were gruelling. A contemporary syllabus gives exercises to be performed 100 times each and positions, such as standing with one leg in the air, to be held for a count of 100. The celebrated Marie Taglioni is reported to have worked for two-hour periods, three times a day, while preparing for her debut.

Ballet hasn't always been performed in today's reverential atmosphere. Sometimes there were episodes of unexpected hilarity, such as the night when ballerina Clara Pilvois decided to revenge herself on a bullying dance master. In the middle of a scene in which she was supposed to be portraying a nun, she launched into a spirited cancan!

The Romantic ballet was a world of enchantment peopled by child-women and nymphs whose stories, with few exceptions, were told from the male point of view. In an age when sex was surrounded by fear of contagion, the moral was that physical union between a man and woman could be fatal, and that only in the afterlife could the sexes safely unite. So it's fitting that the ethereal temptresses of ballet had a quality more troubling than their angelic appearance suggested. Hans Christian Andersen's 1833 review of the *Ballet of the Nuns* at the Paris Opéra describes this kind of female creature:

> By the hundred they rise from the graveyard and drift into the cloister. They seem not to touch the earth. Like vaporous images, they glide past one another. Suddenly their shrouds fall to the ground. They stand in all their voluptuous nakedness, and there begins a bacchanal like those that took place during their lifetimes, hidden within the walls of the convent.

New technology helped emphasize the unearthly nature of ballet's vaporous heroines. Oil lamps and reflectors diffused and softened the light, creating a magical ambience which was heightened by the use of smoke machines, waterfalls and other ingenious new stage effects. The glow of gas lighting gave the plainest of dancers what was called a 'footlights kind of beauty' and there was the same fascinated public interest in them as there is in today's rock stars.

The Romantic ballet, after all, was created for a largely male audience whose prime objective was to ogle the female body on display. Dancers were celebrated in the purple prose of critics who were mainly interested in describing their bodies. Gautier, who wrote the scenario for *Giselle*, took it upon himself to lay down some guidelines and suggested, 'A dancer's smile should play about her mouth like a bird hovering above a rose, unable to land without damaging it.'

Ballerinas worked long hours for little pay and there were risks involved in working in theatres lit by gas or oil lamps with naked flames. Together with dancers' flimsy costumes, this lighting created a fire hazard. At the Paris Opéra ballerinas were ordered to dip their costumes in fireproofing solution. Emma Livry, a member of the corps de ballet, thought this would make her tutu look dull and refused to dip it, and as a result it caught fire. (She wasn't the only dancer to whom this happened.) After months of agony she died from her severe burns.

When the cancan was criticized for revealing a dancer's legs, the French writer Larousse was moved to protest:

> Is there not a huge contradiction between seeing a woman thrown out of a public dance hall for lifting her leg, while 200 dancers, in short dresses, lift them even higher, to the universal applause of an audience in the opera house?

The cancan was a spontaneous affront, a pouring of scorn on acceptable female behaviour. After all, how much more shocking could a woman get than to stand there holding one leg above her head while her gaping skirts drew spectators' eyes to her crotch? Yet the little *rats* of the corps de ballet were doing just the same within the confines of a choreography. Charles Leland, an early tourist who visited Egypt in the 1870s, compared the 'impropriety' of ballet with the dance he saw in Cairo:

> Sometimes two [Egyptian] girls dance a duo; and I have seen this made quite as improper, though not as sickly sentimental, as in any opera house in Europe, when the ballerina falls back into the male object's arms, eyeing him with a leering smile, while she lifts one leg to the gallery.

Today the classical ballerina is still lifting one leg to the gallery; still being carried round the stage in the arms of her partner, parading her crotch before the audience. Only now the skirt of her tutu has become abbreviated to a stiff halo around her knickers, which keeps her partner well away from her pelvis. And what's most peculiar about the whole thing is the art world's reverence for what has become, despite moments of loveliness, essentially an art of high camp.

***

Romantic ballets are oblique lessons in correct behaviour. Like myths and fairy tales they open the door to a garden of enchantment where good and evil, love and lust are engaged in a duel to the death. From the early ballets of the 1830s like *La Sylphide* and *Giselle* down to *Swan Lake,* which appeared in the 1890s, their stories are often stories of class conflict. The hero – an eligible prince – rejects the stifling conventions of his class and goes in search of a more exciting consort than the suitable wife who has been lined up for him. His eye may be caught by a peasant girl, but the pull of class generally overcomes a youthful urge to rebel and our spineless hero ends up abandoning his lower-class mistress, who dies of a broken heart. The situation grows more complicated if he falls in love with another type of ballet heroine: an animated doll or fairy who is under the spell of a wicked magician. These creatures tend to be ultimately unattainable because . . . well, because you can't actually consort with a fairy woman. And the only way of making an enduring connection with a creature who is half-ghost, half-water-sprite is to die and join her in the afterlife.

These allegorical creatures have none of women's messy biology. The *sylphide* is an apparition destined to disappear and leave her prince disappointed as she floats off into the ether. The swan, a favourite of the period, symbolizes an innocent beauty as cold as the water which is her element. *Swan Lake* was created during the era of *fin-de-siècle* decadence, when artists were fascinated by the macabre and the occult as well as by the infant discipline of psychology. A recurring image in Decadent art is woman as mythical creature: sphinx, mermaid, medusa. Sometimes her animal nature is emphasized by the habit of consorting with panthers and snakes.

In *Swan Lake* an evil magician traps the heroine Odette in the body of a swan. By day she is a virginal white swan and it's this vision of icy loveliness which entrances Prince Siegfried, who worships her from afar. Between the hours of midnight and dawn, Odette's place is taken by an imposter, the magician's daughter Odile. She appears as the black swan, whose steps reflect a more earthy sensuality and wantonness. No wonder the prince's eyes light up at the antics of Odile. He's happy to have fun with the black swan, but it's the white swan he loves, or rather, wants to possess. Gradually his control of her grows until we finally see him pinning her arms behind her back, preventing her from taking flight. As we might imagine, the story ends in tears.

These tales were created during a period when men's dominance of ballet was on the wane. Until then men had been the organizers, teachers, creators and theorists, as well as the stars of ballet, and female dancers didn't cut nearly such a dash. In the nineteenth century men lost their pre-eminence as performers, though they continued to dominate in every other department. Gautier declared that men had no place in the ballet: 'A male dancer is something monstrous and indecent which we cannot conceive ... Strength is the only grace permissible to men.' Male dancers gritted their teeth and became 'lifters', obliged to cart their partners around the stage, showing them off to the audience like exquisitely garnished dishes.

It was during this period that the female body took over from the male as the measure of human beauty. For 2,000 years the male nude, shown in vigorous action, had been considered the epitome of strength and nobility and had been central to arts training in the West. The female body which knocked the male off its pedestal represented a different kind of beauty. Rather than active, it was passive and receptive.

In order to prevent spectators having 'impure' thoughts of sex while contemplating it, the female nude in sculpture and painting was placed in an allegorical setting. So we can imagine the stir created by Manet's *Olympia* when it was first exhibited in Paris in 1863. This portrait of a nude woman suggests the opposite of passivity. Nor is she dignified by being placed in the context of a classical morality tale. Olympia lacks the downcast eyes of a virtuous woman. She stares out insolently from the canvas, one hand defiantly covering her crotch, while in the background her black maid carries an offering from a potential customer: a big bouquet of flowers in which – who knows? – perhaps there nestles a case of valuable jewellery.

The painting was exhibited at a time when women were taking a greater part in public life than ever before, especially in entertainment. As stars of the Romantic ballet, they were the working-class heroines of their day. The roles created for them reflected images of women which were common currency then: images on the one hand of delicate flowers and pale, consumptive beauties, and, on the other, of *femmes fatales* who were the bearers of disease and death and whose sexuality was dangerous and rampant.

The wilis in *Giselle* are the ghosts of young girls who were jilted and died before their wedding day. They revenge themselves on men by dancing to death any man they discover roaming around at night. In this way they simultaneously satisfy more than one popular stereotype: not only are they dead women, but even in death they retain the power of the *femme fatale*. Their ghostly frailty – the same popular famished frailty of tubercular women – was also a sign of erotic potency. In *Time and the Dancing Image*, Deborah Jowitt suggests that male members of the audience may well have associated the heroines' hungry look with the idea of sexual appetite.

Ballet has been described as 'sanitized sex' and as 'elevating the pastime of girl watching to a classic art'. And, like other critics, Gautier was an enthusiastic girl watcher: '[Fanny Elssler's] leg, smooth as marble, gleamed through the frail mesh of her silk stockings,' he wrote. Gautier wasn't the only one to dissolve into raptures at the sight of this dancer's dimpled knees or the sheen of her flesh. In 1843 the *Illustrated London Life* recalled with humour:

> We perfectly recollect ... admiring the emotion of several ancient aristocrats in the stalls, on the recent appearance of the legs of Fanny Elssler. We thought that we observed one aged and respectable virtuoso shedding tears; another fainted in his satin breeks and diamond buckles, one appeared to go mad, and bit his neighbour's pigtail in half in sheer ecstasy. Oh! The legs of Fanny displaced a vast deal of propriety, and frightened sober men from their prescribed complacency.

Gautier and his friends were writing about ballet in an age when the soft contours of the female body, a plump knee and well-rounded elbow, were much admired. The French even had a word for this fleshy abundance: *embonpoint.* Today, in many non-Western cultures a woman with *embonpoint* is still appreciated while a skinny body is regarded askance.

In the mid-nineteenth century an Arab sheikh wrote of European women, 'They are winter plants, colourless and tasteless, with sickly faces tormented with hunger. They hardly eat and are thin, poor mad creatures.' Gautier was distinctly anti-ballet at the start of his critical career and contrasted ballerinas unfavourably with the Spanish dancers he had seen in Andalusia:

> They escape that leanness, like that of a horse in training, which gives our ballets such a macabre anatomical touch ... They preserve the rounded contours of their sex; they look like women dancing, not dancing women, which is quite a different thing. In Spain the feet hardly leave the ground; there are none of those grand pirouettes or elevations of the legs which make a woman look like a pair of compasses, stretched to its limits, and which are considered in Andalusia revoltingly indecent.

Gautier mocked one ballerina with the comment that she wasn't even substantial enough to play the part of a shadow, and wrote scathingly of dancers whose shoulder-blades stuck out 'like two bony triangles that resemble the roots of a torn-off wing'. Today bony triangles are considered just perfect for the job; some dancers even use make-up to accentuate their back and collar-bones.

The seeds of anorexia were sown in the late nineteenth century, when Western women began starving themselves in order to imitate the undernourished, feverish look of tuberculosis sufferers. Symbolist paintings of the time show dead women with skeletal bodies and an almost erotic expression of pain on their faces.

The early feminist Abba Goold Woolson commented that women apparently existed on air and moonlight and were reluctant 'to commit the unpardonable sin of eating in the presence of men'. The battle between spirit and flesh gave rise to books like Dr T. C. Duncan's 1878 volume, *How to be Plump,* which urged women to eat: 'The lean are restless and irritable in mind, rarely contented, never quiet … They form the complaining element of society,' he wrote disapprovingly. But for nineteenth-century dance critic Ezra Tharp, 'There is nothing so handsome as a skeleton, as the drop and set and hang of the bones.'

By the beginning of the twentieth century voices were beginning to be raised in protest against the ideal of the animated skeleton. They advocated physical exercise, protested against constricting dress and urged women to eat properly and enjoy their bodies. But by the 1960s the feminist movement was citing the body as a source of oppression. It focused on controlling female reproduction, and the possibility that the body might be a source of pleasure, creativity and physical vitality tended to be overlooked.

Today a different type of repression holds sway, based on the unremitting demand that women display their bodies – but only if they conform to prevailing ideals of female beauty and are of the required stick-insect slimness. Horrifying stories can be found in the press every week in which adolescent girls tell how they have dieted after their boyfriends criticized them for being fat. One fifteen-year-old dutifully dieted, only to be told by the same spotty boyfriend that she was now too thin.

The modern skinny ideal recalls Deborah Jowitt's comment about the link, in the eyes of male observers, between this famished look and a woman's sexual hunger. Meanwhile, the late-twentieth-century fashion photographers' use of adolescent girls with the black-rimmed, hollow eyes of drug addicts had an obvious parallel with the late-nineteenth-century vogue for the look of dying tuberculosis sufferers. Dance historian Walter Sorell comments, 'If we can speak of a near-epidemic disease as fashionable, then consumption was high fashion in the nineteenth century.' Today's fashionable disease is anorexia, and it is provoked by the media, which bombard us with images of food while at the same time promoting the undernourished female as the acme of beauty. On one hand, the siren song of food calls us from every side, from cafés, restaurants and bookshops, from TV programmes and magazines. On the other, the nursery word 'naughty' is used to describe food, turning us into guilty children when we succumb to the entirely natural urge to eat. Starve the body, feed the spirit.

Where once the aristocracy were the creators of fashion, performers have long since taken their place. By the late 1980s the vogue for increasingly skinny dancers was even influencing the world of haute couture. Like today's standard-issue apples, a ballerina's body has to have a certain uniform look.

If she's too tall she'll be chucked out of the barrel. The corps de ballet is a chorus line of identical bodies making identical movements – a reflection of the soothing belief that one woman is much like another. (There's no male chorus line in ballet, nor are male dancers required to conform so exactly to type.) Ballet doesn't accept the glorious diversity of women's bodies: curves ruin a dancer's 'line', which is so important that her health has to be sacrificed to it.

The animated skeleton was Balanchine's ideal and Kirkland records how he tapped her on the ribs and told her he wanted to see her bones. She was happy to oblige:

> I starved by day, then binged on junk food and threw up by night. I stuffed myself with laxatives, thyroid pills and celery juice; I emptied myself with enemas and steam baths. I became an expert with the technique of shoving two fingers down my throat.

The fashion and dance gestapo have a huge investment in exploiting the female body as a commodity, and the media are their most powerful ally. In the recent backlash against the tyranny of the ultra-slim ideal, journalists sprang into defensive mode. The then-editor of British *Elle* said she was irritated by the 'slim girl witch hunt' (conveniently ignoring the fat girl witch hunt which has been raging for years). She claimed that models were 'upset' by the 'current wave of body fascism' (how upset have women been for years when told that nobody will love them unless they lose weight?).

When the British edition of *Marie Claire* offered two different covers – one of Pamela Anderson, complete with silicone-enhanced breasts, the other of buxom Sophie Dahl – the one with Dahl sold most copies. Their editor at the time was an ex-anorexic who later confessed that she had had blackout blinds fitted in her bedroom and wouldn't let her boyfriend see her without her T-shirt on. Following the triumph of the gorgeous Sophie, she wrote that in future, *Marie Claire* would use a greater variety of models. But they have yet to appear in her magazine. The fact is that Sophie Dahl was the token big beauty on the block. The following edition of *Marie Claire* had a skinny model named Gisela on the cover, together with the headline, 'Looking for the new Gisela'. (Why not 'Looking for the new Sophie'?) The same editor told readers that hugging this model was like hugging a bag of bones, but went on to say, 'Even now, if I'm at a fashion shoot I can still find myself thinking, "I want to be like that."' It must have been upsetting for poor Gisela to learn that, in her moment of cover-girl glory, and despite fulfilling the necessary stick-insect criteria, her replacement was already being sought.

Meanwhile British *Vogue*'s editor commented that you don't catch an eating disorder by looking through a copy of her magazine. Journalists like to pass the buck by saying they are simply giving us what we want. But in the modern world we know that the marketing business and the media influence us more than any other institution. It's they who create concepts of beauty which lead women like dim little lemmings rushing for the cliff's edge.

There are many, complex reasons why women punish themselves. But it's still astonishing that so many, especially those who don't depend on their looks for a living, aren't prepared to rebel against conforming to a self-harming body image. It seems that a great many women have had their faculty for self-preservation surgically removed.

***

The idea of the natural female body as a dangerous, imperfect thing which needs to be controlled and altered has never been more alive than it is today, and eating disorders are only the tip of the iceberg. Twenty years ago women's magazines carried few ads for surgical intervention in the name of 'beauty'. Now the back pages are full of them. Twenty years ago few women were prepared to put themselves under the surgeon's knife unless they were ill. Now even teenagers are saving up for operations on their still-developing bodies. It's becoming so normal to stuff your body full of alien substances that this is seen as no different to using make-up. At a recent health and beauty exhibition in Bristol, alongside massage, hair plaiting and all sorts of other benign treats, I found the promotion of collagen, Botox and cosmetic surgery.

While still a teenager Gelsey Kirkland made her first foray into the world of what is euphemistically called 'body remodelling' and had breast implants. She also had her earlobes snipped off and silicone injected in her ankles and lips. At that time the injection of silicone was illegal but, as she says, the most ludicrous aspect of the entire experiment was that the changes were so minuscule they were hardly perceptible from the audience. Kirkland isn't the only dancer who has succumbed to cosmetic surgery, and in a profession which idealizes the unsexed female, ballerinas are just as likely to have surgery to reduce their breasts as to enlarge them.

All that nipping and tucking is the supreme power trip for cosmetic surgeons, most of whom are male. It's a kind of pornography, a form of sado-masochism which illuminates a shadowy hinterland in the psyche where true loathing for woman's body resides. Surgeons start by cutting off a woman's nipples, slicing into her delicate breasts and pumping them full of silicone. There's a problem with silicone? Never mind, they just open them up again and try soya bean oil instead. That ought to do the trick. That's worth another £1,000. And so it goes on.

One article I came across recently even threw out the challenge that, since such practices are now 'common', what reason is there to resist? We can all be Stepford women now. Meanwhile doctors in the British National Health Service are prepared to give adolescent girls 'stretching' operations to make them the required height for a future career as an air hostess or model. Operations like this involve breaking the bones and inserting a metal pin in the legs to give them an extra few inches. And for those who later change their minds and decide they want to become brain surgeons, well, all that pain will just have to be put down to experience.

Equally shocking is the fashion for injecting Botox between the eyes to get rid of wrinkles. One sad little interview I read was with a 41-year-old Botox fan who said it had given a massive boost to her confidence. Her husband told her he loved the fact that if she was cross with him, or feeling ill or unhappy, he couldn't tell any longer as her face muscles were frozen. So now women are happily injecting themselves with a deadly virus, freezing muscles which give expression to the face. You couldn't make it up if you tried.

**

Rebels in ballet are few and far between. Nonconformists usually don't even find a foothold on the ladder. But there's one ballerina who reached the pinnacle of creative success even though she was a born outsider and as unlike the conventional ballerina as it's possible to be. So powerfully did she enter into her roles, she even made you forget she was following the ridiculous convention of dancing on pointe.

At the height of her fame, she danced *Five Brahms Waltzes in the Manner of Isadora*. The words 'the ballet's greatest dramatic dancer' invariably appear in descriptions of her, and though her last great roles were in the 1970s no ballerina has since appeared with an even remotely similar splendour. She gave up dancing many years ago, though she still appears occasionally as guest artist for modern dance companies. No one who has seen her light up the stage could fail to be moved by her artistry for, apart from all the other qualities which make her such a riveting performer, she is that rare thing in the world of ballet: a real woman dancing, rather than a dancing doll.

Lynn Seymour looked different from other ballerinas. Her body was soft and voluptuous, the wrong kind of body for ballet. 'You should have steel wire in the middle of you somewhere. I haven't. I have something more like sponge rubber,' she said in one interview. She had full thighs, gorgeous fleshy shoulders and what one critic called 'Cleopatra arms'. Her movements were unconventional. Rehearsing *Swan Lake*, a coach called out to her once, 'You're not a swan at all. Those legs of yours – why, you're like a snake!' She rejected the pouts and fluttering eyelashes of classical ballet's sugar-coated heroines and in their place substituted what she has described as 'a bit of the hoyden'. In her darker, tragic roles her sensuality disturbed critics who prefer a more antiseptic, androgynous type of female. But those who had no time for the child-women and boy-girls of classical ballet adored her. They rejoiced at seeing a dancer on-stage with a ripe womanly body rather than an animated anorexic.

Seymour's great stroke of luck was to attract the attention of choreographer Kenneth MacMillan, who introduced provocative sexual themes in his work, delved into the female psyche and explored the sadism rather than the sentiment of ballet's fairy stories. MacMillan accepted Seymour's style without trying to change it. She, for her part, put flesh on the bones of his complex heroines, who were far from being fairy creatures on pedestals. They were recognizable women, and Seymour was skilled at finding their inner truth and portraying it with intensity and simplicity. She is described as MacMillan's muse but she was more than a blank canvas: she was his collaborator. Her special style of movement, her dramatic ability and her own creativity made a significant contribution to his work.

Seymour admits that she never fitted into the Barbara Cartland ballet world. She says she could not remake her body and would not remake her personality. For its part the ballet establishment regarded her as a rebel who lived an unconventional life and flouted their unspoken conventions. At a chichi party Seymour once overheard a famous female guest remark to a critic, 'I can't understand why ballerinas have children. It is almost unacceptable.' Clearly the liberated sixties had not yet reached the ballet world.

In Seymour's day ballerinas dressed like debutantes, hobnobbed with the elite and retreated from the world of work to marry men with money and titles: Seymour didn't. Other ballerinas didn't try and combine dancing with having children: Seymour did. As the Royal Ballet's then director Ninette de Valois commented, 'Lynn was a rebel. I'm very fond of rebels. But they must be controlled.'

The most brutal attempt to control Seymour involved MacMillan's *Romeo and Juliet*. She had been intensely involved in its creation and had also made a profound sacrifice in her personal life in order to play the role of Juliet. But when the cast lists were posted, instead of appearing at the premiere she was scheduled to perform last in the role she had helped shape. She was given the job of teaching the role to Margot Fonteyn (who danced the premiere) as well as all the other Juliets who preceded her. Fonteyn didn't care for Juliet's more daring actions, which had been Seymour's contribution, and changed them, with the other Juliets following suit. Instead of stabbing herself in the womb, as Seymour did, Fonteyn stabbed herself in the heart. Instead of dying with her legs splayed, she died with her feet neatly crossed. In this way MacMillan and Seymour's modern Juliet was relegated to the shadows and replaced by the old insipid stereotype.

The decision to let Seymour appear only after the critics had had their say, and after a string of other dancers had had a go at the role, appears to have been a deliberate ploy by management to humble Seymour. She wrote that she felt as if her ego had been removed, leaving her lobotomized and impotent: '[It was] my punishment, for falling in love and getting married and then being careless enough to get pregnant – a greater offence in a young dancer than an abortion.'

In an interview years later she said it had been perfectly reasonable to take the premiere away from her: 'I wasn't a particularly good dancer at the time. I'm terribly painfully aware of that.' But she always had something more compelling than technical proficiency. At the time, the *Romeo and Juliet* debacle led to despair and a breakdown. Seymour says she 'pulled up the old socks' and continued on her way. But after that she was no longer prepared to let ballet consume her life. Never again would she sacrifice herself to the transitory glories of the stage. She continued dancing while bringing up her three sons. Then at the age of forty-two suddenly, dramatically, she quit.

She had returned to the Royal Ballet after having a hysterectomy, flinging herself once more into the breach. The BBC was making a documentary about her and filmed her working out at the barre. We watch her balancing on pointe, her ankle shaking, her face trembling with pain as she struggles to get back into shape. In the middle of rehearsals she tears her Achilles tendon – a particularly serious injury, given that a broken Achilles tendon means not only the end of dancing but even the end of walking normally.

For Seymour the game was up. But in not one of her interviews is there a trace of bitterness in her voice as she talks about the ups and downs of her career. Indeed, she is careful to excuse the harsh treatment by management which floored her emotionally and drove her out after years of dedication. 'I once vowed I would never give up dancing; it would be like severing a limb,' she wrote in her autobiography. 'But sometimes a dancer must lose her life in order to find it.'

***

Every second, somewhere in the world, two Barbie dolls are sold to little girls between the ages of three and ten. Apparently they hang onto their Barbies long after they've thrown their other toys in the bin. 'Ballet is all about fantasy. So is Barbie,' said the company's chief executive after striking a sponsorship deal with English National Ballet in 2001. 'But we certainly don't want to be tacky,' he added. Other ballet companies responded sniffily to the deal and former Royal Ballet board member Lady Deborah MacMillan said it all sounded 'terribly naff. But then little girls are terribly naff too.' The operations director of Arts & Business was beside himself with enthusiasm for the deal: 'Those who enjoy the Barbie brand may well be encouraged to go to the ballet,' he said. 'This Barbie sponsorship is an excellent match.'

So now, all those terribly naff little girls will be clutching their new Barbie dolls in one hand as they go trotting off to see the Sugar Plum Fairy. Their eyes will continue to light up at the sight of the baby-pink tutus and glittering tiaras. The deeper meaning of classical ballet's fairy tales will remain hidden, and nobody will be there to tell aspiring ballerinas that, even if they're fortunate, their brilliant careers will be brief and painful. By the time they're lacing themselves into their blocked satin slippers and making their first tentative steps on pointe they will have passed the point of no return. There's no way they will suspect that they are going to have to pay in spades for putting on the red shoes.

Dance of the Seven Veils

*The paradox was that she was so immediately sensual,
and yet so remote, unapproachable, unobtainable.*
Edward Said

Arabic dance was the door through which I entered the dance world one
winter's night back in 1980. A friend took me to see an Egyptian dancer
perform her solo show in an old London synagogue, which was being
converted into a theatre. We skirted round piles of rubble and piping and
breeze-blocks, clutching our beakers of cheap wine as we crossed the foyer
to the auditorium. Fifty or so people sat bundled in coats, scarves and hats
and I followed suit and kept my outdoor clothes on, for the gas jets set high
on the bare brick walls sent out little in the way of heat. Suspended at the
back of the stage was a hanging depicting a pharaonic banquet scene, but it
was dingy and faded and my heart sank. It would have taken more effort of
imagination than I could muster, that freezing night, to transport myself
mentally to the blazing heat of Egypt.

The hour for the show to begin came and went and we sat there, still
waiting. I asked myself whether it had been a mistake, venturing out to see
someone I'd never heard of perform a dance I knew nothing about. Besides
which, I wasn't even particularly interested in dance at the time!

My musings were cut short by an abrupt fanfare of drums, like a herald
rapping at the door. A corner of the hanging was thrown aside and a small,
dusky figure bounded onto the stage. She wore a calf-length orange *galabia*,
caught in at the hips by a red and yellow striped sash, and her toenails were
painted poppy red. Padding about the stage on the balls of her feet, she
extended an arm in welcome and swept across the floor, hips pumping this

way and that and up and down. She was like a flame shooting up. Sometimes she moved with the soft spring of a panther, sometimes she prowled about the floor with the flexible spine of a cat. Her dancing was a fusion of raw power and fierce, purposeful energy. I was transfixed.

After a while the music changed and the lights dimmed. The dancer stepped into a small circle of light and waited, motionless, as if hypnotized by the languor of the single flute. A sequence of notes on this *nai* sent a shivering motion up and down her spine. Her arms began to lift, at first imperceptibly, then curving out to either side of her body, rippling delicately from her shoulders all the way down to her fingertips. Her arms traced sinuous patterns, hands shifting and stroking the air as they created shapes and carefully placed them. There she stood, lost in her own private world of slow-motion meditation. Then a solo *qanun* began to play, a zither-like instrument which set up a shimmering vibration of notes. Planting herself on the spot, she drove her heels into the floor and set her hips shimmying. The movement travelled up her torso, making it quiver as if she had an electric current shooting right through her.

Then came the low notes of a *tabla*, recalling her to us with a series of complex rhythms to which the audience began clapping in time. Flashing us a wide smile she began playing with these rhythms, drawing on a set of hip movements which even I could see were of dazzling complexity. She wheeled round, presenting us with her bottom, flung a farewell over her shoulder and with a cheeky flick of the hip was gone.

I knew that night that I'd discovered something which was going to involve me with a passion. One thing I grasped very early on, though, in my involvement with Arabic dance, was that I'd entered a kind of underworld. For no dance has been so misunderstood outside its own culture, nor so debased by commercialism. No dance has awoken such a complex response in its audience, nor been described by outsiders in such detail. And while other dances, such as Indian and flamenco, have managed to break free of their former shady associations, Arabic dance has been slow to do so. Even now, to many people's minds, it remains synonymous with stripping and, to many Muslims, being a professional dancer is not unlike being a whore.

Accounts of women's hip dancing in the countries surrounding the shores of the Mediterranean have come down to us from ancient times. It once played a part in fertility rites, celebrating women's creative power, and as we have seen, vestiges of this old symbolic significance still cling to it. One classical Greek dance was distinguished by rotating movements of the hips and belly and was compared to the action of a pestle and mortar – which rather contradicts the popular idea of ancient Greek dancing as being decorous and elegant. A hundred years after the death of Christ, in southern Spain, where merchants from Phoenicia (present-day Lebanon) established themselves, dancers were described 'sinking down to the floor with quivering thighs'. Later on, in the seventh century, a Persian scholar described the skills required by great dancing as 'loose joints and a great agility in twirling and swaying the hips'.

This solo dance of women survived and became a sophisticated art in Egypt, where it is known simply as *raqs baladi* (dance of the people). But *baladi* was seldom written about in its own culture and most descriptions of it until very recently came from the pens of Western travellers. Dancers were the only members of the female sex whom these outsiders freely encountered. They found the open sensuality of the dance, as well as the women's unveiled faces, a surprising sight in a culture where the female body is kept under wraps. Travellers described *baladi* in great detail, its undulating hips, serpentine spine and shimmying torso, its hypnotic effect and inner calm. As French author Charles Gobineau noted:

> Hours pass, and it is difficult to tear oneself away. This is how the motions of the dancing girls affect the senses. There is no variety or vivacity, and seldom is there a variation through any sudden movement, but the rhythmic wheeling exerts a delightful torpor upon the soul, like an almost hypnotic intoxication.

It was from the mid-nineteenth century onwards, the heyday of Orientalism, when all things Eastern were in vogue, that travellers began exploring the region in earnest. In Egypt they met the *ghawazee*. These professional dancers of gypsy blood came from tribes of entertainers who had been expelled from India many generations before, for their thieving and outlaw ways.

The *ghawazee* lived on the fringes of society, along with other immigrants, gypsies and Jews, and while they may have paid lip service to Islam it didn't stop them continuing to practise their customs in private. They performed in the open air for coins tossed at their feet, coins which they sewed into their costumes or converted into jewellery. They wore shawls tied round their hips and in their hair gold coins which, along with their finger cymbals and jewellery, lent the dancing an added air of festive femininity. The *ghawazee* entertained travellers on the steps of Cairo's newly built Shepheard's Hotel and were sometimes hired to entertain in private, where they performed all kinds of circus-like antics, such as dancing with candlesticks or trays of tea glasses on their heads. One particularly supple dancer was described lying on her back with two glasses balanced on her stomach, which she proceeded to clink together in time to the music, using only her muscles. Others had a teasing charm:

> They twined round each other, snake-like, with a suppleness and a grace such as I have never seen before. One of the *ghawazee* took a little glass filled with rosewater between her teeth, and held it so without spilling a drop while she executed the most rapid and difficult movements. Then she stepped up to one of the male spectators, leaned forward and slowly poured the rosewater over his clothes, let the glass drop, kissed his lips and bounded back into the middle of the room.

Some travellers initially found the *ghawazee* distasteful, prompted by an unconscious religious guilt, an inner voice telling them that the women's easy-going sensuality was something they ought not to be watching; that it was dangerous to their moral well-being. But if some were disturbed by what they saw, there were others, refugees from the puritanism of Western culture, whose response was different. They discovered a beauty and vitality in the earthy sensuality of the women and described their dancing in painstaking detail. One thing was certain: no one who saw them remained indifferent though some, like Maupassant, found them unnerving:

> We follow our guide, groping about in the narrow street, lighting matches to see our way. Sometimes we hear muffled voices, strains of music, the murmur of wild festivities coming from far away, a terrifying feeling of deadened sound and mystery. The dancers are decked out in fairy-tale costumes. One of them, aged about fifteen, has two elongated black eyes like that of an idol, a face without expression. Where are we? In a temple of some barbaric religion? Never before have I experienced a sensation so unexpected, so new, so full of colour as I did when I came into this long, low room with these girls decked out, as if for a sacred cult.

From the 1850s onwards it was no longer necessary to visit the Middle East to see the dancers – who by then were one of Egypt's chief attractions, along with the Pyramids and the Sphinx – for they could be found at trade fairs in Europe and the United States. At the 1889 Paris Exposition Arabic dance was all the rage, while in the pleasure gardens attached to the Moulin Rouge, an Egyptian dancer performed (for men only) inside the belly of a plaster elephant. After Edmond de Goncourt had watched an Egyptian dancer perform, he commented in his diary: 'at this point three-quarters of the women in Paris are secretly working on this dance'.

When Middle Eastern dancers started to appear in person at these fairs there was disappointment all round, as well as shock and delight. They were nowhere near as graceful as the travel literature had led readers to believe and their dress was a far cry from the gossamer veils suggested by illustrations in the *Thousand and One Nights*. They danced with expressionless faces, seemingly detached from what they were doing, their faces reflecting the unease of performing in an alien setting which turned them into sideshow freaks.

We will never know exactly how those nineteenth-century dancers moved, though some of the more poetic accounts describe an art of great skill and subtlety. The fact that writers expressed initial disgust and shock probably wasn't only because the women moved their hips freely, or because the travellers came from a culture where movement below the waist wasn't a feature of dance. It was because the performance would have been, depending on circumstances, more or less designed to arouse. It was crude and earthy and it celebrated not the moonlight, candles and roses of romantic love but a more Rabelaisian sensuality.

Something of a romantic image has grown up around the *ghawazee* among Western women learning Egyptian dance today, an image based on those long-ago eulogies. But there must also have been quite a few performers who danced like the one in an 1896 short entitled *Danse du Ventre* or *Passion Dance*. This flickering black-and-white fragment features a woman wearing voluminous pantaloons, a transparent muslin chemise and a bodice which scarcely covers her enormous breasts. On her head a hat is perched at a rakish angle. With her arms open to embrace all comers and a broad grin on her face she sinks to her knees, wobbling her great mounds of lard and thrusting her pelvis at an unseen audience.

Americans queued at slot-machines to see this thirty-second peep-show, and it proved so popular that a self-appointed guardian of public morality decided to take a look. Needless to say, he found it shocking and had it withdrawn. Another short from the same period, *Fatima's Dance*, featured a more skilled performer and was one of the first films to be censored in the history of cinema. White bars were painted across every frame to hide the dancer's undulating hips, leaving only her face visible.

Meanwhile attempts were being made to ban dancers who performed at the great trade fairs. And if all this legal activity seems excessive, it wasn't the first time people had tried to suppress this women's dance. In the Middle East it also had its problems. In 1834 the *ghawazee* were banished from Cairo by Egypt's ruler, Mohammed Ali. He was modernizing the city with the help of Western advisers, and thought the dancers a bad advertisement for his new city. So he sent them up the Nile to Esna while at the same time raising taxes in Cairo to make up for the loss in revenue which resulted from their banishment. For those *ghawazee* who remained in Cairo life was hard. They ended up in hiding, plying their trade in secret. But the sound of drums and finger cymbals alerted police to their whereabouts and every night there were raids, followed by beatings, arrests and the obligatory journey up the Nile.

As in many societies, the line between dancer and prostitute was blurred. In a study of Egyptian dancers' lives, Karin van Nieuwkerk writes that making a move to prostitution was partly caused by the insecure and unsafe existence of entertainers. The celebrated dancer Kutchuk Hanem kept her jewellery with the town *sharif* and had a pimp to protect her. In Upper Egypt dancers were terrorized by bands of Albanian soldiers and by the police who continued to collect taxes from the *ghawazee*. The ruler who instigated this tax (known as 'Pimp Pasha') insisted on his pound of flesh despite the fact that the women's trade was, according to Islam, sinful and its wages therefore unclean. Lucie Duff Gordon, who lived in Egypt during the 1860s for health reasons, wrote:

> I saw one of the poor dancing girls the other day (there are three in Luxor) and she told me how cruel the new tax is on them. It is left to the discretion of the official who farms it to make each woman pay according to her presumed gains, i.e. her good looks.

The desire to remove the *ghawazee* from the public eye is only one indication of their outlaw power. Under Islam the sacred and the secular are indissolubly linked and it follows that recreational pursuits have to be reconciled with ethical principles. In order to earn a living, dancers transgressed a fundamental Muslim code of honour. Rather than remain within the home – the traditional sphere of female power and influence – they intruded on the male environment of public life. Not only that: in a culture where women were compelled to cover their faces in public, dancers did not do so. Worst of all, they danced in front of strangers, something no respectable woman would dream of doing.

Yet, however *déclassée* they may have been (and still are) in their own society, dancers have always been essential to family celebrations, where they bring luck and animate the festivities. Because respectable women didn't dance in public, here was a way for poor girls to earn an independent living. As outsiders they could enjoy benefits which counteracted their precarious social position, as well as a paradoxical freedom denied other women. They had nothing to lose and everything to gain from going where other women feared to tread. Nor were marriage and family life out of reach for them, and it's an interesting reversal of normal conditions in Muslim society that their men were dependent on them for a living.

In the Arab world, then as now, a family generally hopes for the birth of a son rather than a daughter. Yet among tribes of entertainers such as the *ghawazee* it is the women who are the breadwinners. Today the phrase 'son of a dancer' – *ibn al-raqasa* – is one of abuse. The word *ghawazee* translates as 'outsiders', 'invaders', and is also used as something of an insult. But the Maazin Sisters of Luxor, one of the best-known *ghawazee* troupes today, adroitly reverse this meaning when they describe themselves as 'invaders of the heart'. 'Even if they fight us,' says one of them, 'we go inside their heads and their hearts with our dancing. And they cannot forget us.'

***

Some time during the 1910s a set of photographs were taken of a group of Algerian dancers from the Ouled Nail tribe. Some of the dancers are little more than children, and one of them has such a striking face that her image has graced everything from postcards and books to posters and CD covers. In one photo she sits hugging another dancer from behind, as she looks out at the camera with an innocent expression on her face. In another she stares out at the onlooker with merciless eyes. This spirited-looking teenage dancer is still powerfully alive today, through those haunting images, though nobody knows her name.

Ouled Nail dancers inspired many artists during the nineteenth century. They were immortalized in the paintings of Georges Clairin, who depicted them as Amazons, leaning against sun-drenched white walls with cigarettes in their hands. Another French artist from the late nineteenth century, Etienne Dinet, married an Algerian woman and converted to Islam. He went to live in the home of the Ouled Nail, the oasis of Bou Saada, which means 'place of happiness', and devoted many years to creating a pictorial record of the dancers' lives.

In the early 1950s Lawrence Morgan spent a year in Bou Saada. He came to know the dancers well and his fascinating memoir *Flute of Sand* sympathetically describes their everyday lives as well as their dancing. Young girls followed custom handed down from mother to daughter in becoming dancers. The prettiest ones in the family, along with female orphans, left home around puberty and made their way to the oases to begin their life as entertainers. Once they had earned enough money for their dowry they gave up dancing and went back home to marry. Morgan writes that the Ouled Nail were first and foremost entertainers. Any love affairs they might have, he said, and any material benefits they might gain from such liaisons, were purely incidental.

Algeria was at that time under French colonial rule and Europeans were out there prospecting for oil. The dancers were confined to their own neighbourhood, which was inspected weekly by the French chief of police. If they wanted to leave at any time apart from the regular hours on a Thursday, they had to obtain special police permission.

The Ouled Nail quarter once included cafés where the women entertained. But these had disappeared by the time Morgan arrived and the girls were performing in rooms attached to houses where they lived free of rent. These establishments were owned by elderly Ouled Nail women who sometimes – though not always – paid the girls a small sum for dancing. Any gifts bestowed on them by customers were theirs, though, and contributed to their dowry. In the courtyard of one house Morgan came upon the unusual sight of men squatting on the ground washing the women's clothes for them:

> Each room in the quarter is, in fact, a nightclub in miniature. From the early hours of the evening to the early hours of the morning small groups of youths and men would wander from one girl's room

to another, joking, gossiping, making music and singing and, on leaving, give the girl 100 francs or so in payment for the mint tea with which she had entertained them. In a harem society such as this, the group visits to the room of a dancer provided the only opportunity for an Arab boy to talk with a woman who wasn't either his mother, sister or some other relative.

Morgan was right in pointing out that familiarity between the sexes isn't a feature of Muslim society after a certain age. What is less well known is that as children, boys may witness the most intimate secrets of women's lives. They enjoy far greater familiarity with female life than boys growing up in the West, for they are taken to the *hammam* (steam bath) with their mothers rather than their fathers. There they see their female relatives washing, applying henna and removing their body hair with a sugar solution. Only when they reach adolescence are boys excluded from women's company. As soon as the doyenne of the *hammam* notices that a young boy is showing too great an interest in the women's bodies she tells his mother, 'Next time, let him come with his father.' And that is the end of his life among the women. From then on the female sex become strangers to him. In his illuminating study *Sexuality in Islam*, Tunisian sociologist Abdelwahab Bouhdiba comments that young boys soon learn to despise the world of domestic concerns as inferior to the outside world of male interests and preoccupations.

As a European, Morgan was able to form the kind of friendship with Ouled Nail dancers that was impossible for Muslim men. The dancers were curious about the Englishman in their midst, and one by one they invited him to go and visit them. In their rooms he heard the latest gossip and scandal and, little by little, became familiar with the details of their everyday lives. We learn of their love potions and spells, their jealousies and their secret language.

Drinking mint tea with them, Morgan often noticed a dancer going in and out, carrying additional glasses. He thought nothing of this until his hostess demonstrated its hidden significance:

> One glass meant that there was someone waiting to see the girl to whom the glass was brought. If the dancer received the glass by placing it on the table the right way up it meant that she would come in a moment. If she turned the glass upside down the man who

waited was to be sent away. Two glasses meant that she was needed outside the room urgently. And so on. It was a very ingenious technique possessing a competent vocabulary for all kinds of emergencies.

The Ouled Nail paid scant regard to the Muslim prohibition on alcohol. For Europeans stationed in Algeria, alcohol was freely available. In fact the notorious absinthe – a popular nineteenth-century tipple which had devastating effects on the nervous system – is said to be an Algerian drink, originally imported into France by soldiers who had served their time in North Africa.

Some time before Morgan arrived in Bou Saada the colonial administration forbade the importation and sale of alcohol in the Ouled Nail quarter. It was said to cause fights among those who indulged too freely. But, says Morgan, it was the men who couldn't handle their liquor. The dancers, to whom he often gave cigarettes and beer, rarely grew intoxicated and indeed, he says, most of them were capable of drinking him under the table. One day a dancer offered him a smoke of *kif* (marijuana). He declined, with the comment, 'It's illegal, isn't it?' 'Poof!' – she made a gesture of disdain. 'Most things are forbidden, but if everybody obeyed people who take joy in forbidding, what pleasure would there be in life?'

To Europeans working in Algeria a combination of loneliness, lack of their own women and the romance of the desert all conspired to enslave them to these professional charmers. According to Morgan, the Ouled Nail women took them for all they were worth. Nor was fate any kinder to young Algerian men who fell under their spell. For those who came from 'respectable' or religious families, Ouled Nail dancers were no more 'wife material' than the *ghawazee* would have been. Morgan reports on the comic, as well as tragic, incidents that arose when these men became infatuated with one of the dancers. Sometimes there were violent incidents when a new man was replaced in the affections of a Ouled Nail dancer, especially if the replacement was European.

'The man who sleeps with an Ouled Nail will first lose his soul, afterwards his wealth, and finally his life,' Morgan writes, quoting an old Arab proverb. But it was the dancers who lost their lives when violent incidents occurred. Some were beaten up or killed at the hands of jealous ex-lovers; and though the men may have gone to jail, their prison sentences were never over-long. A spell of incarceration certainly didn't prevent a murderer going on to become a respected pillar of the community.

One afternoon a dancer asked Morgan to translate a letter she had received from an absent French lover:

> I read it to myself and then looked at her with renewed interest. What kind of girl was this who could evoke such language from a man, language that must surely move any woman in the world possessing the knowledge that it was addressed to her?

Contemplating the similar situation of a Dutchman and a Swiss man who have fallen in love with the same dancer, Morgan writes:

> What was it that these girls possessed which drew men of a dozen races to them, helplessly and often hopelessly? ... Hollywood has a liking to label certain of its stars as 'sultry and dangerous'. Those women are as middle-aged kindergarten teachers in comparison with the presence and personality of the Ouled Nail dancers.

It was a period of growing revolt against French colonial rule, and towards the end of Morgan's Algerian adventure acts of terrorism began to flare across the country:

> I had heard strange stories of sinister Arabs who were in the habit of calling on [the dancers] late in the evening – men who would not move out of the way if a European tried to pass them in a corridor, men with a glint in their dark eyes and a slim knife in their pockets. There were hints of fanatical nationalists holding secret meetings in the quarter, and, I was warned mysteriously, it would be unwise for a European to crash in on them – I might be mistaken for a French police agent.

Algeria would soon gain its independence. Times were changing for the Ouled Nail as well, and Morgan found himself wondering whether, after all, it might be a good thing that their age-old way of life was ending:

> Wouldn't it be better if this tradition, which condemned children of twelve years old to be brought down to the quarter, was destroyed in every oasis of the Sahara? Amid the gaiety and light-heartedness of the dancers there was a dark thread of human tragedy ... There was

just one bright feature in their lives – freedom ... They chose their own lovers or husbands and the insecurity of easy divorce did not hang over them continually.

In Islam a man may have four wives, as long as he can provide for each of them equally, and he may divorce a woman simply by repeating the words 'I divorce you' three times in succession in front of witnesses. A woman has no such privilege. It's not surprising that some of the Ouled Nail were wary of tying the knot. A dancer called Yacourte, who discarded her lovers with great frequency, at one time had two Europeans dangling on a string (each of them unaware of the other's presence). When Morgan asked Yacourte when she intended to marry, she wrinkled her nose with distaste and replied, 'All you get when you marry is a dress and children. I'll never marry. Never!'

Their status as breadwinners inevitably gave the Ouled Nail the same confidence and authority that Egyptian *ghawazee* and other dancers enjoyed. In North Africa and the Middle East, the names by which dancers were familiarly known described their social origins and freedom of movement, as well as the general perception of them. In Morocco the *chikhat* who travelled from village to village, entertaining at family festivities, were known as 'women who do not want men to tell them what to do'. The *ghawazee* too were branded with a title indicating their position as outsiders. But if, like all outsiders, dancers had to contend with the danger of living beyond the pale, they also enjoyed financial independence and a freedom of movement unknown to other women in Muslim society.

***

For hundreds of years female dancers have been a subversive force in the Islamic world. Before any other women did so, they were the ones who removed their veils and showed their faces to the outside world, flouting the requirement that women be anonymous, faceless beings in public. The origin of female veiling is hotly debated among liberal-minded Muslims of both sexes. They consider that the tradition should long since have vanished and point out that it was not initially meant to rob women of their freedom. However, over time this indeed has been its effect.

Veiling predates the birth of Islam and was a tradition in ancient Greek and Persian society. Aristocratic women veiled in order to indicate their social superiority, and the middle class followed suit for the same reason. By contrast, prostitutes and slaves were forbidden to hide their identity in this way. In Andalusia, which was ruled by the Arabs for nearly 800 years, noblewomen continued to veil in order to distinguish themselves from the poor right up to the 1940s. In most Muslim countries women are no longer obliged to cover their faces, but in Saudi Arabia, where dancing in public isn't even on the agenda, women are still compelled to do so.

One purpose of enforced veiling is to take away a woman's identity and remove from the public domain a sexual presence which might distract men from the course of virtue. If women's faces and bodies are hidden, so the reasoning goes, their potentially disruptive allure ceases to be a danger. Ironically, rather than making a woman less interesting, veiling has quite the opposite effect. For anything which is hidden (and forbidden) immediately becomes all the more sought after. Women know the value of mystery and how to exploit it, and just as European women once used their eyes and fans to convey messages, so too do Muslim women know how to manipulate their veils to best advantage. In Iran today, increasing liberalism has given women the confidence to subtly flout the law to cover up. Though young women may be enveloped in the black *chador* when they go out to shop, beneath it the more rebellious among them wear the shortest of mini-skirts. If they like the look of a man they play the game of pretending that their *chador* has 'slipped' in order to show him what lies beneath it and then, with a laugh, quickly cover up again.

In fashioning woman after his desires man has shown great ingenuity in both advertising and concealing her. In the Christian West men like to see the female body constantly on display. Women are persuaded to go out in public in full regalia, looking as sexy as possible at all times, with fashion highlighting different parts of the body for erotic contemplation. In the Muslim East the opposite is true.

Part of the excuse for veiling women and confining them to the home is that they are delicate flowers, weak creatures, who need as much looking after as children. Keeping them out of public life, away from the world of sin and dirt, is supposed to be for their own protection. It's the same argument used by middle-class Victorians 100 years ago to justify keeping their wives indoors, away from the kind of pursuits which would have expanded their mental horizons. (It also conveniently prevented them from interfering with any pleasurable activities that the men were bent on pursuing elsewhere.)

Apart from infantilizing women, removing their tempting presence reflects the concept that men cannot control their urges and that women are powerless to turn away men's advances. If this concept, so widespread among the Victorians, has partly disappeared in the West these days, it's still going strong in the Muslim world. As a Lebanese friend commented to me wryly, 'Muslim men have no illusions. Islam doesn't believe men and women can overcome temptation and control themselves, so it removes the temptation from their eyes. Having all women the same, alike, not one different or special is very pragmatic.'

This primitive idea has created a social and religious system in which, the better a woman is hidden, the more respectable she is. In Egypt, where women are no longer required by law to cover their faces, many have been persuaded by religious groups to cover their hair, a part of the body historically redolent of sexual suggestion. In Iran women are permitted to show their faces, but in Saudi Arabia it is forbidden. There, women are seen in public only as anonymous bundles of fabric.

Some years ago I was looking for costumes for my show *Dancing Girls* when I found myself in a small village shop selling Middle Eastern artefacts. Climbing the narrow, winding stairs, I turned the corner and came face to face with a dressmaker's dummy covered by an Afghan *burka*. This floor-length garment covers the entire body, back and front, and falls in scores of pleated folds trailing the floor. A fitted headpiece covers the face, with a narrow cotton grille across the eyes which allows a limited view of the outside world.

There are many accounts of women's eyesight being ruined, of disease and failing sight, all the results of a lifetime of struggling to see through the heavy fabric of garments like these. And though, as with any kind of protective mask, wearing a *burka* places a woman in a private space, protecting her from the intrusive glances of strangers, to be hidden is also to be limited. Under the Taliban, who enforced the wearing of this garment in public, there were women who so hated the idea that they voluntarily confined themselves to the house. Needless to say, wearing a *burka* in the heat isn't just uncomfortable; not being able to see properly makes any kind of movement difficult. Within the *burka* there is a sense of being in some way protected; the knowledge that you can't be seen, ogled, known by those on the outside. Yet even this small feeling of safety is illusory. As one Afghan woman comments, 'You become dependent on the *burka* to protect you, in an atmosphere which is threatening and unsafe. So you lose your self-confidence and ability to resist.'

The terrorist crisis of September 2001 brought the tragic reality of women's lives under fundamentalist Islam before the eyes of the world. And it revealed to people who hitherto knew nothing of Middle Eastern life the unpalatable truth behind the romantic cliché of the veiled oriental woman. It is ironic that, when outsiders conjure up images of Arabic dance, the picture which springs to mind is the Hollywood fantasy of women wafting around in veils. But the most enduring stereotype of this dance is to do with *removing* veils.

Travellers have written of seeing North African dancers who covered their bodies in sandalwood oil and slithered across the carpet like snakes, wearing little more than their jewellery. But nude dancing was not a custom, it was a tourist demand. And though dancers often agreed to it, they did so with disdain. Before beginning, they would make their musicians turn and face the wall, so shocking would it have been to dance naked in front of their own men. Accounts of this kind of performance describe how the dancer would look above the heads of her audience, with an expression of contempt on her face.

When Lucie Duff Gordon was in Egypt, a sheikh told her that he once invited a party of Europeans to supper. Halfway through the evening they asked for the dancers to perform nude, an abuse of hospitality which made the sheikh so angry he turned his visitors out of the house. After the incident he was reluctant to welcome Europeans into his home a second time.

During the same period French artist Emile Prisse d'Avennes described seeing Egypt's legendary 'Bee', a kind of humorous striptease in which a dancer comes forward and quivers as if a bee has got into her clothes and stung her. (The Persian 'Ant' dance is similar.) Her companions proceed to dance around her, searching for the insect while stripping off her costume piece by piece. Van Nieuwkirk writes that, according to some travellers who witnessed this dance, 'The bee, hidden in the dancer's clothes, was found before the last garment was parted with. In [another] version, the dancer discovered in time that it was all a mistake.'

During the 1850s Gustave Flaubert visited Egypt and went in search of the dancers. He reported:

> The Bee is a myth, a lost dance whose name alone survives. [Our guide] Joseph claims to have seen it really danced only once, and by a man. As for the present version, it consists of stripping and crying, '*In ny a oh! In ny a oh!*' ('Watch out, the bee! Watch out, the bee!').

When Flaubert met the celebrated dancer-courtesan Kutchuk Hanem, he persuaded her to dance the Bee for him, but unlike her other dances, which enchanted him and which he recorded in detail, he was unimpressed by her Bee. Before she began, Kutchuk closed the door and sent the men away, all but for a young boy and an old man whose eyes she covered. Flaubert noted, 'She danced it very briefly and said she does not like to do this dance.'

A hundred years later Lawrence Morgan saw an Ouled Nail dancer perform nude; once again, she made her musicians turn to face the wall. In contrast to the other dances Morgan had seen, this one made him feel uncomfortable and he wrote that it had an air of sacrifice about it:

> Her gaze was always fixed in front of her, above the heads of the people who watched with self-conscious interest. There was something vaguely false about it. The sense of timelessness and fierce emotion [in the other dances] had gone and been replaced by an importation of sophistication from Montmartre.
>
> As one young girl danced, her eyes quite unseeing, a tourist on the opposite side of the room reached for his camera. She broke off her dance and darted away from him to hide her small, naked body behind one of the curtains over a doorway.
>
> A tall Negro came in and spoke quietly to the man, who was inclined to argue. Finally, his embarrassed young wife took the camera out of his hands.

In *Dancing Girls* I used Colette's account of an experience she had in Algiers in the early years of the twentieth century. Late one night her Arab guide takes her to a dancer's house. Though tired and reluctant to perform, the dancer eventually agrees to do so. Halfway through her performance the guide stops her and insists that she dance nude for her visitors. In the show, the dancer who played this part turned her back to the audience and loosened her dress at the shoulders so that it fell to her waist. Then she turned round and continued dancing, while the music and lights slowly faded. Afterwards, in the bar, an elderly man from the audience came over and said to me, 'The one thing I didn't like in your show was the nude scene. I'll tell you why. When the dancer took her clothes off, all the mystery was gone.'

While nudity leaves nothing to the imagination, it still remains the predominant component of eroticism in the West. 'If you've got it, flaunt it!'

the desperate cry goes up, and there are plenty of women out there heeding the call. At film premieres actresses once known for the elegance of their high-priced gowns now vie with each other to wear as little as possible. They stick double-sided sticky tape to each nipple to keep their breasts from popping out of the gaping openings of their backless frocks, slashed to the thigh and open to the navel. (Today's cloth manufacturers must be nostalgic for the days when it required hundreds of yards of fabric to cover a crinoline.) Sadly, all that this fashion-striptease reveals is how insecure and desperate to please women continue to be.

In the West Arabic dance is often assumed to be little more than striptease. Conversely, in the Middle East, where the most famous performers are celebrated for their skill in reflecting the emotion and passion of the music, any dancer who started removing her costume on-stage would be greeted with shock and disbelief. As we've seen, lightly clad dancers were never the norm in the Middle East and North Africa, and this changed only when cabaret dancers began trying to satisfy the expectations of a Western audience.

Their new costume was influenced most of all by Hollywood. Before the coming of sound, movement and action were what sustained the early 'silents', so dance was a natural subject for film. Heroines were clad in a fantasy of oriental dress consisting of gossamer veils, diaphanous skirts slit to the thigh and sequined bras. Middle Eastern dancers accepted this Hollywood idea of glamour and took it back to Cairo and Beirut with them, and even now this old-fashioned costume is still used by many cabaret dancers, though it's long past its sell-by date. The only veil attached to this outfit is a length of chiffon that the dancer holds aloft as she makes her entrance, circling the stage while the filmy silk billows behind her like a sail. Yet such is the power of the 'seven veils' image that whenever this dance is mentioned, it is still the fantasy most commonly conjured up: a combination of sexy daring with a sly hint of laughter.

***

Until the 1930s Egyptian women danced together largely in private for their own entertainment. A complex language grew up around their dance, using intricate movements of the hips and torso. No teacher had come along to tell women how they ought to move. But in the thirties all this changed. *Baladi* was performed more or less on the spot, and many years later it was said of one of the country's best-loved performers, Tahia Carioca, that she could dance on a single tile. Now, suddenly, dancers found themselves with a large stage to fill. They enlarged their repertoire to include linear movements, extended arms and travelling steps. Some even took to wearing high-heeled shoes – and this, in a dance which until then had been defined by its earthy, rooted stance. At a stroke, a dance which was largely improvised became choreographed, with a new kind of music composed to suit this new East–West hybrid.

Dances of the East tend to explore an inner drama. Western dance, by contrast, is about exploring and conquering space, using an athletic body language centred on movements of the arms and legs, with a big step vocabulary. But you don't need complicated footwork when the focus of a dance lies in the torso. Egyptian dancers were skilled at articulating different parts of the torso, and their step vocabulary was practically non-existent. So the Westernization of *baladi* altered something at the very heart of the dance. The new language grafted onto Egyptian dance wasn't a natural addition. Not only that: any dancer needs training before she can be light on her feet, before she can jump and balance and spin. Egyptian dancers had no such training. The most celebrated cabaret performers – who became film stars through their frequent appearances in Egypt's feature films – took some basic ballet training but they cared little for it.

The thirties films which came out of Cairo have a charm and humour all their own. They also have unwittingly hilarious moments which are the result of this early attempt to produce choreographed, Hollywood-style numbers from a solo dance based on a tradition of improvisation. Behind the principal dancer lurks a chorus line of dumpy women who plod flat-footedly down grand staircases, not sure quite what to do with themselves And when you look closely, you can't help noticing a peppering of slim, blonde Europeans. Such was the demand for chorus lines for these films, there simply weren't enough genuine dancers to go round.

The innovations which began in the thirties took place in a commercial milieu and were largely influenced by popular Western social dance, ballet and Hollywood musicals. The new style, recently dubbed *raqs sharqi* (oriental or Eastern dance) included whirls, twirls and waftings with veils and since then it has developed in various directions. As an aspect of female culture, in a society where women's power still lies primarily in the domestic sphere, this dance has never been taken seriously as an art form. Frivolous and morally suspect, it lacks the status of music, lacks too a more up-market venue than cabarets and clubs. Only folk dance and ballet are thought sufficiently respectable to present at the more prestigious theatre venues. Not the bold, sassy women's solo.

Egyptian dancer Dina has a university degree, studied ballet as a child and danced in a government-sponsored folk troupe early on in her career. Today she is one of the most celebrated cabaret performers in the country. But her family still hasn't accepted her change of direction, despite her fame and popularity at all levels of society. Some years ago she talked of her ambition to open a dance school in Cairo, but said she knew the government would probably not give her a licence, and that even if they did, women would not send their little girls to her. There came a time, though, when it looked as if she was about to fulfil this ambition.

The Egyptian government was so encouraged by Dina's success (as well as her family background) that a plan was drawn up to open just such a school. The first-ever official school for women's dance in Egypt, it would have acknowledged not just the popularity of this much-loved art in the land of its birth, but also its cultural worth. However, it wasn't to be. At the last moment the plans were defeated by religious fundamentalist groups who, for some years now, have waged a concerted campaign to remove female dancing from the public eye. These groups have threatened and flogged unprotected dancers, while more celebrated performers have been famously bribed into taking early retirement.

Despite Dina's ambitions there is nowhere, creatively speaking, where she can take the dance in the Muslim world. More than one celebrated cabaret performer has expressed the opinion that it is in the West that Arabic dance is being kept alive and developing as a theatre art, due to its enormous popularity among women learning it in the thousands of dance studios which now offer courses.

There has always been a dual attitude in the Middle East towards female dancers, who are a prime public expression of the sensuality of human existence. Throughout the Arab world people love participating in and watching dance, but it's still not the correct thing, even today, for women to display themselves in public in front of strangers in such a bold, subversive way. Becoming a professional dancer in Egypt is one of the few ways in which a woman can make a handsome living, and if she is from a middle-class family, like Dina, and has managed to find fame, she is well protected.

However, her very existence, and the continuation of oriental dance cabarets, is considered a threat by religious extremists.

Many years ago Tunisian dancer Leyla Haddad said to me:

> When I told my family I wanted to be a dancer – oh, it was a disaster! I thought they would understand me, but not at all! They were very much afraid because there was no place other than cabarets and restaurants to dance. Apart from these places, where could I do it? They were afraid I would come to a bad end. But now, when they see how we dance in the theatre, they are more secure.

There are few Arab women like Leyla, from educated backgrounds, who are prepared to brave the wrath of their families to pursue a dance career. Leyla herself is based in Europe, where she can choose the theatre as her milieu, an option not available to dancers based in the Arab world. Even so, she still has to contend with opposition – and sometimes it comes from unexpected quarters. Once, performing at an arts festival in Tunis, she encountered a group of Tunisian feminists who asked her, 'Why do you try and take this dance into the theatre? Why not leave it where it belongs? In cabarets and clubs.' Leyla commented, 'For them, intelligent women must only use their heads. They must sacrifice their bodies and deny their sensuality.'

Like Leyla, Venus Saleh has lived in Europe for many years. She left Iran as a child and has never been back. For her, dancing isn't just a way of keeping alive her own cultural heritage, it's a natural way of expressing herself. At one of the women-only parties she took me to, the guests got up one by one to entertain each other, the singing and dancing going on well into the early hours. Some of the dances that night were humorous ones, like *babakaram* ('tough guy') which is performed in shirt and trousers and mocks macho attitudes to women. As Venus says:

> I was brought up in a culture where women tend to be very humorous in their attitude to men. Maybe it's to do with centuries of suppression and prejudice against women. They've used the element of humour to cope with it, especially in their dancing. When they have a party they tend to send men out so that they can be more free, more outrageous, so they can dance and joke more freely without the men looking over their shoulders telling them not to do this, not to do that. If a woman starts to let herself go, her

husband will say, 'Sit down! Sit down! You're embarrassing me, wiggling around in front of my friends!' So we send them out.

In the Middle East it's considered natural for women to entertain their family and friends by dancing for them in private. Since the 1979 Islamic Revolution in Iran, however, women can no longer perform in public. The revolution put paid to Iran's highly Westernized culture and re-established the all-enveloping black *chador*.

When I invited Venus to join my dance company to create a show exploring the humorous aspects of Middle Eastern dance she hesitated. Even though she was keen to take part, she was nervous about performing in public, which would have been something of a statement in itself, for an Iranian woman. However independent she was, she was still concerned about what her Iranian friends – especially the men among them – would think if they heard that she was appearing on-stage. Whenever Venus mentioned to her father that she was in the show he abruptly changed the subject. When she invited him to the theatre to see her, he made the excuse that he was busy on the nights we were performing. Many months later, after a TV company made a documentary about the show, he contrived to miss it on the night it was broadcast. Venus sums up his unspoken attitude with the comment, 'It's okay for other women to perform and dance, but not for one's own wife or daughter.'

Since embarking on a career as a professional dancer, Venus has met with this kind of double-think many times. While planning a performance project, she approached a group of young musicians who had recently arrived in England from Iran. They came from a well-known family of musicians whose reputation in the arts goes back several hundred years. Let's call them the Momo Brothers. They'd seen Venus perform at a gala and told her they liked what she did, but when she approached them to collaborate on her project, things grew complicated. They told her they would love to work for her, but only on condition that she didn't mention their names in the programme or the publicity or in any other way. And of course, no photos of them should appear in connection with the project. Such was the reputation of dancers, they added, they wouldn't get any further engagements if people knew they'd worked for her. Venus said:

> They told me they had a responsibility to their ancestors. So I said, well, in that case, why don't you wear blindfolds and come on as

mystery musicians? Better still, how about disguising yourselves with blonde wigs and dark glasses and calling yourselves the Momo Sisters? [She laughs wryly.] I meet people like this all the time. I think to myself, 'Come on. Get rid of these old ideas. Move on.'

But being trapped in old ideas is the norm rather than the exception. As an Iraqi woman once said to me:

> You know, this dance is such a reflection of how we are in the Arab countries. As a woman you have a need to express yourself, and so you start dancing, you start to show who you are. Then you remember that you shouldn't show so much of yourself, so you withdraw into your own private space.

Ironically, one of the most intriguing aspects of Arabic dance is just that balance between revelation and concealment. It's ironic, too, that the most expressive and meaningful dance of the Middle East is one that, in many parts of the region, women who want to be thought honourable will only perform with other women in private.

It may well be that Middle Eastern women have created, in dance, a counterbalance to the social and sexual constraints of their lives. Away from the intrusive eyes of strangers, they've developed a shared language and a way of expressing themselves which is earthy, humorous and infinitely more moving than any commercial cabaret display. The way they move is a unique barometer of how, when left to their own devices and free from the tyranny of fashion and dance teachers, women choose to express their sensuality – and it isn't in the crotch-thrusting pelvic routines beloved of Western pop videos.

When Brazilian pop star Shakira (whose family is Lebanese) recently broke out in a spot of Arabic dance during her act, Egyptian dance teachers in Europe reported a mini-stampede by young Western women clamouring to join their classes. Perhaps they've had enough of the aggressively sexual styles which currently dominate the dance floor, dances which offer nothing in the way of subtlety or allure or female 'otherness'. For that is, uniquely, what Arabic dance offers. It is what makes it so enjoyable as a way of moving, and so bewitching to watch.

Meanwhile in the Arab world this dance continues to be condemned by its colourful past and long-time connection with prostitution. Yet it is so popular at all levels of society, so deeply rooted as a proud form of sensual expression for women, that it will not be easy to get rid of it.

Afterword: Still Moving …

In 1920 the first English Palais de Danse opened its doors in Hammersmith, West London. Over the next fifty years it remained Britain's most famous ballroom, and it was there that my parents met during the Second World War. My mother loved dancing and throughout her life she retained a sneaking fondness for the Germans because, thanks to the war, she'd had the chance to dance with so many dashing servicemen.

Until the 1950s Europeans and Americans danced in couples. Women often danced together, as an Italian-American friend of mine recalled, looking back on her childhood. She remembers evenings at the social club in her Massachusetts home town, where children, grannies and aunts danced the polka together in one room while the men played cards in another.

By the time the 1960s was in full swing, dancing alone as a form of free expression had replaced couple dancing, and youth culture had taken over and pushed everyone over thirty into the background. Yet a recent British survey shows that, next to eating out, dancing is what people of all ages enjoy doing most in the evening. At regular intervals articles appear in the press telling us we're experiencing a resurgence of interest in dance, with a particular style spearheading the fuss – in general, a high-energy youth style like disco or salsa. But there's nothing new in all this dance activity; it's simply that the searchlight of media interest has swept across a particular dance for a brief moment before moving on to the next body craze. For, just as paganism has never truly been eradicated from Christian culture, neither have people ever really stopped dancing.

For those unwilling to expose themselves on the dance floor, yet desperate to escape the ills of living in a sedentary, mind-dominated culture, there's always the gym. Physical enjoyment isn't part of the gym experience though – not, that is, unless you regard pain as enjoyable. Gyms are big business and they're based on the premise that keeping fit should involve absolutely no spirit of creativity or play. Their dance classes are based on various kinds of aerobics which involve mind-numbing exercises and blaring music and are led by instructors who regard the body as a machine to be maintained. These classes offer none of the traditional benefits of dance, such as grace, skill, self-expression or improved confidence. Getting fit at a gym is all about enduring. It's about pushing oneself beyond one's limits, and women are increasingly buying into this competitive, self-punishing culture which, far from liberating them, is simply one more thing to crush them physically.

Some young women are after something a bit more daring, and they go elsewhere. At the time of writing, pole dancing is being touted for those who are slim and good-looking (no one else need apply). Like stripping, shinning up a pole wearing only a g-string is being sold as an empowering, sexually liberating activity for women. Of course, neither activity is being promoted for anyone over, say, twenty-five, which gives us a good idea just who that sexy display is really for. In a post-AIDS world, where soft porn has become a form of safe sex, the line between social dancing and sexual exhibitionism has vanished entirely. At the start of the twenty-first century, few taboos remain for Western women concerning how they dress and express their sexuality; and on the dance floor, as elsewhere, anything goes.

All those good little bad girls who are obediently stripping off for the punters, and saying and doing what nice girls never used to say or do, have one towering role model: but they have none of her power. They're a far cry from the girl who set out back in the late 1970s, as she says, 'to make something of my life', and who did it by challenging sexual taboos and cultural stereotypes of women.

At the start of her career Madonna hoped to make her name through dancing. She devoted herself to studying ballet and modern dance and even worked for a while in a New York dance company. But she was smart. She realized early on that she was never going to make it unless she combined her love of dancing with something more. In her stage shows she played with androgyny and with every female sexual persona under the sun, creating something quite new for the time. Always in charge, she strutted and posed, stalking and teasing like Jumping Jack Flash. And when she parodied all those bygone goddesses of stage and screen, she drew on the religious imagery which haunts even the most lapsed of Catholic backgrounds.

Madonna once said that dance was her avenue of escape from religion and her middle-class background. So it's interesting that, far from putting religion behind her, she has brought its powerful imagery back into popular culture. Over the years she's run the gamut of sacred iconography, from cross-dressing whip-lady to crucifix-wielding penitent. And in bringing a pagan religious spirit back into mainstream culture Madonna has resurrected the enslaving, destroying goddess and placed her centre stage once more.

What will happen to Madonna the performer as she loses her youthful, well-toned body? Perhaps she's made herself unassailable, unlike ordinary dancers, who have fewer strings to their bow. For they are at the mercy of critics who prefer faces and bodies unmarked by experience and for whom a dancer's 'line' and technique are all.

The obsession with youth and a particular kind of body is a rod that the dance profession has made to beat its own back. In this rarified world, the glorious diversity of the female body is regarded as an irrelevance. Reviewing the company Cumbre Flamenca, English critic Nicholas Dromgoole wrote that the dancers were 'God's gift to the corset industry. Middle-aged spread, or too willing an addiction to paella, is much in evidence.' The essence of female allure in flamenco, according to Dromgoole, is a slim body in a figure-hugging sheath, moving in a sea of frills and flounces: 'When the figure takes a great deal of hugging, when the slim fit reveals that the figure is very far from being slim, much of the illusion is spoilt.' Getting into his stride, he goes on to dismiss the mature performers in the company:

> No dance form is more concerned with spelling out physical attraction. If the dancers are past their prime flamenco can seem dangerously close to becoming a parody of itself . . . Perhaps this company needs to look a little more rigorously at the effects time is wreaking on its high-spirited and cheerfully extrovert dancers.

Flamenco is an art in which the ability to create magic has nothing to do with either youth or the shape of a woman's body, and many of its most celebrated female performers are in their forties and fifties. Audiences who turn out in droves to watch flamenco don't care that a dancer is past her first youth and boasts an ample waistline. What they respond to with rapture is her passionate energy and power of expression.

When Théophile Gautier first set foot in Andalusia in the late nineteenth century he fell in love with the dancers, the women's olive skins, arched noses and sensuous lips. At that early stage of his career, chronicling the charms of women in motion, Gautier preferred flamenco dancers to the gaslight dolls of the Paris Opéra:

> In Spain ... it is the body which moves, the back which undulates, with curving motions of the hips, swaying sides and a waist which twists and turns with the suppleness of a serpent. When the body is thrown back, the dancer's shoulders almost touch the ground.

He described the women's yellow shawls and flounced blue dresses powdered with stars, their amber and coral necklaces, and went on to praise their fluid arms and the way they held themselves erect from the hips. Those were the days when a good dancer was regarded as having 'a lot of honey in the hips' and when a woman was praised for having arms which 'are so beautiful they resemble two sausages hung in the kitchen in winter'.

The word *duende* is often used to describe a memorable flamenco performer. One dancer explains *duende* as a state in which the spirit moves through you, a power which 'climbs up inside you, from the soles of the feet'. An artist with *duende* – or soul – can create the kind of magic on-stage which will live on in the memory of the audience long after the show has ended.

A professional dancer's ability to connect with the audience in this way can be intensified by age and experience. But in much Western dance, by the time a woman hits her mid-thirties the writing's on the wall and she's made to feel she's embarrassing people, still prancing around on-stage. Lynn Seymour retired from ballet when she was at the height of her powers. Years later she reflected:

> When it came to being older, I myself was really on the crest of a wave of having gained so much more technical proficiency that I wanted to explore on. I felt I could dance for a long time. But no one was prepared to offer me these 'furtherances'. It was just repeating stuff I'd been doing for years, including things I thought I shouldn't be doing, like *Juliet*. I just thought it was mutton dressed as lamb by then. This was when I was approaching forty. I thought, well, I've got another good eight years here, I think. So I rejoined the Royal Ballet. But within a week or two I realized it wasn't going to work. I kind of threw in the towel then.

The argument is often made that childbirth and age destroy a dancer's powers. After giving birth three times Seymour confounded the critics by looking and dancing better than ever, performing with the wild, self-challenging bravery of her youth. She danced better as she grew older partly because of the experience and maturity she brought to her roles.

The lack of roles for dancers after a certain age isn't peculiar to dance. Actresses too know they're destined to suffer similar rejection around the age of forty, when the media consider that a woman loses her sex appeal. Occasionally an older dancer features in contemporary pieces, but when she does a very big deal is made of it. Older, like bigger, performers are to dance what Sophie Dahl was to fashion in her glorious voluptuous days. There comes a time in the life of any dancer when she no longer feels comfortable displaying her body on-stage, nor has the same energy for the technical demands of her craft. However, the greater range of expression conferred by age can be far more interesting than dazzling technique, and imperfection is always more intriguing than perfection.

At a festival in Spain I once met a flamenco dancer who was in her seventies. Half her teeth were missing, she smoked like a chimney and had the body of a woman who clearly enjoyed her food. But she was a demon on-stage! In the dressing-room after the show I told her I thought it was amazing that she was still performing at her age. Her eyes glinted dangerously as she looked at me. 'Let me tell you a secret, my dear,' she said, leaning across the table. 'When you dance, there is no such thing as old age.'

Sources

And God Created Devil-Woman

p. 20. 'One theory is': for accounts of goddess faiths see Baring and Cashford, *The Myth of the Goddess*; for images see catalogue of exhibition: *Goddesses: Mediterranean Female Images from Prehistoric Times to the Roman Period* (Institut de Cultura, Barcelona, 2000).

p. 21. For the myth of Cybele see *The Myth of the Goddess*, p. 391; also H. R. Hays, *The Dangerous Sex* (p. 925).

p. 24. 'By their very nature': Leonard Schlain, *The Alphabet Versus the Goddess*, Ch. 9: Hebrews/Israelites.

p. 26. 'In Arabia': Elizabeth Gould Davis, *The First Sex,* (p. 141).

p. 32. 'The evolution of dancing': for a discussion of secular Indian dance see Judith Lynne Hanna, *Dance, Sex and Gender* (p. 103).

p. 34. 'The pink pearls': qu. in Deborah Jowitt, *Time and the Dancing Image* (p. 111).

Sexual Imposters

p. 52. 'When she turned': Leslie Downer, *Geisha: The Secret History of a Vanishing World* (p. 12).

p. 55. 'None have ever begged': Germaine Greer, *The Whole Woman* (p. 64).

p. 57. 'And just when I': Gerard De Nerval, *The Women of Cairo* (p. 65).

p. 57. 'Expressionlessness of their faces': Francis Steegmuller, *Flaubert in Egypt* (p. 70).

p. 61. Interview with Nakamuro Ganjiro 3rd, *He Makes Up Just Like a Woman*, Louise Levene (*Sunday Telegraph*, London, 27 May 2001).

p. 61. 'The women of Japan': Shutaro Miyaki, *Kabuki Drama* (p. 25).

Revolution on the Dance Floor

p. 61. 'In London the new': Hugh Walpole, qu. in A. H. Franks, *Social Dance* (p. 150).

p. 72. 'The waltz is a dance': Mme Celnart, *The Gentleman and Lady's Book of Politeness* (p. 187).

p. 72. 'One might overlook': J. Young, qu. in Elizabeth Aldrich (ed.), *From the Ballroom to Hell* (p. 72).

p. 74. 'We remarked with pain': *The Times* 2 August 1817.

p. 75. 'But let us turn': T. A. Faulkner, qu. in Elizabeth Aldrich (ed.), *From the Ballroom to Hell* (p. 156).

p. 76. For the language of flirtation, see Aldrich (p. 112).

p. 80. 'He presses his partner': Aldrich (p. 76).

p. 81. 'Some girls have a trick': Mrs John Farrar, qu. in Peter Buckman, *Let's Dance* (p. 117).

p. 81. 'The anti-dance lobby': for an investigation of condemnation of social dancing see Ann Wagner, *Adversaries of Dance,* and A. H. Franks, *Social Dance.*

p. 84. 'Emma's heart beat': Gustave Flaubert, *Madame Bovary* (p. 63).

p. 85. 'They started slowly': *ibid.* (p. 66).

p. 87. 'Who that ever sits': Abba Louisa Woolson, *Dress Reform* (p. 149).

p. 88. 'French novelist Colette:' *My Apprenticeships* (p. 16).

p. 89. 'The continual pressure': for a discussion of the myriad ills inflicted by 19th-century corsets see Leigh Summers, *Bound to Please.*

p. 89. 'For some women, tight lacing': David Price, *Cancan* (p. 7).

p. 92. 'Out of laziness': Jules Laforgue, qu. in Dijkstra, *Idols of Perversity* (p. 273).

Forbidden Fruit

p. 96. 'When one see with what': qu. in David Price (p. 29).

p. 99. 'One of the women': qu. in David Price (p. 33).

p. 100. 'The mad, bad, merry music': Pessis and Crépineau, *The Moulin Rouge* (p.16).

p. 102. 'One of the spectators': David Price (p. 42).

p. 104. 'How many times did we': Dijkstra (p. 357).

p. 105. 'Picture carriage parties arriving': Pessis and Crépineau (p. 12).

p. 106. 'La Goulue in black': Yvette Guilbert, qu. in Peter Leslie, *A Hard Act to Follow* (p. 171).

p. 107. 'A wilful, vicious': Georges Montorgeuil, qu. in Leslie (p. 91).

p. 109. 'A month ago': Janet Flanner, *Paris Was Yesterday* (p. 48).

p. 110. 'We had seen quite': Charles Castle, *Les Folies Bergère* (p. 50).

p. 111. 'I have always enjoyed': Colette, *My Apprenticeships* (p. 18).

p. 114. 'I have recovered myself': Colette, *La Vagabonde* (p. 40).

p. 115. 'These sacred scarabs': Jean Cocteau, *Paris Album* (p. 63).

p. 117. 'She filled a costume': Liane De Pougy, *My Blue Notebooks* (p. 30).

p. 120. 'Among the ills': Leigh Summers, *Bound to Please* (p. 118).

p. 121. 'In the 19th century sex': for attitudes towards female sexuality and its representation in fine art, see Dijkstra, Ch. 7.

p. 122. 'Cases of clitoridectomy': for 19th century use of clitoridectomy in both the UK and US, see Dijkstra (p. 178), and Showalter, *Sexual Anarchy* (p. 130).

p. 125. 'A piercing, rolling expression': H. Lippert, qu. in Nickie Davies, *Whores in History* (p. 228).

p. 127. 'She begins to dance': Frank Wedekind, *Journal*, 18 December 1892.

p. 128. 'I've got the pox': Guy De Maupassant, letter to Robert Pinchon, 2 March 1877, qu. in Ed. Brisson, *Le Temps Toulouse-Lautrec*.

p. 128. '"Well," she continued': Maupassant, *Bel Ami* (p. 106).

p. 129. 'There was no applause': Emile Zola, *Nana* (p. 44).

p. 130. 'She was draped': Edmund and Jules de Goncourt, *Journals,* qu. in Showalter (p. 148).

p. 132. 'Her poses suggested sighs': Gustave Flaubert, *Three Tales* (p. 120).

p. 132. 'Wwho exhorts a cry': J. K. Huysmans, *Against Nature* (p. 65).

Twentieth-Century Goddess

p. 135. 'She rode the wave': Max Eastman, *Heroes I Have Known* (p. 86).

p. 136. 'She was a nomad': Flanner (p. 31).

p. 136. 'If you could see': Edward Gordon Craig, letter to Martin Shaw, as qu. in Steegmuller, *Your Isadora: The Love Story of Isadora Duncan and Gordon Craig* (p. 63).

p. 138. 'You enter. The audience': as qu. in Ann Daly, *Done Into Dance* (p. 156).

p. 139. 'Her sole costume': Fredrika Blair, *Isadora: Portrait of the Artist as a Woman* (p. 32).

p. 140. 'All that day': Isadora Duncan, *My Life* (p. 42).

p. 141. 'While the conference': Mary Desti, *Isadora Duncan's End* (p. 34).

p. 142. 'I found her': Lois Fuller, as qu. in Fredrika Blair, *Isadora* (p. 52).

p. 143 'When we went to': Julia Levien, as qu. in Blair (p. 239).

p. 143. 'After lunch': Kathleen Bruce as qu. in Blair (p. 70).

p. 144. 'Dear Sir,': *ibid.* (p. 65).

p. 145. 'She moves often': review in *The Boston Transcript*, 28 November 1908.

p. 146. 'Our meeting, first of all': Craig, as qu. in Steegmuller (p. 279).

p. 147. 'Darling Love': letter from Isadora to Craig, Steegmuller (p. 76).

p. 147. 'You need not write': letter from Isadora to Craig, Steegmuller (p. 84).

p. 148. 'She came to move': Craig, a talk for BBC Radio, *The Listener*, 5 June 1952.

p. 149. 'Of course people will respond': *My Life* (p. 135).

p. 149. 'I believe': *ibid.* (p. 136).

p. 150. 'Dearest, When I opened': letter from Isadora to Craig, Steegmuller (p. 139).

p. 151. 'It was a queer cry': Kathleen Bruce, as qu. in Steegmuller (p. 146).

p. 155. 'No-one had reckoned': Irma Duncan, *Duncan Dancer* (p. 27).

p. 158. 'The English people': *My Life* (p. 177).

p. 158. 'With all his money': Sewell Stokes, *Isadora Duncan, an Intimate Portrait* (p. 139).

p. 159. 'I have never seen': Desti (p. 56).

p. 160. 'How I wanted': *My Life,* (p. 198).

p. 161. 'I believe that': *ibid.* (p. 191).

p. 162. '[She] was then in': *ibid.* (p. 50).

p. 163. 'All she knew': Lily Dikovski, interview with the author, recorded August 1993.

p. 164. 'With her hands bound': as qu. in Daly (p. 196).

p. 166. 'Then she bent down': Stokes (p. 81).

p. 167. 'I used to believe': Stokes (p. 92).

p. 168. 'I'll do one more': *ibid.* (p. 83).

p. 169. 'She did not narrow': Jean Cocteau, *Paris Album* (p. 108).

Black Bottoms

p. 171. 'It has been said': for the history of jazz see the excellent TV documentary series by Ken Burns, *Jazz*.

p. 173. 'For the last two': as qu. in Lynn Fauley Emery, *Black Dance in the United States from 1619–1970* (p. 150).

p. 174. 'The quadroons are almost': Emery, *ibid.* (p. 149).

p. 175. 'I must avow': *ibid.* (p. 153).

p. 176. 'Bernays took on board': see BBC TV documentary series *Century of the Self* (2002).

p. 178. 'I walked into the Knickerbocker': Irene Castle, *Castles in the Air* (p. 85).

p. 180. 'Can it be said': *New York Herald*, 1913, as qu. in Ken Burns, *Jazz*.

p. 182. 'We were the most powerful': F. Scott Fitzgerald, *Echoes of the Jazz Age* (p. 5)

p. 185. 'Don't you go': Ann Wagner, *Adversaries of Dance* (p. 259).

p. 185. 'With each passing year': Wagner (p. 273).

p. 186. 'Half the population': Irene Castle, *Castles in the Air* (p. 85).

p. 186. 'Now negroes go': Rudolph Fisher, as qu. in Ken Burns, *Jazz*.

p. 188. 'They danced, Rose': Claude McCoy, as qu. in Emery (p. 222).

p. 188. 'Flooding the little cabarets': Langston Hughes, *When the Negro Was in Vogue*, pub. in *The Langston Hughes Reader* (p. 369).

p. 190. 'From knee to neck': as qu. in Buonaventura, *Serpent of the Nile* (p. 123).

p. 192. 'Marbury and her colleagues': Marybeth Hamilton, *When I'm Bad I'm Better* (p. 78).

p. 193. 'We went to the Elite': Mae West, *Goodness Had Nothing to Do with It* (p. 66).

p. 196. 'Witnesses of her triumph': Flanner, as qu. in Phyllis Rose, *Jazz Cleopatra* (p. 32).

p. 197. 'Our romanticism is desperate': André Levinson, *ibid.* (p. 23).

p. 197. 'There seemed to emanate': *ibid.* (p. 31).

p. 200. 'In the big dining room': Arnold Shaw, *The Jazz Age* (p. 227).

p. 201. 'We play, taking turns,': Henry Grew Crosby, *ibid.* (p. 286).

p. 203. 'The thing that makes': Frank Boyd, *Rent Parties*, pub. in *A Renaissance in Harlem* (p. 65).

p. 203. 'They spin, tug and': *ibid.* (p. 65).

p. 204. 'We had an edge': Norma Miller, *Swingin' at the Savoy* (p. 77).

Battle of the Sexes

p. 214. 'In this agitated dance': Vicente Rossi, qu. in Marta Sevigliano, *Tango and the Political Economy of Passion* (p. 44).

p. 214. 'The compañera threw her': *ibid.* (p. 41).

p. 216. 'In Buenos Aires tango': Collier (ed.), *Tango* (p. 69).

p. 216. 'Her body bent pliantly': Ricardo Guiraldes, qu. in *Tango* (p. 73).

p. 217. 'I went to the Rue': *ibid.* (p. 79).

p. 218. 'Knotted couples. Their shoulders': Jean Cocteau, *ibid.* (p. 80).

p. 218. 'It is a miracle': *ibid.* (p. 120).

p. 219. 'It was against the law': Irene Castle, *op. cit.* (p. 31).

p. 220. 'I am one of': *The Times*, 20 May 1913.

p. 223. 'The patrons were all': Luciana Devis, qu. in *Tango* (p. 117).

p. 223. 'Those broads': lyrics of song, *Champagne Tango* by Pascual Contursi.

p. 224. 'I was never blinded': lyrics of song, *Thinking About Old Age*, by Eduardo Méndez.

p. 225. 'I'm afraid I'm not': Dorothy L. Sayers, *Have His Carcass* (p. 141).

Dance Macabre

p. 234. 'An interview with': Sarah Wildor, qu. in article by Clifford Bishop, 'Not Drowning But Dancing' (magazine of *The Sunday Times*, London, 22 October 2000).

p. 238. 'In her leisure time': Albert Smith, qu. in Derek & Julia Parker, *The Natural History of the Chorus Girl* (p. 16).

p. 239. 'I've often seen girls': Colin Jones, picture review in 'Portfolio' (magazine of *The Independent*, London 11 November 2000).

p. 241. 'Your body doesn't want': Patricia Ruane, as qu. in article 'The Dancing Tourists' by Janet Watts (magazine of *The Observer*, London 8 November 1981).

p. 244. 'It is wonderful': Theophile Gautier, from the Goncourt *Journal*, 1 March 1862 (p. 68).

p. 245. 'I have seen maidens': Derek & Julia Parker (p. 33).

p. 246. 'By the hundred': Hans Christian Andersen, as qu. in Deborah Jowitt, *Time and the Dancing Image* (p. 37).

p. 248. 'Sometimes two [Egyptian] girls': Charles Leland, *Egyptian Sketchbook* (p. 131).

p. 251. 'They escape that leanness': Théophile Gautier, *A Romantic in Spain* (p. 77).

p. 251. 'The seeds of anorexia': for a discussion of the fashion for the starving, tubercular female, see Dijkstra, Ch. 2.

p. 253. 'I starved by day': Gelsey Kirkland, *Dancing on My Grave*, (p. 131).

p. 258. 'The BBC was making': Omnibus documentary *When the Dancing Had to Stop* (BBC television 1981).

p. 258. 'Ballet is all about': Richard Brooks, article 'Ballet Signs Barbie For Nutcracker' (*The Sunday Times,* 9 September 2001).

Dance of the Seven Veils

p. 263. 'Hours pass': Charles Gobineau, *The Dancing Girl of Shamahka and Other Asiatic Tales* (Jonathan Cape, London, 1926) (p. 43).

p. 264. 'They twined round each other': Paul Lenoir, as qu. in Zarifa Aradoon, *The Oldest Dance* (Dream Place Publications, California, 1979).

p. 264. 'We follow our guide': Guy de Maupassant, as qu. in Judy Mabro, *Veiled Half-Truths* (p. 239).

p. 268. 'Each room in the quarter': Lawrence Morgan, *Flute of Sand* (p. 50).

p. 269. 'One glass meant that': *ibid.* (p. 97).

p. 271. 'I had heard strange stories': *ibid.* (p. 177).

p. 271. 'Wouldn't it be better': *ibid.* (p. 190).

p. 276. 'Her gaze was always fixed': *ibid.* (p. 48).

Afterword: Still Moving …

p. 287. 'It looks at its best': Nicholas Dromgoole, review of Cumbre Flamenca in *The Sunday Telegraph*, London, 25 September 1994.

Further Reading

Among the many books which I consulted for this work, those listed below are all worth a good read

And God Created Devil-Woman

Baring, Anne and Cashford, Jules. *The Myth of the Goddess* (BCA/Penguin, London, 1991).

Bouhdiba, Abdelwahab. *Sexuality in Islam* (Saqi Books, London, 1998).

Eliade, Mircea. *Myths, Dreams and Mysteries* (Fontana, London, 1970).

Davis, Elizabeth Gould. *The First Sex* (Penguin Books, New York, 1971).

Hays, H. R. *The Dangerous Sex: The Myth of Feminine Evil* (Putnam, New York, 1964).

Hoare, Philip. *Wilde's Last Stand: Decadence, Conspiracy & the First World War,* (Duckworth, London, 1997).

Schlain, Leonard. *The Alphabet Versus the Goddess* (Allen Lane, The Penguin Press, London, 1998).

Taylor, Timothy. *The Pre-History of Sex* (Fourth Estate, London, 1996).

Thomas, Keith. *Religion and the Decline of Magic* (Penguin Books, Harmondsworth, 1971).

(Exhibition Catalogue) *Goddesses: Mediterranean Female Images from Prehistoric Times to the Roman Period* (Institut de Cultura, Barcelona, 2000).

Sexual Imposters

Barker, Roger. *Drag* (Cassell, London, 1994).

Dalby, Lisa. *Geisha* (Vintage, London, 2000).

Downer, Leslie. *Geisha: The Secret History of a Vanishing World* (Headline, London, 2000).

Gibson, Joy Leslie. *Squeaking Cleopatras* (Sutton Publishing, Stroud, 2000).

Greer, Germaine. *The Whole Woman* (Doubleday, London, 1999).

Hanna, Judith Lynne. *Dance, Sex and Gender* (University of Chicago Press, 1988).

Jaffrey, Zia. *The Invisibles: A Tale of the Eunuchs of India* (Weidenfeld & Nicolson, London, 1997).
Miyaki, Shãtaro. *Kabuki Drama* (Japan Travel Bureau, Tokyo, 1938).
Paglia, Camille. *Sexual Personae* (Penguin Books, Harmondsworth, 1991).
Scott, A. C. *The Kabuki Theatre of Japan* (George Allen & Unwin, London, 1955).
—— *The Theatre In Asia* (Macmillan, London, 1972).

Revolution on the Dance Floor
Aldrich, Elizabeth (ed.), *From the Ballroom to Hell: Grace and Folly in Nineteenth-Century Dance* (Northwestern University Press, Illinois, 1991).
Buckman, Peter. *Let's Dance* (Paddington Press, London, 1978).
Ellis, Havelock. *The Dance of Life* (Houghton Mifflin, New York, 1923).
Flaubert, Gustave. *Madame Bovary* (Penguin Books, Harmondsworth, 1976).
Franks, A. H. *Social Dance* (Routledge, London, 1963).
Murray, Venetia. *High Society in the Regency Period* (Penguin, London, 1998).
Summers, Leigh. *Bound to Please: A History of the Victorian Corset* (Berg, Oxford, 2001).
Woolson, Abba Gould. *Dress Reform* (lectures) (Roberts Brothers, Boston, 1874).

Forbidden Fruit
Baldick, Robert (ed.), *Pages from the Goncourt Journal* (Oxford University Press, 1962).
Brisson, Dominique (ed.), *Le Temps Toulouse-Lautrec* (Réunion Des Musées Nationaux, Paris, 1991).
Castle, Charles. *La Belle Otero* (Michael Joseph, London, 1981).
—— *The Folies Bergère* (Methuen, London, 1982).
Christiansen, Rupert. *Tales of the New Babylon* (Sinclair-Stevenson, London, 1994).
Cocteau, Jean. *Paris Album 1900–1914* (W. H. Allen, London, 1956).
Colette. *The Vagabond* (Penguin, Harmondsworth, 1960).
—— *My Apprenticeships and Music-Hall Sidelights* (Penguin, Harmondsworth, 1979).
Dijkstra, Bram. *Idols of Perversity: Fantasies of Feminine Evil in Fin-de-Siècle Culture* (Oxford University Press, New York, 1986).
Goncourt, Edmund and Jules. *The Goncourt Journals, 1850–1890* (Oxford University Press, 1962).
Huysman, Joris-Karl. *Against Nature* (Penguin Books, Harmondsworth, 1959).
Leslie, Peter. *A Hard Act to Follow* (Paddington Press, London, 1978).
Maupassant, Guy de. *Bel Ami* (Hamish Hamilton, London, 1974).
Parker, Derek and Julia. *The Natural History of the Chorus Girl* (David & Charles, Newton Abbot, 1975).
Pessis, Jacques and Crépineau, Jacques. *The Moulin Rouge* (Alan Sutton Publishing, Stroud, 1990).

De Pougy, Liane. *My Blue Notebooks* (Andre Deutsch, London, 1979).

Price, David. *Cancan* (Cygnus Arts, Londo, 1998).

Roberts, Nickie. *Whores in History* (Grafton, London, 1993).

Seymour, Bruce. *Lola Montez: A Life* (Yale University Press, New York, 1996).

Showalter, Elaine. *Sexual Anarchy* (Virago, London, 1992).

Sweetman, David. *Toulouse Lautrec and the* Fin de Siècle (Hodder & Stoughton, London, 1999).

Thurman, Judith. *Secrets of the Flesh: A Life of Colette* (Bloomsbury, London, 1999).

Zola, Emile. *Nana* (Penguin Books, Harmondsworth, 1981).

Woolson, Abba Goold. *Woman in American Society* (Robert Brothers, Boston, 1873).

Twentieth Century Goddess

Blair, Fredrika. *Isadora: Portrait of the Artist as a Woman* (Equation, Northamptonshire, 1986*)*.

Current, Richard Nelson & Marcia Ewing. *Lois Fuller: Goddess of Light* (Northeastern University Press, Boston, 1997).

Daly, Ann. *Done into Dance: Isadora Duncan in America* (Indiana University Press, 1995).

Desti, Mary. *Isadora Duncan's End* (Gollancz, London, 1929).

Drinnon, Richard. *Rebel in Paradise: A Biography of Emma Goldman* (Harper Collins, New York, 1961).

Duncan, Irma. *Duncan Dancer* (Wesleyan University Press, Connecticut, 1965).

Duncan, Isadora. *My Life* (Gollancz, London, 1928).

Schneider, Ilya Ilyich. *Isadora Duncan: The Russian Years* (Harcourt Brace, New York, 1968).

Steegmuller, Francis (ed.), *Your Isadora: The Love Story of Isadora Duncan and Gordon Craig* (Macmillan, London, 1974).

Stokes, Sewell. *Isadora Duncan: An Intimate Portrait* (Cedric Chivers, Bath, 1968).

Black Bottoms

Bascom, Lionel C. (ed.), *A Renaissance In Harlem: Lost Essays of the W. P. A.* (Harper Collins, New York, 1999).

Castle, Irene. *Castles in the Air* (Doubleday, New York, 1958).

Driver, Ian. *A Century of Dance* (Hamlyn, London, 2000).

Emery, Lynne Fawley. *Black Dance in the United States from 1619–1970* (California National Press, 1972).

Fitzgerald, F. Scott. *The Jazz Age* (New Directions Publishing Corp., New York, 1996).

Flanner, Janet. *Paris Was Yesterday: 1925–1939* (Viking, New York, 1972).

Hamilton, Marybeth. *When I'm Bad I'm Better: Mae West, Sex and American Entertainment* (University of California, Berkeley, 1997).

Hughes, Langston. *A Langston Hughes Reader* (George Brazillier, New York, 1958).

Levinson, André. *André Levinson on Dance* (Wesleyan University Press of New England, 1991).

Malnig, Julie. *Dancing Til Dawn* (Greenwood Press, Connecticut, 1992).

Martin, Carol. *Dance Marathons* (University Press of Mississippi, Jackson, 1994).

Miller, Norma and Jensen, Evette. *Swingin' at the Savoy: The Memoir of a Jazz Dancer* (Temple University Press, Philadelphia, 1996).

Rose, Phyllis. *Jazz Cleopatra: Josephine Baker in Her Time* (Chatto & Windus, London, 1990).

Shaw, Arnold. *The Jazz Age* (Oxford University Press, 1987).

Stuart, Andrea. *Showgirls* (Jonathan Cape, London, 1996).

Wagner, Ann. *Adversaries of Dance* (University of Illinois, 1997).

West, Mae. *Goodness Had Nothing to Do with It* (Englewood Cliffs, New Jersey, 1959).

Battle of the Sexes
Collier, Simon (ed.), *Tango* (Thames & Hudson, London, 1998).

Ferrer, Horacio. *The Golden Age of Tango* (Manrique Zago Ediciones, Buenos Aires, 1998).

Savigliano, Marta E. *Tango and the Political Economy of Passion* (Westview Press, Boulder, 1995).

Washabaugh, William (ed.), *The Passion of Music and Dance: Body, Gender and Sexuality* (Berg, Oxford, 1998).

Danse Macabre
Adair, Christy. *Women and Dance: Sylphs and Sirens* (Macmillan, London, 1992).

Barnes, Sally. *Dancing Women* (Routledge, London, 1998).

Foster, S. (ed.), *Corporealities: Dancing Knowledge, Culture and Power* (Routledge, London, 1996).

Guest, Ivor. *The Ballet of the Second Empire* (Black, London, 1955).

—— *Victorian Ballet Girls* (Black, London, 1957).

Jowitt, Deborah. *Time and the Dancing Image* (University of California Press, Berkeley, 1988).

Kirkland, Gelsey Kirkland and Laurence, Greg. *Dancing on My Grave* (Doubleday, New York, 1986).

Seymour, Lynn. *Lynn* (Panther Books, London, 1985).

Dance of the Seven Veils
Buonaventura, Wendy. *Serpent of the Nile: Women and Dance in the Arab World* (Saqi Books, London, 1989).

Tr. Darwood, N. A. *The Koran* (Penguin, London, 1990).

Mabro, Judy. *Veiled Half-Truths: Western Travellers' Perceptions of Middle Eastern Women* (I.B. Tauris & Co. Ltd., London, 1991).

Mernissi, Fatima. *Beyond the Veil* (Saqi Books, London, 1985 and 2003).

Morgan, Lawrence. *Flute of Sand* (Cinnabar Books, Bristol, 1999).

Nieuwkerk, Karin Van. *A Trade Like Any Other: Female Singers and Dancers in Egypt* (American University in Cairo Press, 1996).

Steegmuller, Francis (ed.), *Flaubert in Egypt* (Academy, Chicago, 1979).

Walther, Wiebke. *Women in Islam* (Markus Wiener, Princeton, 1993).

Index

Abraham, 25
Acosta, Luciana (La Moreira), 214–16
Adam and Eve, 26
Adversaries of Dance (Wagner, A.), 184
aerobics, 286
Afghanistan, 274
Africa, 11, 17–18, 175
African-American culture, 176, 179–80, 201–5
Agra, 32
Akhnaton, 24
alcohol, 189, 270
Algeria, 267–72
Algiers, 98
Alhambra Music Hall, London, 103
Allen, Maud, 33–7
Allen, Theo, 36
Almack's Club, London, 69–70, 73
amazones, 123
Amberley, Lady, 116
America *see* United States
American Ballet, 240
American Dress Reform Society, 90
American Tobacco Corporation, 176–7
amphetamines, 242
Anatolia, 21–2
Andalusia, 98, 109–10, 251, 273
Andersen, Hans Christian, 246
Anderson, Pamela, 253
androgyny, 43, 177
anorexia, 116, 242, 251
'Ant' dancing, 275
Antes del 1900 (Bioy, A.), 215
anti-dance movements, 81–2, 120

Arabic dance, 261–83
Argentina, 12, 207–31
arsenic poisoning, 117–18
art, modeling for, 96
arthritis, 241
artificial insemination, 121–2
d'Arvilly, Blanche, 117–18
Asquith, Herbert, 34
athletics, ballet and, 236
Atlantic, female fashion casualties, 90
Augustin Daly Company, 139
Austrian Empire, 76–7
Avril, Jane, 105
Ayama, Yoshizawa, 39, 54

Baartman, Saartje, 196
babakaram ('tough guy'), 58
Babe Gordon (Hamilton, M.), 193
Babylon, 33
Backstage at the Paris Opéra (Degas), 245
Baker, Josephine, 194–9
Baker-Brown, Isaac, 122
Bakst, Leon, 160
Bal Mibelle, Paris, 100, 102, 127
baladi see raqs baladi
Balanchine [Georges], 168, 240, 241–2, 253
ballet, 12, 139, 145, 233–59
Ballet of the Nuns (Paris Opéra), 246
ballet rebels, 255–6
Ballets Russes, 194
ballroom dancing, 178–80
ballroom tango, 219–21

bals musettes, 96–102
Balzac, Honoré de, 135
Banbury, Earl of, 72
bandoneón, 221–2
Bara, Theda, 159
Barbie dolls, 258–9
Bath, 68
Baudelaire, Charles, 198
BBC (British Broadcasting Corp.), 258
Beaton, Cecil, 178–9
beauty, pain and, 237–9, 240–1, 243
Beaux Arts [Ecole des], Paris, 160
'Bee' dancing, 275–6
Bel Ami (de Maupassant, G.), 128–9
belly-dancing, 28, 60–3 see also danse du
    ventre
Berenson, Edward, 130
Berlin, 144, 146, 198
Berlioz, Hector, 78, 136
Bernays, Edward, 176–7
Bernhardt, Sarah, 118
Biblical quotations, 17, 18
Bierce, Ambrose, 81
big band sound, 205
Billing, Noel, 36–7
Bioy, Adolfo, 215
Birmingham, 34
Blisset, George, 172–3
body fascism, 253
body modeling, 254–5
Bokova, Jana, 220–1
Bolitho, William, 56
Bolshevism, 164–5
boogie-woogie, 184
The Book of Beauty (Beaton, C.), 178
bootlegging, 189
Borges, Jorge Luis, 224, 229
Boston, 116
Boston Weekly, 79
Botox, 13, 118, 254–5
Botticelli, Sandro, 156
Bou Saada oasis, 268–72
Bouhdiba, Abdelwahab, 269
Boullay, Gustave, 79
Bound to Please (Summers, L.), 89, 121
Bow Bells magazine, 118
Brazil, 172
Brill, Dr A.A., 189–90
Britain, 29, 35, 255 see also England

Broadway Melody, 201
Brooks, Louise, 199
Brown, Mary, 230–1
Bruce, Kathleen, 143, 150–1
Buddhism, 23, 44, 46–7
Buenos Aires, 207–31
Bull, Deborah, 230, 241
bunny hug, 183
burka of Afghanistan, 274
burlesque halls, 190–1
Byrd, Frank, 203
Byron, George Gordon, Lord, 73

Café Anglais, Paris, 99, 124
Cairo, 12, 59, 60, 247–8, 264–7, 278–9
Campaneando la Vejez, 224
cancan, 10, 11, 12, 13, 96–102, 105–9,
    195, 196, 243, 247
candomblé, 212
Caribbean, 172
Carioca, Tahia, 278
Carmichael, Hoagy, 182
Carpeaux, Jean-Baptiste, 102–3
Casino de Paris, 194, 199
Castle, Irene and Vernon, 178–9, 181,
    186, 190, 219–20
Castlereagh, Robert Stewart, Viscount,
    76
castration, 33, 42
Century Theatre, New York, 136
chador, 273, 281
Chanel, Coco, 177
Channel, Kate, 230
La Chanson de Ma Vie (Guilbert, Y.),
    106–7
Chappell, Clovis G., 189
Charles, Jacques, 194–5
Charles II, 44
charleston, 183, 187, 199, 204
Cheltenham, 68
Chicago Trade Fair (1893), 190
childbirth, 151–2, 289
China, 10, 40–1, 55
chitons, Greek-style, 154–5
Chopin, Frédéric, 78, 135
Christ see Jesus Christ
Christianity, 18, 24, 25, 26, 81–2, 285
Christiansen, Rupert, 95, 103
Clairin, Georges, 268

claquers, 78–9
Clayton-Powell, Rev Adam, 186
Clermont-Tonnerre, Duchesse de, 217
clog-dance, 175
cocaine, 189, 242
Cocteau, Jean, 115, 169, 218
Colette, 88, 111, 112–14, 116, 130–1, 132, 135, 276
Colin, Paul, 195
Collier's magazine, 185
Columbia, South Carolina, 179
Comédie Française, 114
commedia dell'arte, 10
Comte, Auguste, 121–2
Confitería Ideal, 207, 227
Confucianism, 48
The Constant Sinner (Hamilton, M.), 193
consumerism, 176, 253
consumption *see* tuberculosis
Copes, Juan Carlos, 207
corsets, 87–93, 115, 119–21, 219
cosmetic surgery, 240, 255
Cotton Club, Harlem, 188
courtesans, 123–5, 129–30
courtly dancing, 69–71
Craig, Edward Gordon, 136, 138, 146–53, 161
Creoles, 175
crinolines, 11, 86–7, 101
Crosby, Henry Grew, 201
cross-dressing, 43, 56–7, 58–9, 101, 130–1
culottes, 11
Cumbre Flamenca, 287
Curie, Marie, 142
Cuvier, Baron, 198
Cybele, 21–2, 26
Czechoslovakia, 76

Dahl, Sophie, 253, 289
La Dame aux Camélias (Dumas, A.), 127
dance
    classes in, 61, 80–1, 162–6
    dangerous force of, 10–11
    evolution, spiritual to secular, 30–2
    professionalism in, 12–13
dance floor
    dangers of, 75, 80
    as meeting place, 10, 80

turbulent change on, 11–12
dance halls, 10–12, 80, 182–3, 204–5, 208–9, 215–16, 226–8, 285
dance styles
    Arabic dance, 261-83
    ballet, 12, 233–59
    ballroom dancing, 178–80
    belly-dancing, 28, 60–3
    boogie-woogie, 184
    bunny hug, 183
    cancan, 10, 11, 12, 13, 96–102, 105–9, 195, 196, 243, 247
    candomblé, 212
    charleston, 183, 187, 199, 204
    clog-dance, 175
    courtly dancing, 69–71
    danse du ventre, 108, 191, 196, 265
    exhibition dancing, 180–1
    fandango, 98
    flamenco, 13, 262, 287–9
    grizzly bear, 183
    habanera, 212
    hip dancing, 262–3
    hoochie coochie, 190
    hula, 10
    jig, 175
    minuet, 70–1
    pole dancing, 286
    polka, 98, 175
    rock 'n' roll, 184
    saraband, 10
    'shimmy-shawobble,' 193
    'spieling,' 192
    storytelling dance, 31
    tango, 11, 12, 79, 184, 196, 208–31
    turkey trot, 183, 184, 186
    waltz, 10–12, 71–85, 83–7, 175
Dancing Girls (Buonaventura, W.), 13, 274, 276
Dancing On My Grave (Kirkland, G.), 240
danse du grand écart (La Goulue), 124
danse du ventre, 108, 191, 196, 265 *see also* belly-dancing
danse sauvage (Josephine Baker), 195
Daru, Vicomte Paul, 245
death, fashion and, 118–19
debutantes, 69–70
Degas, Edgar, 104, 245–6

Delhi, 32
Delmonico's, New York, 189
Delsarte, François, 137–8
department stores, 83, 103
Derval, Paul, 114
Desti, Mary, 141, 159–60
Devadasis, 31–2
Devon, 158
Diana, Princess of Wales, 18–19
Dijkstra, Bram, 116
Dikovski, Lily, 162–3, 165–6, 167
Dina (Egyptian dancer), 279
Dinet, Etienne, 268
Downer, Lesley, 50–3
dreams, myths and, 20
Dresden, 217
dress reform movement, 154–5
dressmakers, underpaid, 119
Dromgoole, Nicholas, 287
Du Camp, Maxime, 124
Dudley, Earl and Countess of, 34
Duff Gordon, Lucie, 266, 275
Dumas *fils,* Alexandre, 126–7
Duncan, Dr T.C., 251–2
Duncan, Irma, 154–6, 163, 167
Duncan, Isadora, 14–15, 115, 135–69,
    185, 194, 237
    adventurous life, 135–6
    birth and early life, 136–40
    birth of daughter, 151–2
    chitons, Greek-style, 154–5
    dancing schools, 162–5
    death of children Deirdre and
    Patrick, 160–1
    dress reform programme, 155–6
    and Edward Craig, 146–53
    later years and death, 166–9
    modesty, lack of false, 143
    mood and music, immersion in,
    153–4
    Paris Singer and, 157–9
    Sergei Esenin and, 165–6
    struggle for attention, 140–2
    success, 143–6
Duncan, Raymond, 141, 159
Dunning, Jennifer, 242
Duplessis, Marie, 127
Durand's, Paris, 124

earth mother, 20–1
Easter Parade, New York, 177
Eastman, Max, 135
economic transformation, 103–4, 176–7
Edward, Prince of Wales, 108, 124
Edward VII, 34
Egypt, 12, 13, 24, 28, 261, 263–7, 274,
    275–6
Egyptian dance, 277–9
Eiffel Tower, 105
Elite Number One, Chicago, 193
Elizabethan theatre, 43
Elle magazine, 253
Ellis, Havelock, 65, 122
Elssler, Fanny, 250
Eltinge, Julian, 56
Elysée, Montmartre, 104–5
Emery, Lynne Fauley, 175
England, 43–4, 68–70, 74–6, 158 *see also*
    Britain
English National Ballet, 258
Esenin, Sergei, 165–6
Esna, Egypt, 59, 266
eunuchs, 42
European culture, 65–71
evangelism, 82
Eve, the original temptress, 22, 26
exhibition dancing, 180–1

family celebrations, 28, 267
fandango, 98
fashion
    animated skeletons, 251–4
    bourgeois preoccupation with, 86–7
    changes in, 11, 66–7, 114–15
    corsets, 87–93, 115, 119–21, 219
    crinolines, 86–7
    dance and, 11
    evolution in Europe of, 66–7
    female body and, 237
    tango's effect on, 219
Fashion Aid, 39
fashion models, 39–40
Fatima's Dance, 266
Faulkner, T.A., 75
female assertiveness, 130–3, 176–8
female body and sexual obsession, 9–10,
    14
female fashion casualties, 90–1

female impersonation, 41–3, 53–5, 56–7, 59–60
female natural invalids, 116–19
female physique, 251–5
female public performance, 43–4
female sexuality, 121–33
   constraints on, 28–9, 282
   male fear of, 13–14
female social casualties, 92–3
fertility rituals, 21
Le Figaro, 100, 110, 200
filles de marbre, 123
film, dance in, 145, 228–9 *see also* Hollywood
Finette (Creole dancer), 99
Fisher, Rudolph, 186–7
Fitzgerald, F. Scott, 182, 200
Five Brahms Waltzes in the Manner of Isadora Duncan, 256
flamenco, 13, 262, 287–9
Flanner, Janet, 109, 136, 195–7
flapping, 56, 183, 192
Flaubert, Gustave, 59–60, 84–5, 92, 132, 275–6
Flute of Sand (Morgan, L.), 268
Folies Bergère, 109–112, 113–14, 126, 194, 199
Fonteyn, Margot, 233, 238, 257
foot-binding, 40–1
Fowler, Orson, 119
France, 44, 79, 95–103, 104–112, 112–15, 162, 210
Franco-Prussian War, 124
French Revolution, 58, 65, 71, 76, 77, 243
Freud, Sigmund, 22, 33, 126, 176, 189
From Dance Hall to White Slavery, 184
Fuller, Loie, 141–2

Galbraith, Dr Anna, 121
Ganjiro 3rd, Nakamuro, 53–5
Gardner, Augustus, 119
Gautier, Théophile, 237, 245, 247, 249, 250–1, 287–8
geisha, 49–53
Genthe, Arnold, 143
Germany, 62, 73, 77, 79, 162, 200, 210
ghawazee, 263–7
gigolos, 226
Giselle, 247, 248, 250

Gobineau, Charles, 263
goddess cults, 21–3
de Goncourt, Edmond, 130, 265
Goncourt brothers, 244
La Goulue, 106–9, 124
Gramont-Caderousse, Duc de, 99
La Grande Chaumière, Paris, 102
grandes cocottes/horizontales, 123, 126, 129
Greece, ancient, 156, 272
Greek dance, 262–3
Greer, Germaine, 57
Grimaldi, Barry, 237
Grisi, Carlotta, 237
grizzly bear (dance), 183
Guilbert, Yvette, 106–7, 110–11
Güiraldes, Ricardo, 216–17
Gumbo Ya-Ya, 172
gym experience, 285–6
gynaecological complaints, corsets and, 120–1

habanera, 212
Haddad, Leyla, 280
hair styles, 53, 178–9
Hamilton, Emma, Lady, 155–6
Hamilton, Marybeth, 56–7, 192–3
hammam (steam bath), 269
Hammersmith Palais de Danse, 285
Hanem, Kutchuk, 266, 276
Hansen's Coffee, 215
Happy Days Are Here Again, 200
Harberton, Lady, 90
Harlem, New York, 187–91, 193, 202
Harlow, Jean, 34
Haussmann, Baron, 104
Have His Carcase (Sayers, D.L.), 225–6
Hawaii, 10
Hebrews, 24–6, 27
Hellman, Lillian, 192
Herod Antipas, 22, 33–4
Herodias (Flaubert, G.), 132
Heuzé, Edmond, 107
hijras, 41–2
Hinduism, 29–32, 48
hip dancing, 262–3
historical perspectives
   Arabic dance, 263–7, 277–8
   ballet, 235–6, 243–8

China, 40–1
European culture, 65–71
fashion, development of, 86–93
female public performance, 43–4
Japan, 44–6
nineteenth century, 11–13
prehistoric times, 20
US, early twentieth century, 176, 180, 182–3
Hoare, Philip, 37
Holland, 150
Hollywood, 36, 277
homosexuality, 35
hoochie coochie, 190
Hottentot Venus, 196, 198
Houdini, Harry, 56
How to be Plump (Duncan, T.C.), 251–2
Hughes, Langston, 188, 204
hula, 10
Hungary, 76
Huysmans, J. K., 132

Idols of Perversity (Dijkstra, B.), 116
illness, female beauty and, 116–19
Illustrated London Life, 250
immigration, 209–12
India, 22, 29–32, 41–3, 221
Indian dance, 30–2, 262
Indo-Aryans, 30
Industrial Revolution, 85–6, 95
injuries in ballet, 234
Iran, 43, 58, 273, 281
Iraq, 30, 282
Ishtar, 33
Islam, 13, 18, 24, 26, 28, 42–3, 48, 58–9, 266–7, 269–70, 272–4
Istanbul, 59
Italy, 10, 77, 217, 244

Jack the Ripper, 36
Jaipur, 32
James, Henry, 118
Japan, 32, 41, 44–55
Jardin de Paris, 124
jazz, 171–2, 175, 184, 187–8, 194, 200, 210
Jazz Cleopatra, 199
Jesus Christ, 26, 263
jig, 175

Jockey Club de Paris, 245
John the Baptist, 32–7, 132
Jones, Colin, 239
Jowitt, Deborah, 250, 252
Judaism, 18, 24–6, 27
juke joints, 179

kabuki, 46–8, 50–1, 53–5
Kali (the Black Mother), 22
Kama Sutra, 29
Karma, Law of, 30
karyukai, 50–3
Kellogg, J.D., 122
Kessler, Harry, 198
Khajuraho, India, 29–30
Kirke, Oscar, 200
Kirkland, Gelsey, 240, 241–2, 253, 254–5
Knickerbocker Hotel, New York, 178
knickers, 101–2
Kostenbaum, Wayne, 57
Kyoto, 44, 46, 48, 53

La Boca, Buenos Aires, 209–12, 215–16, 221
Ladies Companion, 92
Laforgue, Jules, 92
Leland, Charles, 247
Leningrad, 166
de Leon, Millie, 190–1
Leroux, Hughes, 109–10
lesbianism, 35, 131, 177
Levien, Julia, 143
Levinson, André, 197–8
Linton, E. Lynn, 117
Lippert, H., 125
literature, Western, 233
Little Egypt, 190
Livry, Emma, 247
London, 34, 36, 66, 68–9, 103, 123, 140
Lopez, Vincent, 189
Lorrain, Jean, 107
Los Angeles, 37
Louis XIV, 44
Luxor, 266, 267

Maazin Sisters of Luxor, 267
McCay, Claude, 188
MacKaye, Steele, 137
MacMillan, Kenneth, 256–7

MacMillan, Lady Deborah, 258
Madame Bovary (Flaubert, G.), 84–5, 92
Madonna, 286–7
make-up, ingredients of, 117
male impersonation, 58
Manet, Edouard, 104
Manning, Frank, 202
Manu, Law of, 30–1
Marbury, Elizabeth, 192
Marie Claire magazine, 253
marijuana, 270
Markova, Natalia, 241
masked balls, 185
masturbation, 122
Mata Hari, 132
de Maugny, Comte, 245
de Maupassant, Guy, 127–9, 264
Mediterranean, 23
Meo, Elena, 148–9
Mesopotamia, 30
Metternich, Klemens Fürst von, 70, 76
Middle East, 12–13, 21–2, 23, 25–6, 28,
    41, 43, 58–63 *see also* Arabic dance
Miller, Norma, 204
milonga, 212–13
milongas (tango dance halls), 208–9
milonguitas, 215, 222–5
Mimi La Sardine (Buonaventura, W.), 17
minuet, 70–1, 74
misogyny, 133
Miyaki, M., 53–4
Modes, Le Cabinet des, 67
Mohammed Ali, 59, 266
La Môme Fromage, 108
monotheism, 23–4
Montez, Lola, 117
Montmartre, 104–112
Montorgueil, Georges, 107–8
Montparnasse, 98
Moore, Doris Langley, 37
Moreau, Gustave, 132
Morgan, Lawrence, 268–72, 276
Morgen Post, Berlin, 144
Morrison, Jim, 135
Moscow, 159, 163, 165–6
mother goddess, 20–1
Moulin Rouge, 105–9, 126, 194–5
Mughal invasion of India, 31–2, 42–3
Muhammad, 26

mulattos, 175
Mumford, Ethel Watts, 181
Munich, 62, 143
Murray, Venetia, 70
muscularity, 116
Muslim culture *see* Islam
My Apprenticeships (Otero, C.), 111
My Life (Duncan, I.), 140, 145, 148, 149,
    157, 160
myths, dreams and, 20

Nana (Zola, E.), 129–30
Napoleon, Louis, 124–5
Napoleonic Wars, 76
National Health Service (UK), 255
A Natural History of the Ballet Girl, 238
nature, supremacy of, 28–9
necrophilia, 37
Negresco Hotel, Nice, 168
Nerval, Gérard de, 59
New Orleans, 171, 173–5
New Testament, 32
New York Herald, 180
New York Times, 242
New Yorker, 109
Nice, 112, 166–9
Nieves, María, 226–7
Nini-la-Belle-en-Cuisse, 97
Noh theatre, 46
Noverre, Jean-Georges, 236
nudity, 102–3, 107, 142–3, 195, 249–50,
    276–7
Nurofen, 241
nymphomania, 122–3

Observations on Modern Dancing
    (Saint-Laurent), 98
obstetrics, 121
Okuni (creator of *kabuki*), 46, 49
Old Testament, 17, 25, 26–7
Oller, Joseph, 106
Olympia (Manet), 249–50
onnagata, 41, 44, 47, 50–5
Opéra Ball, Paris, 99, 101, 102, 114,
    124–5, 126
Opera House, London, 234
Orientalism, 58–63, 114, 157, 191, 263
osteoarthritis, 237
Otero, Caroline, 109–12, 115, 124, 132

Ouled Nail, 267–72, 276

Padong, 237
Paglia, Camille, 23, 62–3
Palais de Glace, Paris, 115
paradise ('walled garden'), 28
Parent-Duchâtelet, Dr, 126
Paris, 13, 35, 67, 95–115, 123–4, 131, 141, 160, 163–4, 194, 201, 217–18
Paris by Night, 123
Paris Exposition (1889), 130
Paris Exposition (1900), 141–2
Paris Opéra, 244, 246, 247, 288
La Parisienne, 130
Passion Dance, 265
Pavlova, Anna, 238
Pekin Restaurant, New York, 189
Penn, William Evander, 82
Père Lachaise cemetery, Paris, 135
Le Père Pudeur, 105
Period Piece, Memoir of a Victorian Childhood (Reverat, G.), 91
Persia, 43, 58, 272–3
personal hygiene (18th-century Europe), 67–8
petticoats, 102, 114–15
Philadelphia Minerva, 80
Philadelphia North American, 190–1
Phoenicia, 263
Piedmont, King of, 124–5
Pilvois, Clara, 246
'Pimp Pasha,' 266
Pinchon, Robert, 128
Plutarch, 102
Poe, Edgar Allan, 116
pointework, 238–9, 243
Poiret, Paul, 157
Polaire, 115
Poland, 77, 210
pole dancing, 286
polka, 98, 175
Popham, Peter, 42
Porter, J.W., 184
post-natal depression, 152
Potter, Sally, 228–9
de Pougy, Liane, 117
de Pourtales, Countess Melanie, 217
power, gender aspects, 23, 228–9, 235
pregnancy, 91, 92

Price, David, 89
Primavera (Botticelli), 156
Prisse d'Avennes, Emile, 275
Prohibition, 189, 201
Pronko, Leonard C., 50
prostitution, 48–50, 96, 123, 125–9, 188
Proverbs, Book of, 17, 25
psychoanalysis, 22
Puckler-Muskau, Prince, 69
purdah, 42
The Pure and the Impure (Colette), 116

quadroon balls, 174
The Quran, 28

Ranelagh Gardens, London, 68–9
raqs baladi (dance of the people), 263, 278
Raucho (Güiraldes, R.), 216
Raverat, Gwen, 91
ready-made clothes, 177
A Rebours (Huysmans, J. K.), 132
Rector, George, 180
Regency period, 70, 74
La Reine Pomaré, 101
religious fundamentalism, 23, 275, 281–2
rent parties, 202–3
Renuka, 42
Revue Nègre, 194–5, 197, 200
Richepan, Jean, 218
Rig Veda, 30, 31
Rigolboche, 97, 99–100
rock 'n' roll, 184
Rodin, Auguste, 14, 143
Rojo, Tamara, 239
Romanticism, age of, 77–8
Romeo and Juliet (MacMillan), 257
Rose, Phyllis, 199
Rose Adagio *(pas de deux),* 243
Roseland Ballroom, New York, 183
Royal Albert Hall, London, 39
Royal Ballet, London, 234, 235, 257, 258
Ruanne, Patricia, 241
Russia, 103, 136, 159–60, 162, 164–6, 210
Russian Revolution, 164–5

Sade, Marquis de, 193
sadism, 37
Said, Edward, 261

Saint-Laurent, Vicomte de, 98
St Paul, 26
Saleh, Venus, 58, 280–2
Salome, 22, 32–7, 82, 132–3
San Francisco, 36, 136–7
saraband, 10
Sarah (black madonna), 26
Sarah the Kicker (Wiry Sal), 103
Saudi Arabia, 273, 274
Saures, Carlos, 27
Savoy Ballroom, New York, 202, 204–5
Saxe-Weimar Eisenach, Duke of, 174, 175
Sayers, Dorothy L., 225–6
Schneider, Hortense, 124
Schneider, Ilya Ilyich, 156
Scott, A.C., 41
Scovel, Sylvester F., 82
sculpture (Carpeaux), 102–3
Sem (journalist), 218
sensuality, 265
Sevigliano, Marta, 225
Sex and Character (Weininger, O.), 125
sex-change operations, 57
sex magazines, 9, 14
sexual desire, 121–33
sexual liberation, 191–3
sexual obsession, 9–10, 14
sexual stereotypes, 56
Sexuality in Islam (Bouhdiba, A.), 269
Seymour, Lynn, 256–8, 288–9
Shakespeare, William, 43, 137
Shakira, 282
Shakti, 30
Shaw, Martin, 153
Shepheard's Hotel, Cairo, 264
'shimmy-shawobble,' 193
Shintoism, 46
shirabyoshi, 49
Shiva, 22, 30
Shlain, Leonard, 24–5
Shuffle Along, 194
Simenon, Georges, 198
Singer, Paris, 157–9, 163–4
slavery, 172–3
social dance, 68–9, 70, 162, 180–7
Song of Songs, 27
La Sonnambula (Balanchine), 242
South America, 22, 207–31
Spain, 10, 13, 26, 210, 221, 263, 288, 289

'spieling,' 192
steam baths, 68, 269
steam engines, 83–4
Stokes, Sewell, 166–7, 168–9
'stomach-dance' (Josephine Baker), 195
storytelling dance, 31
Stowe, Harriet Beecher, 120
Strabo, 31
Strauss, Johann the elder, 77–9, 83
Strauss, Richard, 36
Strictly Dancing, 230–1
striptease, 275, 286
Summers, Leigh, 89, 121
Sunday, Billy, 191–2
suttee (wife's ritual suicide), 31
Swan Lake, 248, 249, 256
swing, orchestrated sex, 186, 201–2, 205
La Sylphide, 248–9
Sylvestre, Armand, 104
syphilis see venereal disease

Taglioni, Marie, 246
Tales of the New Babylon (Christiansen, R.), 103
Taliban, 274
Talmey, Bernard, 122–3
tango, 11, 12, 79, 184, 196, 208–31
The Tango Lesson (Potter, S.), 228–9
tango music, 221–5
Le Tango (Richepan, J.), 218
Tanguay, Eva, 171
Tanguero magazine, 209
tantrism, 30
taxi dancing, 185–6
tea-dancing, 181, 189
Terry, Ellen, 149, 162
Thailand, 237
Tharp, Ezra, 252
theatre
    dances in, 138–9
    role of women in, 43–4
Théâtre des Champs Elysées, 194
The Thousand and One Nights, 265
Thurman, Judith, 116, 130
Time and the Dancing Image (Jowitt, D.), 250
The Times, 73, 74, 220
Times Square, New York, 187
toe shoes, 239

Tolstoy, Leo, 121
Tomlin, Liz, 230
312   Toulouse-Lautrec, Henri de, 98, 107
trance dancing, 17–18
transvestism, 41, 57–8, 101
Travels With My Tutu (Channel, K.), 230
tuberculosis, 118–19, 127
Tunisia, 18–19, 280
Turkey, 21–2, 59
turkey trot, 183, 184, 186
tutus, 244, 247, 248

ukiyo, 44
underwear, evolution of, 101–2
United States, 79–83, 103–4, 136,
    171–205, 230
Universal Exposition, Paris (1870), 105
US Code Noir, 173
US *nouveaux riches*, 182

The Vagabond (Colette), 113
vagina dentata, 22, 130
de Valois, Ninette, 235, 257
van Nieuwkerk, Karin, 266
Variétés Theatre, Paris, 96
Vauxhall Gardens, London, 68–9
veiling women, 273–4
venereal disease, 126, 127–8, 184
Venus figurines, 20
Vernon, Rev Dr S., 120
Verón, Pablo, 228–9
Versailles, 65
Victoria, Queen, 35, 124
Victorian social life, 92–3, 273–4
Vienna, 34, 77–9
Vienna, Congress of, 76–7
The Vigilante, 37, 173
Vigilante Society, 36–7
vinegar, 118
Virgin Mary, 26
Vision of Salome (Allen, M.), 33–4
Vogue magazine, 254
Voisin's, Paris, 124
von Thaulow, Fritz, 143

Wagner, Ann, 184
Wagner, Cosima, 156
Wagner, Richard, 78
Wall Street crash, 200
Waller, Maureen, 66
Walpole, Horace, 69
waltz, 10–12, 71–85, 83–7, 175
Wedekind, Frank, 127
Weininger, Otto, 125
Wellington, First Duke of, 69
West, Mae, 55–7
When I'm Bad, I'm Better (Hamilton,
    M.), 192
Wilde, Oscar, 33, 35, 36–7, 135
Wilde's Last Stand (Hoare, P.), 37
Wildor, Sarah, 234
Wilhelm II, Kaiser, 217
Woman magazine, 89–90
Women (Talmey, B.), 122–3
women's movement, 136, 146, 150
Woolson, Abba Goold, 116–17, 251
World War I, 58, 124, 176, 180, 187, 205
World War II, 200, 285

Yacourte (Ouled Nail dancer), 272
Yellen, Jack, 200

Zidler, Charles, 106
Zola, Emile, 104, 126, 129–30